SECONDARY CLASSROOM MANAGEMENT

LESSONS FROM RESEARCH AND PRACTICE

SECONDARY CLASSROOM MANAGEMENT

LESSONS FROM RESEARCH AND PRACTICE

Carol Simon Weinstein

Rutgers, the State University of New Jersey

THE McGRAW-HILL COMPANIES, INC.

New York   St. Louis   San Francisco   Auckland   Bogotá   Caracas
Lisbon   London   Madrid   Mexico City   Milan   Montreal   New Delhi
San Juan   Singapore   Sydney   Tokyo   Toronto

McGraw-Hill

A Division of The **McGraw·Hill** *Companies*

This book was developed by Lane Akers, Inc.

This book was set in Times Roman by Ruttle, Shaw & Wetherill, Inc.
The editor was Lane Akers; the production supervisor was Diane Ficarra.
The cover was designed by Joseph Gillians.
Project supervision was done by Tage Publishing Service, Inc.
R. R. Donnelley & Sons Company was printer and binder.

Photo credits: Suzanne Karp Krebs

SECONDARY CLASSROOM MANAGEMENT

Lessons from Research and Practice

This book is printed on acid-free paper.

1 2 3 4 5 6 7 8 9 0 DOC DOC 9 0 9 8 7 6 5

ISBN 0-07-069156-8

Library of Congress Cataloging-in-Publication Data

Weinstein, Carol Simon.
     Secondary classroom management: lessons from research and
practice / Carol Simon Weinstein.
       p.   cm.
    Includes bibliographical references and index.
    ISBN 0-07-069156-8
    1. Classroom management.   2. Education, Secondary.   3. Classroom
environment.   I. Title.
LB3013.W46   1996
371.1'024—dc20   95-37068

ABOUT THE AUTHOR

CAROL SIMON WEINSTEIN is a professor of education and chair of the Department of Learning and Teaching at Rutgers, the State University of New Jersey. She received her doctorate from Harvard Graduate School of Education in 1975, where she first became interested in the impact of classroom design on students' behavior and attitudes. Her fascination with this topic resulted in numerous journal articles and an edited book (with Tom David), *Spaces for Children: Child Development and the Built Environment.*

Her current interests focus on teacher education and the process of learning to teach; most recently, she has studied prospective teachers' beliefs about teaching and classroom management. With her friend and colleague, Andrew J. Mignano, Dr. Weinstein has written a book on managing elementary classrooms, published by McGraw-Hill in 1993. Dr. Weinstein has also been one of the leaders in Rutgers' redesign of its teacher education programs and co-chaired a task force to develop a professional development school with the New Brunswick school district.

CONTENTS IN BRIEF

CONTENTS

PREFACE

For several years I have asked prospective secondary teachers to consider two questions: "What makes a good teacher?" and "Why do you think you'll be a good teacher?" Invariably, one of the major themes to emerge from their responses is the capacity for caring. Prospective secondary teachers see caring about students as one of the major hallmarks of good teaching. Moreover, they believe they have the capacity to care deeply and to create strong bonds with students. They imagine themselves nurturing students' self-esteem, rejoicing in their successes, and watching over their well being. They envision classrooms characterized by warmth, affection, and mutual respect.

And then these prospective teachers actually enter the classroom. Suddenly, the desire to establish caring relationships clashes with the need to establish order. Talk of caring is overshadowed by talk of control, authority, discipline, and punishment. At times, it may even seem as though caring and order were irreconcilable goals.

These two goals are not mutually exclusive. Indeed, I am convinced that if caring relationships are to flourish in classrooms, teachers must be able to create an organized, orderly environment. I am also convinced that one of the ways teachers create that kind of environment is through their acts of caring. The question is not whether the two goals of caring and order can co-exist in classrooms, but how to achieve their co-existence. This question provides the starting point for my book.

Secondary Classroom Management represents an unusual collaboration among a university professor and the four secondary teachers whose experiences are described here: Fred Cerequas, Donnie Collins, Sandra Krupinski, and Carmen Sanchez. Readers will come to "know" these four real teachers—to see the ways they apply the principles of classroom management and to hear their thinking on various issues. I believe this approach is more effective than using fictitious anecdotes or vignettes collected from large numbers of different teachers. I realize, however, that my portrayal of these four teachers may convey the idea that their ways are the only ways of managing classrooms. This is certainly not my intention. The case materials are not meant as recipes for correct practice that are to be imitated. Classroom management isn't that simple: readers must devise their own strategies and solutions to problems.

I wish to acknowledge the enormous debt I owe these four teachers. They have allowed me to observe in their classrooms and to ask them endless questions during lunch periods and prep periods, after school, and even on weekends. They read drafts of each chapter and provided down-to-earth suggestions. Over suppers of Chinese food and pizza, they shared the lessons they have learned in their combined 110 years of teaching.

Fred, Donnie, Sandy, and Carmen are all deeply committed to their students and to their work. This commitment drives their constant efforts to become better teachers. They seize opportunities to extend their knowledge and skills. All four of them recognize that learning to teach is an ongoing, lifelong process—despite the fact they have already achieved reputations as outstanding teachers. This book would not have been possible without them, and I am very grateful.

In addition to the four teachers, numerous others contributed to the making of this book. I thank Peter Bastardo, superintendent of schools in Highland Park; Ronald Larkin, superintendent of schools in New Brunswick; and Willa Spicer, assistant superintendent in South Brunswick, for welcoming me into their districts and taking the time to read and respond to the manuscript. I also thank Penelope Lattimer, assistant superintendent in New Brunswick, for leading me to Donnie Collins and Carmen Sanchez. I am deeply grateful to the student teachers and beginning teachers who shared their experiences and their journal entries with me; special thanks go to Geoffrey Alpaugh, Cynthia Braslow, Patti Hearn, Dave Pellicare, Sandra Roth, and Dixie Shafer. It should be noted that in several cases, details have been changed to avoid embarrassment to anyone, and at times, composite journal entries have been created.

I also want to acknowledge the help of Carol Lefelt and Liz Marquez, two outstanding secondary teachers who read *Elementary Classroom Management* (Weinstein and Migano, 1993) and suggested changes for the secondary book. I appreciate the thoughtful, thorough, and supportive comments made by the following reviewers: Greta Morine-Dershimer, Michael B. Ross, and Barbara Wasik. In addition, the feedback provided by the classes of teacher education students who read and reacted to various drafts was both insightful and encouraging; thanks to their instructors, Stanley Flood (Rutgers) and Rita Silverman (Pace University) for making this possible.

I wish to acknowledge that Chapter Twelve, "Helping Students with Serious Problems," benefitted from the input and advice of Carol Lowinger and Andreé Robinson at South Brunswick High School, Tonia Moore at Highland Park High School, and Gail Reynolds at New Brunswick High School. Edward Chobrda, vice-principal of Roosevelt School, and Nancy Carringer, guidance counselor at South Brunswick High School, shared materials that were used in Chapter Six. Deeply felt thanks also go to Fred Cerequas and Sandy Krupinski, who spent precious vacation days helping to write the activities at the end of each chapter. The three of us owe a lot to Andrew Mignano, who created the activities for the elementary classroom management book, and who allowed us to use them as our inspiration and starting point.

To Suzanne Krebs, whose photographs grace these pages, I express my sincerest gratitude and my awe at her ability to capture the spirit of the teachers and their classes. I also thank Neil Weinstein, who read every page of the manuscript. His criticism was not always welcome, but it was always constructive. Finally, I thank my editor, Lane Akers. He has the qualities of an effective classroom manager: he is patient, understanding, and caring, but he knows how to set limits.

Carol Simon Weinstein

PART I

INTRODUCTION

Chapter One

The Secondary Classroom Environment

For many prospective and beginning teachers, entering a secondary classroom is like returning home after a brief absence. So little has changed: desks with oversized arms are still arranged in straggly rows; the musty odor of chalk still permeates the air; bells still signal the end of classes; and bulletin boards still display faded copies of bell schedules and fire drill instructions. The familiarity of these sights, sounds, and smells makes us feel comfortable and at ease; in fact, it may lead us to conclude that the transition from student to teacher will be relatively easy. Yet, ironically, this very familiarity can be a trap; it can make it difficult to appreciate what a curious and demanding place the secondary classroom really is. Looking at the classroom as if we have never seen one before may help us recognize some of its strange characteristics and contradictions.

Viewed from a fresh perspective, the secondary classroom turns out to be an extremely crowded place. It is more like a subway or a bus than a place designed for learning, and it is hard to think of another setting (except prison, perhaps) where such large groups of individuals are packed so closely together for so many hours. Nonetheless, amid this crowdedness, students are often not permitted to interact. As Philip Jackson (1968) has noted, "students must try to behave as if they were in solitude, when in point of fact they are not. . . . These young people, if they are to become successful students, must learn how to be alone in a crowd" (p. 16).

There are other contradictions in this curious place. High school students are expected to work together in harmony, yet they may be strangers—even rivals—and may come from very different cultural backgrounds. Students are urged to help one another, but they are also told to keep their eyes on their own papers. They are encouraged to cooperate, but they are often in competition, especially if they are concerned about class rank and college admission. They are lectured about being independent and responsible, yet they are also expected to show complete, unquestioning obedience to the teacher's dictates. (This peculiar situation is cap-

"I expect you all to be independent, innovative, critical thinkers who will do exactly as I say."

FIGURE 1-1
Students are urged to be independent and responsible, yet they are also expected to show complete obedience to the teacher. *(Reprinted by permission.)*

tured in the cartoon that appears in Figure 1–1.) They are urged to work slowly and carefully, but they are often reminded that 42-minute periods require adherence to a rigid time schedule.

In addition to these contradictions, Walter Doyle (1986) has pointed out some features of the classroom setting that make it even more complex. First, classrooms are characterized by *multidimensionality*. Unlike a post office or a restaurant, places devoted to a single activity, the classroom is the setting for a broad range of events. Within its boundaries, students read, write, and discuss. They work on projects, view videotapes, and listen to lectures. They also form friendships, argue, and evaluate last Saturday's basketball game. Teachers lead whole-class discussions, coordinate small-group activities, and administer tests. They also take attendance, settle disputes, and counsel students with problems. Somehow, the classroom environment must be able to accommodate all these activities.

A second characteristic of classrooms is the rapid pace at which things happen. Classroom events occur with an *immediacy* that makes it impossible to think through every action ahead of time. An argument erupts over a perceived insult; a student complains that a neighbor is copying; a normally silent student makes a serious, but irrelevant, comment during a group discussion. Each of these incidents requires a quick response, an on-the-spot decision about how to proceed. Furthermore, classroom incidents like these cannot always be anticipated, despite the most careful planning. This *unpredictability* is a third characteristic of classrooms. It ensures that being a teacher is rarely boring, but unpredictability can also be exhausting.

A fourth characteristic of classrooms is the *lack of privacy.* Classrooms are remarkably public places. Within their four walls, each person's behavior can be observed by many others. Teachers talk of feeling as though they are always "on stage" or living in a "fishbowl" (Lortie, 1975). Their feelings are understandable. With 20 or 30 pairs of eyes watching, it is difficult to find a moment for a private chuckle or an unobserved groan. But the scrutiny goes two ways: teachers constantly monitor students' behavior as well. And in response to this sometimes unwelcome surveillance, students develop an "active underlife" (Hatch, 1986) in which to pursue their own personal agendas. With skills that increase as they progress from grade to grade, students learn to pass notes, comb their hair, and do homework for another course, all—they hope—without the teacher's ever noticing. Yet, even if they avoid the teacher's eyes, there are always peers watching. It is difficult for students to have a private interaction with the teacher, to conceal a grade on a test, or to make a mistake without someone noticing.

Finally, over the course of the academic year, classes construct a joint *history.* This fifth characteristic means that classes, like families, remember past events—both positive and negative. They remember who got yelled at, who got away with being late to class, and what the teacher said about homework assignments. They remember who was going to have only "one more chance" before getting detention, and if the teacher didn't follow through, they remember that too. The class memory means that what happens today affects what happens tomorrow. It also means that teachers must work to shape a history of shared experiences that will support, rather than frustrate, future activities.

Crowded, competitive, contradictory, multidimensional, fast-paced, unpredictable, public—this portrait of the classroom highlights characteristics that we often overlook. I have begun the book with this portrait because *effective organization and management require an understanding of the unique features of the classroom.* Many of the management problems encountered by beginning teachers can be traced back to their failure to understand the complex setting in which they work.

Past experiences with children and adolescents may also mislead beginning teachers. For example, you may have tutored an individual student who was having academic difficulties, or perhaps you have been a camp counselor or a swim-club instructor. Although these are valuable experiences, they are very different from teaching in classrooms. Teachers do not work one-on-one with students in a private room; they seldom lead recreational activities that participants have themselves selected. Teachers do not even work with people who have chosen to be present. Instead, *teachers work with captive groups of students, on academic agendas that students have not helped to set, in a crowded, public setting.* Within this setting, teachers must gain the cooperation of students and get them involved in educational activities. This is not a simple task. As Tracy Kidder (1989) has noted:

> The problem is fundamental. Put twenty or more children of roughly the same age in a little room, confine them to desks, make them wait in lines, make them behave. It is as

if a secret committee, now lost to history, had made a study of children and, having figured out what the greatest number were least disposed to do, declared that all of them
should do it. (p. 115)

The purpose of this book is to help prospective and beginning teachers understand the special characteristics of the classroom setting and their implications for
organization and management. I hope to provide concepts and principles that you
can use to think about the managerial tasks you will encounter as a teacher. For example, once you recognize that students are a captive audience, you are better able
to see why it's necessary to stimulate interest in lessons. Comprehending the norms
of the traditional classroom leads you to appreciate the difficulty that students have
in cooperative learning situations. Being aware of the crowded, public nature of
classrooms helps you to understand the importance of dealing with behavior problems in an unobtrusive way.

GUIDING ASSUMPTIONS

Five underlying assumptions have guided the content and organization of this book.
First, *I assume that most problems of disorder in classrooms can be avoided if
teachers use good preventive management strategies.* Thus, I emphasize the prevention of misbehavior, rather than strategies for coping with misbehavior. This
emphasis is consistent with classroom-management research conducted within the
last two decades. In a now classic study, Jacob Kounin (1970) set out to explain the
differences between orderly and disorderly classes by examining how teachers responded to misconduct. To his surprise, he found that the reactions of effective and
ineffective managers were quite similar. What accounted then for the differences in
order? Kounin eventually determined that the orderly classes were more the result
of a teacher's ability to *manage the activities of the group* than of particular ways of
handling student misconduct. Kounin's research changed the way we think about
classroom management. The focus is no longer on ways of disciplining students,
but rather on ways of getting them involved in academic lessons and activities.

*My second assumption is that the way teachers think about management
strongly influences what they do.* Recent research has provided some fascinating
examples of the links between teachers' beliefs about management and their behavior. Consider, Sarah, for example, a first-year teacher who was having difficulty
managing her class (Ulerick and Tobin, 1989). Sarah's behavior in the classroom
seemed to reflect her belief that effective teachers should use charm and humor to
engage students in learning and gain their cooperation. In short, her thinking about
management reflected a metaphor of "teacher as comedian." Eventually, Sarah
reconceptualized the role of teacher, discarding the comedian metaphor and adopt-
ing a metaphor of teacher as "social director." As "social director," the teacher's job
was to "invite students to appropriate, interesting, and meaningful learning activities" (p. 12), and to assist students in directing their own learning activities. This
change in Sarah's thinking about classroom management led to changes in her behavior and to dramatic improvements in the atmosphere of her classes.

In a similar study, Carter (1985) reviewed narrative descriptions of life in the classrooms of an effective and an ineffective classroom manager. Carter's analysis led her to conclude that the two teachers thought about classroom management in very different ways. The effective manager saw her managerial role as "a driver navigating a complex and often treacherous route" (p. 89). From this perspective, her responsibility was to guide classroom events smoothly and efficiently; she emphasized the academic tasks that students needed to accomplish and did not allow minor misbehaviors and interruptions to get her off course. In contrast, the ineffective manager seemed to see her role as "defender of a territory." Constantly vigilant for threats to order, she was careful to catch all misbehaviors whenever they occurred and used reprimands and appeals to authority in order to control inappropriate behavior.

Taken together, these studies suggest that teachers who view classroom management as a process of guiding and structuring classroom events tend to be more effective than teachers who stress their disciplinary role or who see classroom management as a product of personal charm (Brophy, 1988). This perspective on classroom management is also consistent with an emphasis on prevention.

A third assumption of this book is that the need for order must not supersede the need for meaningful instruction. It is commonly acknowledged that management and instruction are complementary, with good classroom management a prerequisite for good instruction. Certainly, instruction cannot take place in an environment that is chaotic and disorderly. On the other hand, an excessive focus on management can sometimes *hinder* instruction (Doyle, 1986). For example, a teacher may wish to divide the class into small groups for a cooperative learning activity. Yet her anxiety about the noise level and her fear that students may not work well together could make her abandon the small-group project and substitute an individual workbook assignment. Academic work that is more intellectually and socially challenging may also be more challenging from a managerial perspective. Yet, it is crucial that teachers not sacrifice the curriculum in order to achieve an orderly classroom. As Doyle (1985) comments, "A well-run lesson that teaches nothing is just as useless as a chaotic lesson in which no academic work is possible" (p. 33).

My fourth assumption is that the tasks of classroom management vary across different classroom situations. Ecological psychologists remind us that the classroom is not a "homogenized glob" (Kounin and Sherman, 1979, p. 150). Rather, it is composed of distinct "subsettings"—teacher presentations, whole-class discussions, transition times, small-group activities, laboratory investigations—and what constitutes order may be different in each of these subsettings. For example, "calling out" may be a problem during a teacher-directed question-and-answer session (often referred to as "recitation"), but it may be perfectly acceptable in a more student-centered discussion. Similarly, students may be prohibited from helping one another during an independent writing assignment, but they may be encouraged to work together during a cooperative learning activity. Students have the right to know what is expected of them in these different classroom situations. This means that teachers must think about the unique management needs of each classroom subsetting and make a point of teaching students the appropriate ways of behaving in each one. In order to assist in this task, *Secondary Classroom Management* discusses the specific management "hazards" associated with seatwork, groupwork, recitations, and discussions (Carter, 1985) and suggests ways of preventing these hazards from occurring.

The final assumption is that managing classrooms is a decision-making process. Despite numerous books that provide "101 guaranteed ways of creating classroom order," classroom management cannot be reduced to a set of recipes or a list of "how to's." As we have seen, the classroom environment is crowded and complex. Pat answers won't work. Teachers must be able to anticipate problems, analyze situations, generate solutions, and make decisions—sometimes within seconds. And they must become familiar with relevant research that can help to inform these decisions.

PLAN OF THE BOOK

Secondary Classroom Management focuses first on "beginning-of-the-year" tasks, such as designing the physical environment of the classroom and developing rules and routines for behavior. It then moves to longer-term issues—for example, gaining students' cooperation, using time wisely, and managing various subsettings of the classroom. Finally, the book examines issues that extend beyond the classroom environment; it discusses ways of working with families and the special resources that are available for special problems.

Throughout the book, concepts and principles derived from research are woven together with the wisdom and experiences of four real secondary teachers. These teachers share with you their thinking about the challenges of classroom management. You learn about the classes they teach and about the physical constraints of their rooms; you hear them reflect on their rules and routines and watch as they teach them to students. You listen as they talk about motivating students and fostering cooperation, and as they discuss appropriate ways to deal with misbehavior. In sum, *this book focuses on real decisions made by real teachers as they manage the complex environment of the secondary classroom.* By sharing their stories, I do not mean to suggest that their ways of managing classrooms are the only effective ways. Rather, my goal is to illustrate how four reflective, caring, and very different individuals approach the tasks involved in classroom management.

Now, let's meet the teachers.

SUMMARY

This chapter examined some of the contradictions and special characteristics of classrooms. It argued that effective management requires an understanding of the unique features of the classroom environment and stressed the fact that teachers work with captive groups of students on academic agendas that students have not helped to set. It then discussed five assumptions that guided the content and organization of the book.

Contradictions of the Classroom Environment

- Classrooms are crowded, yet students are often not allowed to interact.
- Students are expected to work together harmoniously, yet they may not know or like each other.
- Students are urged to cooperate, yet they often work in individual or competitive situations.
- Students are encouraged to be independent, yet they are also expected to conform to the teacher's dictates.
- Students are instructed to work slowly and carefully, but they have to be aware of the "press of time" in a 42-minute period.

Characteristics of the Classroom Environment

- Multidimensionality
- Immediacy
- Unpredictability
- Lack of privacy
- History

Guiding Assumptions of the Book

- Most problems of disorder can be avoided if teachers use good preventive management strategies.
- The way teachers think about management influences the way they behave.
- The need for order must not supersede the need for meaningful instruction.
- Behavioral expectations vary across different subsettings of the classroom.
- Managing classrooms is a decision-making process that should be informed by relevant research.

In an effort to illustrate various ways of managing classrooms effectively, the book focuses on real decisions made by real teachers as they manage the complex environment of the secondary classroom.

REFERENCES

Brophy, J. (1988). Educating teachers about managing classrooms and students. *Teaching and Teacher Education, 4*(1), 1–18.

Carter, K. (March–April 1985). Teacher comprehension of classroom processes: An emerging direction in classroom management research. Paper presented at the annual meeting of the American Educational Research Association, Chicago.

Doyle, W. (1985). Recent research on classroom management: Implications for teacher preparation. *Journal of Teacher Education, 36*(3), 31–35.

Doyle, W. (1986). Classroom organization and management. In M. C. Wittrock (Ed.), *Handbook of research on teaching*. New York: Macmillan, 392–431.

Hatch, J. A. (March 1986). Alone in a crowd: Analysis of covert interactions in a kindergarten. Presented at the annual meeting of the American Educational Research Association, San Francisco. ERIC Document Reproduction Service No. 272 278.

Jackson, P. (1968). *Life in classrooms.* New York: Holt, Rinehart & Winston.

Kidder, T. (1989). *Among schoolchildren.* Boston: Houghton Mifflin

Kounin, J. S. (1970). *Discipline and group management in classrooms.* New York: Holt, Rinehart & Winston.

Kounin, J. S., and Sherman, L. (1979). School environments as behavior settings. *Theory into Practice, 14,* 145–151.

Lortie, D. (1975). *Schoolteacher.* Chicago: University of Chicago Press.

Ulerick, S. L., and Tobin, K. (March 1989). The influence of a teacher's beliefs on classroom management. Paper presented at the annual meeting of the American Educational Research Association, San Francisco.

Chapter Two

Meeting the Teachers

Two of our teachers work in New Brunswick, a relatively small urban district in central New Jersey. Here, *Donnie Collins* teaches mathematics at the high school, and *Carmen Sanchez* teaches art at Roosevelt School, which houses kindergarten through eighth grade. Across the Raritan River from New Brunswick is Highland Park, where *Sandra Krupinski* is a high school chemistry teacher. Finally, *Fred Cerequas* ("Serakwas") teaches social studies in nearby South Brunswick. This chapter introduces all four teachers and briefly describes the districts within which they work. We begin with New Brunswick.

Of the 4,448 students who attend this district's ten schools, 50 percent are African-American and 44 percent are Hispanic. Many of the children come from families who live in poverty, evidenced by the fact that 82 percent of the students qualify for the federal free or reduced lunch program. The poverty breeds other problems typical of urban areas—drugs, a high drop-out rate, transiency, homelessness, teenage pregnancy, physical abuse.

About fifteen years ago, after receiving some of the lowest scores in New Jersey on a statewide standardized test, New Brunswick instituted a highly structured curriculum. Objectives were developed for every subject at every grade level, along with timelines for teaching each objective. Teachers must submit plan books and grade books to building principals, who closely monitor when each objective is taught and evaluated and how students are progressing.

Critics argue that the new curriculum restricts creativity and burdens teachers with unnecessary paperwork, but academic achievement has steadily increased in the last decade. Nonetheless, a sizable number of students still have difficulty passing the High School Proficiency Test that New Jersey requires for graduation. Fall 1994 results indicate that 59.8 percent of eleventh graders passed the reading portion of the test; 58.3 percent passed the math portion; and 72.3 percent passed the writing portion. Although these percentages seem low, they compare favorably with other urban school districts in the state, and teachers and administrators are convinced that New Brunswick is moving in the right direction. Financial support from local corporations (in particular, Johnson and Johnson, whose world head-quarters is located in the city) and collaborative projects with Rutgers, the state university, have also aided the district's quest for improvement.

DONNIE COLLINS

New Brunswick High School is a few miles from the heart of downtown, a low brick building set back from the street on a wide expanse of lawn. Built in the 1960s, the school currently accommodates 720 students in grades nine through twelve. A large sign just inside the main entrance proclaims "Care and Excellence—Our #1 Goal," and fancifully painted murals honor the school's mascot, the zebra. The long hallways are lined with metal lockers in banks of red, green, blue, orange, and yellow. On the walls are posters advertising school clubs and activities; one announces a meeting of WWF—Working With Fathers—an organization for adolescent fathers.

On the second floor, in a corner classroom opposite the math department office, we find Donnie Collins, a ninth- through twelfth-grade mathematics teacher. A 50-year-old mother of one, Donnie began teaching math in 1964 in Birmingham, Alabama. She moved to New Brunswick in 1969 and has been teaching in the district ever since, first on the junior high level and then at the high school.

Being a teacher was Donnie's childhood dream. "As a child I always wanted to play school," she recalls, "and I always wanted to be the teacher, never one of the pupils." Reflecting on this early dream, Donnie acknowledges the influence of her grandmother, who had been an elementary teacher before she opened a beauty school and shop. Although Donnie's parents were farmers, they recognized that farming was not for her. As Donnie puts it, "My calling was to be a teacher."

Donnie was influenced not only by her grandmother, but also by two of her own teachers. Her fifth-grade teacher, Mrs. Poole, was intimidating at first, but Donnie soon realized that she needn't be frightened. Mrs. Poole wasn't mean; she was just concerned about students' achievement and well-being. "From Mrs. Poole, I learned about the importance of maintaining discipline, about the need to be firm and fair, and the value of keeping in touch with parents." Later, in high school, Donnie encountered Miss Anchrum, a young math teacher fresh out of college, with lots of new ideas about how to make math exciting: "Miss Anchrum made math real, and she would accept nothing less than our best." From her, Donnie learned the importance of motivating students and holding high expectations.

Donnie eventually earned both a bachelor's degree and a master's degree in mathematics, along with certification to teach. But the impact of Mrs. Poole and Miss Anchrum has stayed with her, and her teaching reflects the lessons she learned from them. When asked about her goals, she answers without hesitation:

> I want the same things my teachers wanted. I want my students to become creative, independent thinkers; I want them to be able to function effectively in our everyday world; I want them to make a positive contribution to society. I continually stress that there is always more than one way to solve a problem and I encourage them to find alternative solutions. I believe strongly in the importance of groupwork and peer tutoring

Donnie Collins

so that students can learn to work together and to take constructive criticism. When students say, "Oh, Ms. Collins, I don't need to know this; all I need to know is how to count my money," I tell them: "But first you have to *make* the money, and once you've made your money, you have to *keep* it." And you have to know math to do that.

Donnie's goals are not achieved easily. She is frustrated by those students "who can't see beyond today," who cause disruption, and create problems for those who do want to learn. She is also concerned about a lack of parental involvement (a topic we will discuss in Chapter 11), and the problems that her students face. As she puts it, "Education is just not a priority for many of my students. *Survival* is the priority." Sometimes she has to forego a math lesson in order to discuss the more immediate problems of her students: conflicts with families, pregnancy, parenting (New Brunswick High School has a day care center for the children of its students), running away from home, violence in the community, drugs. With a certain amount of resignation, Donnie comments:

If you try to go ahead with a math lesson when they're all riled up about something that has happened at home or in the neighborhood, you're doomed. There's just no point to it. It's better to put away the quadratic equations and **talk.**

In a continuing effort to meet the needs of her students, Donnie has served as a trainer in New Brunswick High School's Peer Leadership Program. During a week-long retreat, fifteen to twenty high school seniors are taught interpersonal, communication, and problem-solving skills so that they can then help freshmen make the adjustment from junior high to senior high. Donnie is also committed to her own professional development; she frequently attends workshops and courses on a variety of topics, such as classroom management, dealing with diverse students, sensitivity training—even Teaching the Holocaust. But it is the daily help provided by her colleagues for which she is most grateful: "It's important to know that you're not alone in dealing with a student. I am lucky to have colleagues I can go to for advice and support."

Despite the difficulties of teaching in an urban district, Donnie is still enthusiastic and optimistic about her chosen career. One of the major satisfactions is the fact that each day brings something new. Another is "seeing the light come on," and knowing that a student suddenly understands what the lesson is all about. Particularly satisfying is sharing the successes of former students—and knowing that you played a part:

> I was recently given a surprise birthday party, and one of my former students was invited. He's currently working for the General Electric Corporation, and there he was at my party, talking about having had me in eighth grade and the impact I had had on his life. That's the real reward of teaching.

Listening to Donnie Collins speak about the goals she has for her students and the satisfactions she derives from teaching, it is obvious that the legacy of Mrs. Poole and Miss Anchrum lives on in this New Brunswick High School mathematics teacher.

CARMEN SANCHEZ

Since New Brunswick's elementary schools house children from kindergarten through eighth grade, it is at Roosevelt School, near the heart of downtown New Brunswick, that Carmen Sanchez teaches art to students of junior-high age. Surrounded by single- and multifamily dwellings, Roosevelt is an old but well-cared-for building with capacity for 700 students. The art room is on the first floor; it is bright, spacious, and overflowing with posters and paraphernalia. Once a week, children from first grade through eighth grade come to Carmen's room for instruction in art. In addition to teaching Roosevelt's fifteen "mainstream" classes, Carmen also provides art instruction for the children in the eight bilingual classes, the five special education classes, and a "port-of-entry" class for older children who have just arrived from a non-English speaking country.

Carmen was born in New York, the daughter of a construction worker who had emigrated from Spain when he was fifteen and a homemaker whose parents had also come from Spain. Neither of Carmen's parents completed high school, and when a guidance counselor suggested that Carmen go to art school after high school graduation, her parents vehemently vetoed the idea: their daughter would go to a

Carmen Sanchez

"real" college. It was at the State University of New York at New Paltz that Carmen first became excited about the possibility of teaching art. When she graduated in 1965, with a bachelor's degree in art education, she taught for three years in a nearby urban community. She then moved to New Jersey, obtained a master's degree in fine arts from Rutgers in 1970, and began teaching in New Brunswick. Carmen has been at Roosevelt for the last 22 years—which means that her classes now include the children of some of her former pupils.

Teaching art in an elementary school poses special challenges. Unlike junior high school, there is no three-minute break between Carmen's classes: one class gets "dropped off" as another gets "picked up." This means that Carmen has absolutely no chance between classes to organize supplies, set up displays—even to catch her breath. Furthermore, since students come only once a week for 40 minutes, maintaining continuity and sustaining interest in long-term projects can be difficult. The limited class time also puts frustrating constraints on what Carmen can accomplish: "I'd love to bring in films, slides, videos, music. But then there'd be no time for students to do any hands-on art, and that's my highest priority." In addition, Carmen's role as a once-a-week teacher of a special subject carries the risk that youngsters won't take her class seriously. Students at Roosevelt have only two "specials" each week—art and physical education—and all too often, nonacademic subjects like these are viewed as opportunities to play around. Finally, Carmen has responsibilities as the school's "resident artist." During her "free" periods, at lunch time, and after school, she can be seen working with children to create hallway exhibits or stage designs for all sorts of special festivities, such as American Education Week, Hispanic Culture Month, the African-American History Program, the spring festival, the Academic Fair, and, of course, the eighth-grade graduation.

Somehow, Carmen not only surmounts these challenges, she also manages to make it look easy. The steps of every art project are outlined on large sheets of heavy cardboard, which also display the project at various stages of completion. This allows Carmen to move quickly through the instructions and enables students to pick up easily from where they left off the week before. Every day, supplies are set out for each class before school begins, so there is no wasted time during the all-too-brief art period. During classes, Carmen is an intense, but gentle whirlwind: she circulates constantly through the room—prodding, assisting, praising, and questioning—and always, of course, reminding students to watch the clock.

Carmen's goals for her classes focus more on thinking, feeling, and talking than on knowledge of specific techniques:

> First of all, I want them to *think* about what they're doing—to become invested in each project—not just take the easy way out by copying what someone else is doing. Second, I want them to do things that they'll get *excited* about, so that they'll remember art as being a positive experience, even if they don't continue to do it once they're out of school. So many times I hear adults say, "I hated art class. My teacher made me draw a dog, and I couldn't do it." I don't ever want my students to feel that way. I want them to explore a lot of different materials and try a lot of different techniques. I try to give them choices so they won't have to make excuses about why they can't do something. Finally, I want my students to *talk* more about art, to ask questions, to verbalize their preferences and feelings. They tend to be too quiet, so one of my goals is to get discussions going about the art we're doing.

For the seventh and eighth graders, Carmen also has specific goals related to the art history curriculum she has developed. An art timeline stretches across one wall of the classroom, and each art project is carefully chosen to represent a particular period of art history:

> For many of my students, this will be the only time they'll ever learn about art history. We don't go real deeply, but I want them to understand that people have made art all through history, and to have some sense of the chronology. So when we learn about prehistoric cave paintings in France, they make their own paintings on large sheets of brown paper; when we talk about the achievements of ancient Egypt, they make mummies out of Paris Craft; when we discuss the Renaissance, they make Venetian masks. And whatever the period, I try to connect what they do now with what people did then. For example, with the Venetian masks, we talk about how they differ from Halloween masks, or the masks that people wear during Mardi Gras.

Like Donnie, one of Carmen's greatest satisfactions is knowing that she has had an impact on her students' lives. Since she lives in New Brunswick, Carmen frequently sees her former students when she walks home or goes shopping. It warms her heart when grown men and women stop to say hello and to tell her about a particular project they remember doing in her class. "Some of them want to know if I still have their art work," she laughs. At times like these, Carmen knows that she has succeeded in making art class a positive experience for her students. Clearly, none of Carmen Sanchez's students will ever lament, "She made me draw a dog, and I couldn't do it."

SANDRA KRUPINSKI

The tree-lined borough of Highland Park lies on the other side of the Raritan River from New Brunswick. The population of this small community is extremely diverse. The district's three schools serve children who live in homes valued at $500,000 as well as those from low-income apartment complexes. The student population of 1,450 is 63 percent white, 17 percent African-American, 11 percent Hispanic, and 9 percent Asian-American. About 10 percent of the children qualify for the federal free-lunch program. HSPT results from Fall 1994 indicate that 90 percent of eleventh graders passed the reading portion of the test; 91.4 percent passed the math portion; and 98.6 percent passed the writing portion. These results reinforce Highland Park's reputation as a district that works hard to promote academic excellence, no mean accomplishment in the face of recent budget problems and changing demographics.

Highland Park High School currently houses 450 students in grades seven through twelve. Built in 1925, the building is badly in need of repairs, and many facilities need to be modernized. Fortunately, the community recently passed a $15-million-dollar bond referendum, which will allow the district to make long overdue capital improvements.

In the science wing on the second floor is the chemistry classroom where Sandra Krupinski, a 44-year-old mother of two, teaches three classes of chemistry—"regular," honors, and advanced placement. Sandy's love of science was awakened when she herself was a student at Highland Park High School, and teaching seemed like the obvious, logical career. "At that time," Sandy remembers, "women just weren't encouraged to consider other options. It was either teaching or nursing." Her father, a construction worker, and her mother, an office manager for an insurance company, applauded the decision to be a teacher, proud that Sandy would be the first in her family to attend college.

Although Sandy recognizes that becoming a teacher was not the result of thoughtful deliberation, she is confident that she pursued the right course. After 16 years of teaching, she still doesn't regard it as "just a job." Even in the summer, after only a few weeks of vacation, she finds herself gravitating back to school so she can begin to prepare for classes.

Sandy is very clear about what she is trying to achieve with her students. She sees chemistry as a vehicle for helping students develop problem-solving skills, self-discipline ("a new experience for some"), and self-confidence:

> Chemistry is seen as a difficult subject, and some students begin the year thinking they'll never be able to master it. They'll come up to me with a blank paper and say, "I

Sandy Krupinski

couldn't do this, Mrs. K." I can't stand that. My hope is that by the end of the year these students will have the confidence to attack problems and the ability to develop appropriate strategies. That's much more important to me than getting the right answers.

In order to achieve this goal, Sandy tries hard to create an accepting, nonthreatening atmosphere in her class. On the first day of school, for example, she gives her students an index card and asks them to answer four questions: (1) How do you learn best? (2) What do you expect to be excited about in chemistry? (3) What do you expect to be nervous about? and (4) What can I do to help? Their responses are revealing, particularly to the third and fourth questions. One student shares his fear of talking in front of the class and asks her not to call on him. Several confide that they are anxious about the difficulty of the course, particularly the mathematics and the need to memorize "lots of itsy, bitsy facts"; they ask her to be patient and to take extra time. One girl with limited proficiency in English writes about the fact that her "language is not good," and asks Sandy to speak slowly and to "sometimes explain something for me."

When students return on the second day of class, Sandy addresses each concern that has been raised (telling students that these are the fears expressed by "two or more students"). She thanks them for sharing information that will help her to help them and reassures them that she will be patient, that they will proceed slowly, and that she will always be available for extra help outside of class. Afterwards, thinking about why she takes the time to do this, Sandy comments:

> As I talk about each fear they've expressed, I can actually see their shoulders drop, and I can feel the anxiety level in the class go down. Doing this also gives me information that I can use to help them. For example, take the boy who's afraid of speaking in front of the class. Today, students were putting problems on the board that they had done for homework. Normally, I don't particularly want people with the right answers to put the problems up on the board, because I want them to see that what's important is developing a strategy, not just getting the correct answer. In this case, however, it was important for him to feel confident about going up to the board. So, as I walked around the room, I glanced at his paper and saw that he had a particular problem correct. I told him he had done a good job with it and asked him to put it on the board. Instead of getting anxious, he smiled at me! This couldn't have happened if I hadn't asked students to share their concerns with me.

Sandy may be sensitive to students' anxieties about chemistry, but she still communicates high expectations and a no-nonsense attitude. This year, during an unexpectedly long "vacation" brought about by a fierce blizzard, Sandy called all of her Advanced Placement students to give them an assignment "so they wouldn't fall behind." Her students weren't surprised; one of them told her, "Oh, Mrs. K, we just *knew* you'd call!"

Sandy's no-nonsense attitude is also apparent in an incident that occurred during very different weather many months earlier. Last year, on a hot spring day when temperatures in the chemistry lab hovered around 100 degrees Fahrenheit, Sandy glanced out the window and saw one of her students lying on the lawn. The girl was blatantly cutting class. Sandy called the dean of discipline and asked her to bring the student to the classroom. "Are you sure you don't want me to take her to the detention room?" asked the dean. "Of course not," Sandy told her. "I want her in here, where I can teach her something!"

Sandy is troubled by incidents like this; it is hard for her to accept the fact that she doesn't succeed with every student, and she continually takes courses and workshops to find ways to reach even the least motivated youngster. Yet, it is incidents like this that have helped to build Sandy Krupinski's reputation as a teacher who is passionate about chemistry and fiercely committed to students' learning—a teacher who manages to be both demanding and caring.

FRED CEREQUAS

Not far from New Brunswick is the community of South Brunswick. The school district has a reputation for innovation. Indeed, a 1989 issue of *Newsweek* magazine featured South Brunswick's initiatives in early childhood education. Recently, with a substantial grant from the R. J. R. Nabisco Foundation, the district has begun to explore new ways to assist at-risk children. South Brunswick is also known for its commitment to "whole language," in which the language arts—reading, writing, speaking, and listening—are integrated with one another and with other areas of the curriculum.

This well-regarded school district currently has about 5,000 students and is gaining more than 200 a year. The student population is becoming increasingly diverse; it is now 69 percent white, 15 percent Asian-American, 11 percent African-American, and 6 percent Hispanic. Over 100 children—representing about 40 different languages—require instruction in English as a second language, and like Highland Park, the socioeconomic range is striking. Although people think of South Brunswick as a middle- to upper-middle class community, a sizable number of its children live in low-cost mobile home parks. About 10 percent are eligible for the federal free-lunch program. The HSPT results from Fall 1994 show that 92.1 percent of the eleventh graders passed the reading portion of the test; 89.8 percent passed the math; and 92.5 percent passed the writing.

Fred Cerequas, a 52-year-old father of three, is a member of the ten-person social studies department at South Brunswick High School. Although designed to accommodate 1,000 students, the high school currently houses 1,200, and the numbers are constantly growing. Indeed, South Brunswick is in the midst of planning a new high school to meet the needs of the rapidly expanding student population.

Fred's route to teaching was circuitous. As the son of factory workers who had to leave school for economic reasons, Fred went into the United States Army after high school. He worked as an information specialist in Alaska, where he had a radio and television show, narrated troop information films, and wrote for several army newspapers. When he was discharged in 1962, he began to work his way through college by driving a school bus for high school students. It was then that he discovered he was able to "connect with kids" and decided to earn a teaching certificate "just in case." A successful and gratifying student-teaching experience led him to decide that this was the career he wanted to pursue. His first teaching position was in South Brunswick, and he's been there ever since—a total of 28 years. Far from being burned out, Fred still believes he learns as much from his students as they do from him. In fact, he proclaims that last year was the most interesting and exciting of his career—and that this one looks even better.

Fred currently teaches five classes: two sections of U.S. History I (honors); one section of the Institute for Political and Legal Education (IPLE), a practicum in law, government, and politics for a heterogeneous group of seniors; and two sections of Contemporary World Issues, a non-western history course for seniors (one honors and one "regular"). It is the Contemporary World Issues course that excites Fred the most; here, students study non-western cultures and examine the impact—positive and negative—of western influence.

Fred articulates his goals for his students by telling the story of Tanida, a senior he had in class last year. After learning about the problems of women and children in the third world, Tanida organized her classmates to sponsor a little girl in Africa through *Save the Children*—all without prompting from the teacher. To Fred, Tanida's efforts represent a combination of knowledge and compassion, and it is this combination that he strives for in his classes. He tells us:

I believe *real* teachers are cultivators. They nurture the seeds of wisdom in their students by helping them become independent, eager learners who combine experience and knowledge with the genuine concern for others that gives life its meaning . . .

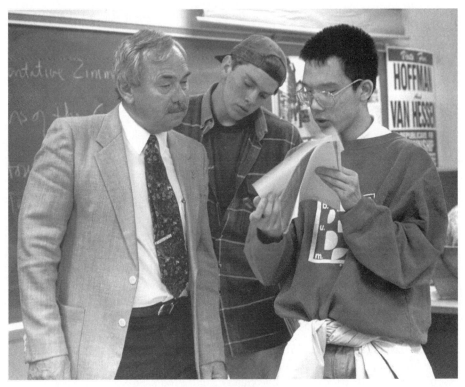

Fred Cerequas

Fred admits that his goals are not easily achieved in today's typical high school, where an "Industrial Revolution mentality" dominates:

> Buildings like factories; seats in rows; rigid schedules; production quotas; quality controls. . . . The whole system seems geared to efficiency rather than humanity. At times, it seems to me that schools as they are designed actually inhibit education. . . .

Despite the obstacles to learning that he sees in our current system of schooling, Fred is energetic and optimistic, and he continually seeks better and more interesting ways to teach. In 1992, he participated in a summer institute at the National Humanities Center in North Carolina, along with 20 other outstanding teachers from around the country. The following summer, he was named a Dodge Foundation Fellow and received a grant from the National Endowment for the Humanities to study ways of integrating literature more effectively into a history curriculum. He regularly works with student teachers from Rutgers and Princeton.

Professional activities like these fuel his determination to connect with kids and to "nurture wisdom." Early in the fall, for example, Fred led a discussion in Contemporary World Issues on the social institutions common to all cultures. Although

students were generally cooperative, about one-half of the class wasn't fully engaged—a fact that did not escape his notice. Fred stopped the lesson and addressed
the students' apathy in his characteristically direct, down-to-earth manner:

> Listen, we don't study junk in here. What we're doing in here is trying to understand
> processes of change. This *affects* us; this stuff can make a *difference in your life.* And if
> you can be more than just bored seniors, we can do some really important stuff in
> here.

After class, Fred sat in the teachers' room reflecting on the students' resistance.
He reviewed the class roster, noting which youngsters had participated and which
had remained silent. He spoke of the skepticism and detachment frequently displayed by students, particularly seniors; he acknowledged the difficulty of convinc-
ing them that what they were studying held meaning for their lives. Nonetheless, he
vowed to "convert" them, and looked ahead to the day when he would actually
have to chase them out after class. Given Fred's commitment and passion for teaching, there was little doubt that he would succeed. After all, according to Fred,
"Teacher is not a word that describes what I do for a living; rather, it defines who I
am."

CONCLUDING COMMENTS

Donnie, Carmen, Sandy, and Fred teach different subjects in very different settings.
Grade levels range from seventh to twelfth. The racial composition of the four
teachers' classes differs dramatically: Sandy's and Fred's classes are predominantly
white, while Donnie's and Carmen's classes are predominantly African-American
and Hispanic. Sandy and Fred work in districts where 10 percent of the children are
eligible for free lunch, compared with the 80 percent figure in Donnie and Carmen's district. And while Donnie and Carmen must follow a carefully prescribed
curriculum, Fred and Sandy are given a great deal of freedom. In order to be effective, our four teachers must be sensitive and responsive to these differences in age,
race, culture, socioeconomic conditions, and district policy.

Despite these differences, Donnie, Carmen, Sandy, and Fred are alike in many
ways. Obvious similarities emerge when they talk about the tasks of classroom
management. Chapter 1 discussed the assumption that the way teachers think about
management strongly influences how they behave. I cited research suggesting that
teachers who view classroom management as a process of guiding and structuring
classroom events tend to be more effective than teachers who stress their disciplinary role. Interestingly, when Donnie, Carmen, Sandy, and Fred speak about classroom management, they rarely use the words "discipline" or "punishment," "con-
frontation" or "penalty." Instead, they emphasize mutual respect; they talk about
the importance of being organized and well prepared; they stress the need to develop a "caring community," in which all individuals are contributing, valued
members (Schaps and Solomon, 1990); they speak about involving students and
helping them to achieve.

It's important to remember that Donnie, Carmen, Sandy, and Fred are real human beings working in the complex, uncertain environment of the secondary classroom. Although they are intelligent, skillful teachers who are extremely effective at preventing misbehavior, their classrooms are not free of problems. (In fact, Chapter 6 focuses specifically on the ways they deal with misbehavior.) Like all of us, they make mistakes; they become frustrated and impatient; they sometimes fail to live up to their own images of the ideal teacher. By their own testimony, they are all "still learning how to run more effective classrooms."

It is also important to remember that these four teachers do not follow recipes or prescriptions for classroom management, so their ways of interacting with students often look very different. Nonetheless, underlying the differences in behavior, it is often possible to detect the same guiding principles. The chapters that follow will try to convey the ways these four excellent teachers tailor the principles to fit their own particular contexts.

Finally, it is necessary to point out that these teachers do not work in schools where conditions are so bad that classes have to be held in stairwells or storage closets, where windows remain broken for years, and where 40 students in a class have to share a handful of books. Nor do they teach in schools that have installed metal detectors, where students regularly carry weapons, and where gang activity is common. In recent years, New Brunswick, Highland Park, and South Brunswick have all experienced a frightening increase in the number of serious problems, but violence is not an everyday occurrence. Whether the strategies discussed here are generalizable to severely troubled schools is not clear. Nevertheless, I hope that *Secondary Classroom Management* will prove to be a useful starting point for teachers everywhere.

SUMMARY

This chapter introduced the four teachers whose thinking and experiences will be described throughout the rest of the book. They work in three school districts in central New Jersey.

• **New Brunswick:** an urban district of 4,448 students (50 percent African American and 44 percent Hispanic); 82 percent of the students qualify for the federal free- or reduced-lunch program

> **Donnie Collins:** a mathematics teacher at the high school
> **Carmen Sanchez:** an art teacher at Roosevelt Elementary School (K–8)

• **Highland Park:** a small district of 1,450 students (63 percent white, 17 percent African-American, 11 percent Hispanic, and 9 percent Asian-American); about 10 percent of the students qualify for the federal free-lunch program

> **Sandra Krupinski:** a chemistry teacher at Highland Park High School

• **South Brunswick:** a district of about 5,000 students and growing fast; student population is 69 percent white, 15 percent Asian-American, 11 percent African-American, and 6 percent Hispanic; about 10 percent of the students are eligible for the federal free-lunch program

Fred Cerequas: a social studies teacher at South Brunswick High School

Although these four teachers teach different subjects in very different settings, they are alike in many ways. In particular, they speak about classroom management in very similar terms: they emphasize the prevention of behavior problems, mutual respect, involving students in learning activities, and the importance of being organized and well prepared.

Since the teachers work in very different contexts, their ways of interacting with students often look very different. Nonetheless, underlying the differences in behavior, it is often possible to detect the same guiding principles. The chapters that follow will try to convey the ways these four teachers tailor the principles to fit their own particular situations.

REFERENCE

Schaps, E., and Solomon, D. (1990). Schools and classrooms as caring communities. *Educational Leadership, 48*(3), 38–42.

PART II

ESTABLISHING AND MAINTAINING AN ENVIRONMENT FOR LEARNING

Chapter Three

Designing the Physical Environment

Discussions of organization and management often neglect the physical character-istics of the classroom. Unless it becomes too hot, too cold, too crowded, or too noisy, we tend to think of the classroom setting as merely an unimportant backdrop for interaction. This general tendency to ignore the physical environment is espe-cially prevalent in secondary schools, where many teachers are like nomads, mov-ing from room to room throughout the day. In this unfortunate situation, it is diffi-cult to create a classroom setting that is more than simply adequate. Nonetheless, it is important to recognize that the *physical environment can influence the way teachers and students feel, think, and behave.* Careful planning of this environ-ment—within the constraints of your daily schedule—is an integral part of good classroom management.

Environmental psychologists point out that the effects of the classroom setting can be both *direct* and *indirect* (Proshansky and Wolfe, 1974). For example, if stu-dents seated in straight rows are unable to carry on a class discussion because they can't hear one another, the *environment is directly hindering their participation.* Students might also be affected *indirectly* if they infer from the seating arrangement that the teacher does not really want them to interact. In this case, the arrangement of the desks is sending a message to the students about how they are supposed to behave. Their reading of this message would be accurate if the teacher had deliber-ately arranged the seats to inhibit discussion. More likely, however, the teacher gen-uinely desires class participation, but has never thought about the link between the classroom environment and student behavior.

This chapter is intended to help you develop *environmental competence* (Steele, 1973)—awareness of the physical environment and its impact and the ability to use that environment to meet your goals. Even as nomads, environmentally competent teachers are sensitive to the messages communicated by the physical setting. They plan spatial arrangements that support their instructional plans. They know how to evaluate the effectiveness of a classroom environment. They are alert to the possibility that physical factors might contribute to behavioral problems, and they modify at least some aspects of the classroom environment when the need arises.

As you read this chapter, keep in mind the discussion of classroom management in Chapter One. (You might find it helpful to refer back to pages 6–8.) Classroom management is not simply a matter of dealing with misbehavior. Instead, effective management means *gaining students' cooperation and promoting their involvement in educational activities.* My discussion of the classroom environment reflects this perspective: I am concerned not only with reducing distraction and minimizing congestion through good environmental design, but also with ways the environment can foster students' security, increase their comfort, and stimulate their interest in learning tasks. Throughout this chapter, I will illustrate major points with examples from the classrooms of the four teachers you have just met. Interestingly, all of them happen to teach their classes in one room this year, although Donnie, Sandy, and Fred share their room with other teachers. For Donnie and Fred, teaching in one room is a substantial improvement from past years, when they had to move from room to room. Last year was particularly difficult for Fred: he taught his five classes in four different rooms!

SIX FUNCTIONS OF THE CLASSROOM SETTING

Chapter One emphasized the wide variety of activities that occurs in classrooms. Although we normally think of the classroom as a place for instruction, it is also a place for making friends, for taking attendance, and passing notes. It is a setting for social interaction, for trying out new roles, and for developing trust, confidence, and a sense of personal identity. Fred Steele (1973) has suggested that physical settings serve *six basic functions:* security and shelter, social contact, symbolic identification, task instrumentality, pleasure, and growth. These six functions provide a useful framework for thinking about the physical environment of the classroom. They make it clear that designing the physical setting is far more than decorating a few bulletin boards.

Security and Shelter

This is the most fundamental function of all built environments. Like homes, office buildings, and stores, classrooms should provide protection from bad weather, noise, extreme heat or cold, and noxious odors. Sadly, even this most basic function is sometimes not fulfilled, and teachers and students must battle highway noise, broken windows, and leaky roofs. In situations like this, it is difficult for any of the other functions to be met. Physical security is a *precondition* that must be satisfied, at least to some extent, before the environment can serve students' and teachers' other, higher-level needs.

Physical security is a particularly important issue in classes like science, home economics, woodworking, and art, where students come into contact with potentially dangerous supplies and equipment. It is essential that teachers of these subjects know about their state's safety guidelines regarding proper handling, storage, and labeling. Sandy goes even further; she tries to anticipate where accidents might occur and to arrange supplies in a way that minimizes risk. For example, when her students are doing a lab that involves two chemicals that are harmful together, she sets one chemical out and keeps one under her control. In this way, students have to ask her for it ("I'm ready for my nitric acid"), and she can double-check that they are following correct lab procedures. Similarly, Carmen pays special attention to safety. On the wall of her room is a large chart listing "Art Room Safety Tips" (see Figure 3-1), and Carmen is careful to store supplies according to state specifications. She also keeps informed about regulations regarding the kinds of materials she can order; pointed scissors and rubber cement, for example, are definitely out!

Often, school environments provide *physical* security, but fail to offer *psychological* security—the feeling that this is a safe, comfortable place to be. Psychological security is becoming increasingly crucial as more and more youngsters live in impoverished, unstable, and sometimes unsafe home environments. For them, in particular, schools must serve as a haven.

One way of enhancing psychological security is to make sure your classroom contains some "softness." Many classrooms are examples of "hard architecture" (Sommer, 1974). With their linoleum floors, concrete block walls, and formica surfaces, they are designed to be "strong and resistant to human imprint" (p. 2). But youngsters (and adults) tend to feel more secure and comfortable in environments that contain items that are soft or responsive to their touch. In elementary classrooms, we sometimes find small animals, pillows, plants, beanbag chairs, and area rugs, but these are generally absent in secondary classrooms. If you are lucky enough to have your own classroom, think about ways to incorporate elements of softness into the environment. Also keep in mind that warm colors, bright accents, and varying textures (e.g., burlap, wood, and felt) can also help to create an atmosphere of security and comfort.

Another way of increasing psychological security is to arrange classroom space so that students have as much freedom from interference as possible. In the crowded environment of the classroom, it is easy to become distracted. You need to make sure that students' desks are not too near areas of heavy traffic (e.g., the pencil sharpener, the bookcase, the front door). You can also enhance psychological security by allowing students to select their own seats. Often, students want to sit near their friends, but some individuals have definite spatial preferences as well (e.g., they prefer to sit in a corner, near the window, or in the front row). All four teachers

FIGURE 3-1
Art Room Safety Tips

> 1. After selecting a scissor, walk with blade part down.
> 2. Use crayons, pencils, and other art materials as they should be used—properly!
> 3. Be careful of paper cuts.
> 4. Keep away from window areas.
> 5. Art materials are to be used for art projects and not for eating.

allow students to sit where they wish—as long as they behave appropriately, of course—but Carmen tells her students to "sit next to a worker," and Fred advises his students to "sit next to someone smart."

If you have your own room, you might also set up a few cubicles where students who want more enclosure can work alone, or provide folding cardboard dividers that they can place on their desks. All of us need to "get away from it all" at times, but research suggests that opportunities for privacy are particularly important for youngsters who are distractible or have difficulty relating to their peers (Weinstein, 1982).

Social Contact

Interaction Among Students   As you plan the arrangement of students' desks, you need to think carefully about how much interaction among students you want there to be. Clusters of desks promote social contact since individuals are close together and can have direct eye contact with those across from them. In clusters, students can work together on activities, share materials, have small-group discussions, and help each other with assignments. This arrangement is most appropriate if you plan to emphasize cooperative learning activities. But it is unwise—even inhumane—to seat students in clusters and then forbid them to interact. If you do that, students receive two contradictory messages: the seating arrangement is communicating that it's okay to interact, while your verbal message is just the opposite!

As a beginning teacher, you may want to place desks in rows until you are confident about your ability as a classroom manager. Rows of desks reduce interaction among students and make it easier for them to concentrate on individual assignments (Axelrod, Hall, and Tams, 1979; Bennett and Blundell, 1983; Wheldall, Morris, Vaughan, and Ng, 1981). Rows also direct students' attention toward the teacher, so they are particularly appropriate for teacher-centered instruction. You might also consider putting desks in horizontal rows. (See Figure 3-2). This arrangement still orients students toward the teacher, but provides them with close "neighbors" on each side.

FIGURE 3-2
A Horizontal Arrangement

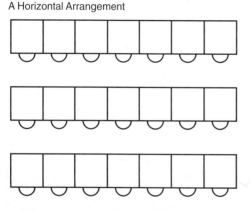

Figures 3-3 to 3-6 illustrate the way Carmen, Sandy, Fred, and Donnie have arranged their classrooms. As you can see, both Carmen's classroom and Sandy's classroom are divided into whole-group instructional areas and laboratory or work areas. Since Sandy's room is equipped with laboratory tables that can't be moved, her spatial options are limited. Nonetheless, she tries to find a way around the constraints; when she wants to use cooperative learning, for example, she has students sit on stools around the lab tables.

Fred has chosen to arrange his desks in rows; however, students often move into clusters for small-group work, a circle for whole-class discussions, or even a circle within a circle. In Donnie's classroom, the two-person tables are new this year. She has arranged them in groups of two, forming horizontal rows, but continues to experiment with other arrangements (see Figure 3-7). She even allows individual students to move their tables into configurations they feel are more comfortable. Interestingly, although Donnie's tables are attractive and facilitate small-group work, she actually prefers desks, which are easier to arrange in a horseshoe.

Interaction Between the Teacher and the Students   The way students are arranged can also affect the interaction between teacher and students. A number of studies have found that in classrooms where desks are arranged in rows, the teacher interacts mostly with students seated in the front and center of the classroom. Students in this "action zone" (Adams and Biddle, 1970) participate more in class discussions and initiate more questions and comments.

Educational researchers have tried to tease out the reasons for this phenomenon. Do students who are more interested and more eager to participate select seats in the front, or does a front seat somehow produce these attitudes and behaviors? This issue has not yet been fully resolved, but the weight of the evidence indicates that a front center seat does encourage participation, while a seat in the back makes it more difficult to participate and easier to "tune out." During a discussion with students in Sandy's class, it was clear that they were aware of this phenomenon. As one student said, "When there are only three rows, you know that the teacher can see you real easily. That helps keep you awake!"

Although research on the action zone has only examined row arrangements, it is easy to imagine that the same phenomenon would occur whenever teachers direct most of their comments and questions to the students who are closest to them. Keep this in mind and take steps to ensure that the action zone encompasses your whole class. Some suggestions are to: (1) move around the room whenever possible; (2) establish eye contact with students seated farther away from you; (3) direct comments to students seated in the rear and on the sides; and (4) periodically change students' seats (or allow students to select new seats) so that all students have an opportunity to be up front.

Symbolic Identification

This intimidating term simply refers to the information provided by a setting about the people who spend time there. The key questions are: What does this room tell us

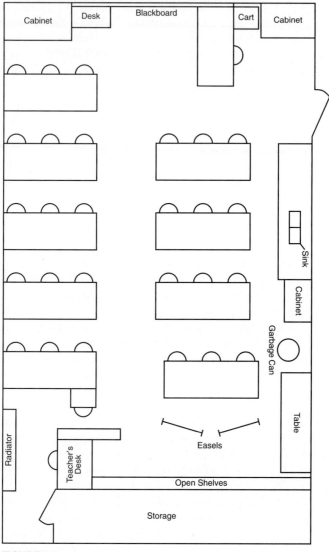

FIGURE 3-3
Carmen's Room Arrangement

about the students—their classroom activities, backgrounds, accomplishments, and preferences? And what does the classroom tell us about the teacher's goals, values, views of the content area, and beliefs about education?

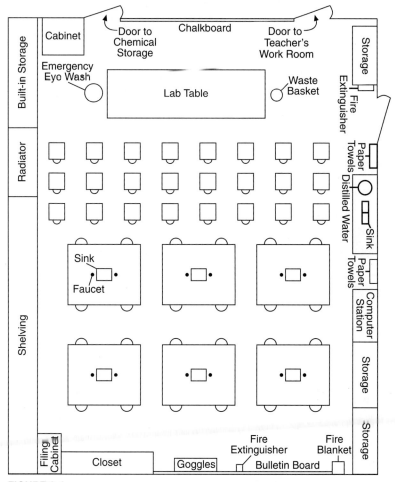

FIGURE 3-4
Sandy's Room Arrangement

    Too often, classrooms resemble motel rooms. They are pleasant but impersonal, revealing nothing about the people who use the space—or even about the subject that is studied there. This "anonymity" is exacerbated in junior and senior high school when six or seven classes may use the space during the day (and then an adult class uses it in the evening—as in Fred's situation!). Nonetheless, it's important to think about ways of personalizing your classroom setting. Before using wall space or bulletin boards, however, be sure to negotiate "property rights" with the other teachers who are using the room.
    All four teachers attempt to personalize their classrooms, within the constraints

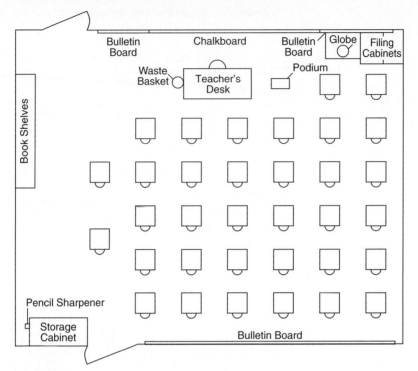

FIGURE 3-5
Fred's Room Arrangement

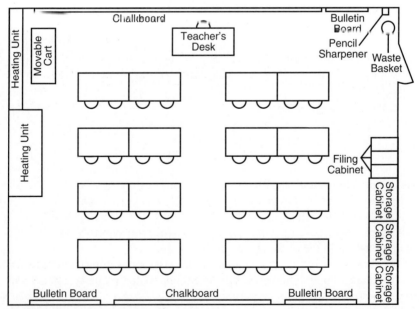

FIGURE 3-6
Donnie's Initial Room Arrangement

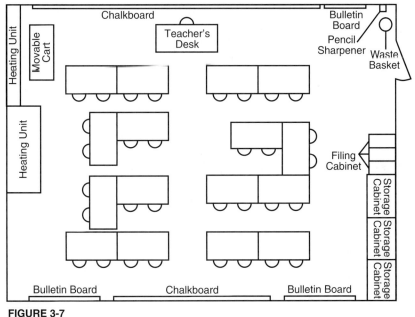

FIGURE 3-7
Donnie's Rearrangement

of their individual circumstances. Since Carmen has her own classroom, she is able to mount students' art work all over the walls; this practice clearly communicates the symbolic message that youngsters' work is special and valued. Donnie has the use of only two bulletin boards, but she tries to have them reflect her students' activities and accomplishments. She watches the newspaper and regularly posts stories about her current and former students. One bulletin board is usually devoted to a "Math Honor Roll" (students who have received A's or B's for the marking period). Sometimes, she even takes photographs of the students in her classes and displays them in honor of special events (e.g., when a student does particularly fine work, when a student has had outstanding attendance, etc.).

Sandy also posts photographs of her students conducting laboratory investigations, although never without explicit permission. Occasionally, Sandy also displays students' outstanding work, but she offers words of caution:

> High school students often don't want their work posted on the bulletin board, because they don't want to "stand out" from their peers in any way. If I do put work up, I make sure to put their names on the *back* of the paper.

Sandy's major exception to this rule of thumb is on "Mole Day" (October 23) when students decorate the bulletin boards and the walls with poetry, murals, riddles, and recipes—all celebrating the "mole," a basic chemical concept. Begun by a group of chemistry teachers (National Mole Day Foundation, Inc.), Mole Day is intended to promote enthusiasm for chemistry. The impressive exhibits of student work not only suggest that this goal is being achieved, they also serve the function of symbolic identification by providing information about what goes on in Room 221.

In addition to communicating information about students and the subject matter, you can also use the environment to communicate something about *yourself.* In Fred's class, for example, the bulletin board in the rear of the room displays some of his student-teacher's favorite quotations: "Study history—or be history," "The best way to make your dreams come true is to wake up" (Paul Valery), and "May the force be with you" (Obi Wan Kenobi). In Sandy's classroom, Millie Mole, a small stuffed animal, often perches on the front lab table, particularly during the Mole Day festivities. Not only does Millie stimulate interest in the study of moles, she allows students to see that Mrs. Krupinski is a "real" person.

Task Instrumentality

This function concerns the many ways the environment helps us to carry out the tasks we need to accomplish. Think about the tasks and activities that will be carried out in your classroom. Will students work alone at their desks on writing assignments? Will they work cooperatively on activities and projects? Will you instruct the whole class from the chalkboard? Will you work with small lab groups? Will students do research using encyclopedias and trade books?

For each of these tasks, you need to consider the physical design requirements. For example, if you plan to gather students around you for whole-group instruction before they work individually, you have to think carefully about where to locate the instructional area vis-a-vis the work area. Do you want it near a chalkboard or a bulletin board? In any case, its location should allow all students to see and hear your presentations without being cramped. You also want the work areas to be well organized so that individuals or small groups do not interfere with one another.

Whatever tasks will occur in your classroom, there are a few general guidelines you need to keep in mind:

Frequently used classroom materials should be accessible to students. Materials like calculators, scissors, dictionaries, textbooks, and rulers should be easy to reach. This will minimize the time spent preparing for activities and cleaning up. Decide which materials will be kept in locked or closed cabinets and which will be kept on open shelves.

Shelve and storage areas should be well organized so that it is clear where materials and equipment belong. It is useful to label shelves so that everyone knows where things go. This will make it easier to obtain materials and to return them. You should also have some sort of system for the distribution and collection of students' work (e.g., in–out boxes).

Pathways throughout the room should be designed carefully to avoid congestion and distraction. Paths to the pencil sharpener, supply closet, and wastebasket should be clearly visible and unobstructed. These high traffic areas should be as far from students' desks as possible.

The seating arrangement should allow students to have a clear view of instructional presentations. If possible, students should be able to see instructional presentations without turning their desks or chairs around.

The location of the teacher's desk depends on where you will be spending your time.   If you will be constantly moving about the room, your desk can be out of the way, in a corner perhaps. If you will use your desk as a conference area or as a work station, then it needs to be more centrally located. But be careful: With a central location, you may be tempted to remain at your desk for long periods of time, and this cuts down your ability to monitor students' work and behavior. Moreover, if your desk is in a central location, holding student conferences there may be distracting to other students.

Decide where to store your own personal teaching aids and supplies.   If you move from room to room, arrange to have a desk drawer or a shelf in a storage cabinet for your own personal use. At the very least, you will probably need storage for pens and markers, paper clips, a stapler, rubber bands, chalk, tape, tissues, attendance forms, and file folders. An alternative strategy is to carry your personal supplies with you, perhaps in one of the plastic carrying bins often used for home cleaning supplies. Some teachers even use a movable cart.

Pleasure

The important question here is whether students and teachers find the classroom attractive and pleasing. To the already overworked teacher preoccupied with covering the curriculum, raising test scores, and maintaining order, aesthetic concerns may seem irrelevant and insignificant (at least until parent conferences draw near). Yet given the amount of time you and your students spend in your classroom, it is worth thinking about ways to create a pleasing environment. It is sad when students associate education with sterile, uncomfortable, unpleasant places.

The classic study on environmental attractiveness was conducted by Maslow and Mintz (1956). These experimenters compared interviews that took place in an "ugly" room with those that took place in a "beautiful" room. Neither the interviewer nor the subject knew that the real purpose of the study was to assess the impact of the environment on their behavior. Maslow and Mintz found that interviewers assigned to the ugly room complained of headaches, fatigue, and discomfort. Furthermore, the interviews *finished more quickly* in the ugly room. Apparently, people in the ugly room tried to finish their task as quickly as possible in order to escape from the unpleasant setting.

More recent studies have also demonstrated that aesthetically pleasing environments can influence behavior. For example, two college-level studies have indicated that attractive classrooms have a positive effect on attendance and feelings of group cohesion (Horowitz and Otto, 1973) and on participation in class discussions (Sommer and Olson, 1980). The classrooms in these studies had specially designed seating, soft lighting, plants, warm colors, and carpeting, hardly the kinds of aesthetic improvements that can be implemented by most secondary school teachers. Nonetheless, it is worth thinking about the kinds of environmental modifications that *are* possible—for example, plants, mobiles, banners, bulletin board displays. Donnie has furnished her classroom with plants all along the windowsill, and her bulletin boards are covered with brightly colored paper and a contrasting border. In Carmen's room, a timeline of art history and prints of famous paintings are posted along the walls (along with students' own work, of course).

Growth

Steele's last function is particularly relevant to classrooms, since they are settings specifically intended to promote students' development. This function is also the most difficult to pin down, however. While it's easy to see that environments should be functional and attractive, it's less obvious that they can be designed to foster growth. Furthermore, growth can refer to any number of areas—learning the subject matter; increasing your self-confidence; learning to cooperate. For simplicity, we will restrict our discussion to ways in which the environment can promote students' *intellectual development.*

Psychologists have found that the opportunity to explore rich, stimulating environments is related to cognitive growth. Ideally, your classroom setting should support your instructional program by inviting students to observe, think, investigate, test, and discover. This means that in addition to the standard texts and workbooks, your classroom should contain a wide variety of materials appropriate to the content area. Donnie's math class, for example, contains calculators, rulers, protractors, and compasses; Fred's history classes have access to globes, maps, and other resource materials. In Sandy's chemistry room, students work with balances, bunsen burners, test tubes, and centrifuges. And Carmen's classroom is filled with an assortment of art books, *National Geographic* magazines, calendars, print portfolios, and postcards from art museums, in addition to a vast array of art materials.

A relatively new addition to the classroom environment is the microcomputer. Computers can provide opportunities for students to complete practice exercises, to engage in problem solving and exploration through games and simulations, and to experience the writing process—to compose, edit, revise, and publish (Weinstein, 1991). Unfortunately, in many schools there is only one computer per classroom. This means that teachers have to think carefully about the location of this scarce but precious resource. If students are going to work at the computer in pairs or in small groups, place it in an area where clusters of students can gather around without creating traffic congestion and distraction. Also keep in mind that computer use is often "a social event" (Genishi, 1988); both the novelty of the computer and the upright position of the screen invite comment and inquiry from students walking past or sitting nearby. How you feel about this spontaneous interaction should be a factor in your decision about the computer's location.

THE TEACHER AS ENVIRONMENTAL DESIGNER

Steele's six functions give you a way of thinking about the environment, but they don't provide you with an architectural blueprint. If you think about the various roles that settings play, you will realize that the functions not only overlap, they may actually conflict. Seating that is good for social contact may be bad for testing, as Donnie can attest: She often prepares two to three versions of a test, since students are sitting so close to one another! Similarly, room arrangements that provide students with privacy may be poor for monitoring and maintaining order. As you think about your room and your own priorities, you will have to determine which functions will take precedence over others. You also need to think about what is possible for you to achieve if you are a "nomad."

This section of the chapter describes a process you can follow as you design your classroom.

Think About the Activities the Room Will Accommodate

The first step in designing a classroom is to decide on the activities your room is to accommodate. For example, if you are teaching a lab science, you may need to accommodate whole-group instruction, "hands-on" lab work, media presentations, and testing. If you are teaching history, you may want to have small-group research projects, debates, simulations, and role plays in addition to the standard lecture, recitation, discussion, and seatwork formats. List these activities in a column and, next to each activity, note if it poses any special physical requirements (e.g., computers need to be near electrical outlets and away from chalkboards).

Draw a Floor Plan

Before actually moving any furniture, draw a number of different floor plans and select the one that seems most workable. (Figure 3-8 depicts symbols that may be useful.)

In order to decide where furniture and equipment should be placed, consider the special requirements noted on your list of activities, as well as the room's "givens"—the location of the outlets, the chalkboard, the windows, and the built-in shelves, cabinets, or lab tables. Also keep in mind our discussion of psychological security, social contact, and task instrumentality.

It may be helpful to begin by deciding where you will conduct whole-group in-

FIGURE 3-8
Drawing a Floor Plan: Some Useful Symbols

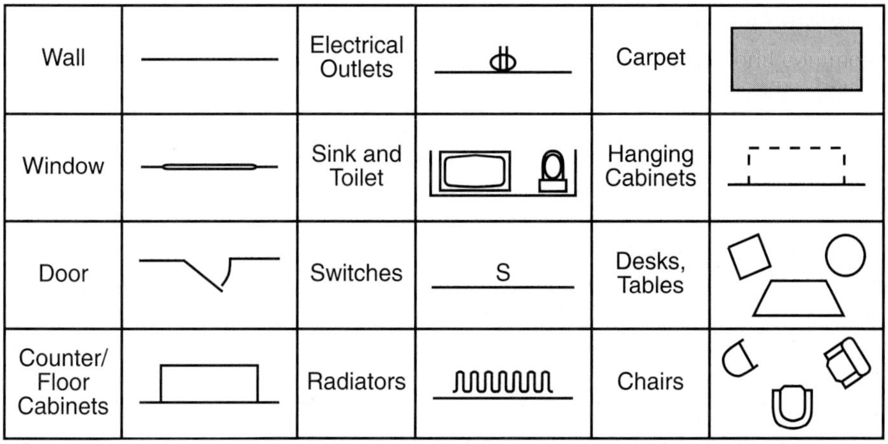

struction (if at all) and the way students will be seated during this time. Think about where the teacher's desk should be; if frequently used materials are stored on shelves or in cabinets that are accessible to you and your students; and if pathways are clear. Remember, there is no one right way to design your classroom. The important thing is to make sure that your spatial arrangement supports the teaching strategies you will use and the kinds of behaviors you want from your students.

Involve Students in Environmental Decisions

Although a great deal can be done before the start of school, it is a good idea to leave some things undone, so your students can be involved in the design process. Although their suggestions are occasionally beyond the means of the normal public school—planetarium-type ceilings and rope ladders (Hill, 1968)—it is likely that many of their ideas will be reasonable. Listen to Arthur, a student at an inner-city junior high, speaking of his ideal classroom (Coles, 1969):

> I'd like comfortable chairs, like ones that had cushions so your back doesn't hurt and your bottom either. I'd like us sitting around—you know, looking at each other, not in a line, not lined up. I'd like a sink, where you could get some water to drink, and you wouldn't have to ask the teacher to go down the hall. . . . There'd be a table and it would be a lot nicer homeroom than it is now. . . . (pp. 49–51)

If you teach four or five classes in one room, it is obviously impossible to involve everyone in all environmental decisions; however, you might solicit ideas for room design from your various classes, and then select those that seem most feasible. You might also rotate responsibility for some aspect of the environment among your classes (e.g., each class could have an opportunity to design a bulletin board display). Inviting students to participate in environmental decision-making not only helps to create more responsive physical arrangements, it also prepares students for their roles as active, involved citizens who possess environmental competence.

Try the New Arrangement, Evaluate, and Redesign

Use Steele's six functions of the environment as a framework for evaluating your classroom design. For example, does the desk arrangement facilitate or hinder social contact among students? Do displays communicate information about the subject matter and students' work? Are frequently used materials accessible to students? Does the room provide pleasure? Does it contain materials that invite students to extend their interests and abilities?

As you evaluate the effectiveness of the classroom setting, stay alert for behavioral problems that might be caused by the physical arrangement. For example, if a student suddenly becomes inattentive when his or her desk is moved next to the pencil sharpener, it is likely that an environmental change is in order, rather than detention. If the classroom floor is constantly littered despite your appeals for neatness, the underlying problem may be an inadequate number of wastebaskets.

Improving your room does not have to be tedious and time-consuming. In fact, small modifications can bring about gratifying changes in behavior. This was demonstrated by Krantz and Risley (1972), who found that when kindergartners crowded around a teacher who was reading a story, they were inattentive and disruptive. Just spreading the children out in a semi-circle markedly improved their attentiveness. In fact, this simple environmental modification was as successful as a complicated system of rewards and privileges that the experimenters had devised!

DESIGNING AN ART ROOM

This chapter has tried to provide you with a way of thinking about classroom environments and an outline of the design process. Now we'll take a closer look at Carmen's art room (see Figure 3-3). Carmen's reflections illustrate the way one teacher thinks through the process of designing the classroom environment. Her comments also point out the frustrations teachers can feel when they have to share their rooms.

> When I first came to Roosevelt, the school was a fifth- to sixth-grade middle school, and the art room was arranged very differently. I wasn't pleased with the way it was arranged, but I shared the room with another art teacher and she had seniority—so it stayed that way! The two teachers' desks were in the front of the room by the chalkboard, and they interfered with kids entering and leaving the room. Also, the students' work tables were arranged in groups of two. With six students sitting together, facing one another, there was just too much socializing going on. I figured it would be better to separate the tables, but I had to go along with the teacher who had designed the room.

A view of Carmen's art room.

Eventually, the other art teacher left, Roosevelt became a K-8 building, and I was able to rearrange the furniture. It was a real challenge: the room now had to accommodate children from first grade to eighth grade! I had to think about where the instructional areas would be, where the work areas would be, and where I would keep supplies. I decided to create two different instructional areas, one for kids in grades one through six and one for the seventh and eighth grades. I put the teacher's desk all the way in the back—I never sit at it (except to eat breakfast) and it's only in the way—and I created an instructional area for the older kids in the "front" of the room by the chalkboard. They bring their chairs and gather around me so that I can explain and demonstrate the art projects they'll be doing, and we can talk more informally. It's nice having the chalkboard here, because I can post my timeline on it and keep up all the displays, reproductions, pamphlets, and books that we use for the art history curriculum. Sometimes I'll also sit here during the class period and work with students who need special help. It's great when the younger kids come in and see everything and ask about it; I tell them, "Just wait, you'll get to learn about this when you're in seventh and eighth grade." The instructional area for the younger kids is in the "back" of the room. Since I don't have a chalkboard there (which I'd love), I put two easels side-by-side (I robbed everyone who didn't want their easels), and I use them to demonstrate art projects. They're easy to remove to make more space when we need it.

I separated the groups of tables, and put the tables in rows. This way there are three students at a table, and I find that works well. There's plenty of opportunity to talk and work together, but it doesn't get as wild as it did with six. For a while I tried having the tables facing the windows, but it was just too bunched up that way, so I turned them around to face the "back" of the room. Staring at that ugly yellow wall wasn't very nice, so I got some wallpaper for it; it looks a lot nicer now. I also mount displays on cardboard and prop them up on the windows and around the room; I'm "cardboard crazy"—I use it to display kids' work, reproductions, lettering styles, art careers, safety rules. I only have one bulletin board, which is a real constraint in an art room! I use a clothesline strung across the side of the room for extra display space.

I've tried to make the room "homey." I have photographs of my husband and my cat—he's blind in one eye and the kids love to hear about him—and also photos of the kids that they have given me. There are also little toys, a stuffed bear, and gifts from Puerto Rico and Santo Domingo that kids have brought back. The kids like to look at everything and talk about their pets and their toys.

One problem is that there's never enough storage for materials or unfinished proj-ects. I have to use the hallway for drying kids' paintings. I have lots of open boxes around with all kinds of materials—scraps of fabric, and paper, and yarn, etc. It looks messy, but that's what happens in an art room. Actually, I like to have open boxes so that the kids can see the materials and get ideas. But I'd love to have a few more cabinets with doors; I only have two—one for clay and the other for storage of ongoing projects. It would be nice to have separate storage shelves for each class; I could label them with the name of the class, and the kids would know exactly where to go to get their projects when they came in. This way I have to get out the projects and call the students to come and get them.

I've tried my best with the room. I've tried to create a space that meets the needs of all the different grade levels; a room that's colorful and inviting; a room that encourages kids to work together but not so that it gets out of hand; a room that's organized and everybody knows where things are, but that's not super-neat. It works pretty well, and the kids seem to like it. When it stops working, then I'll see what changes have to be made.

SOME THOUGHTS ON HAVING TO SHARE ROOMS

When we sat down as a group to discuss the role of the physical environment in classroom management, it became clear that Donnie, Sandy, and Fred—the three teachers who do not have their own room—feel frustrated by the limited control they have over the physical setting. Sandy emphasized the difficulties that are created when access to the classroom is limited:

> When *I'm* not in my room, someone *else* is; that means that I can't get into the room during the school day to prepare labs—and we do six labs a week. I have to prepare labs before or after school, and that's also when I carry out the other responsibilities associated with being a chemistry teacher, like organizing materials, disposing of old chemicals, making sure all the equipment is in working order, and of course, working with kids who are having trouble. Although I'd like to pay attention to creating a more attractive environment, that's got to be a lower priority.

The teachers also expressed irritation over other common problems—for example, inadequate storage space, inappropriate furniture, and insufficient numbers of desks. They traded war stories about materials that disappear (Fred's gone through three staplers this year) and the lack of personal work areas (it took Sandy three years to get a desk where she could sit during free periods to plan lessons and grade papers; when she finally got one, it was in a storage closet!). They also talked about the problems that arise when the other teachers sharing the room are inconsiderate "roommates" who fail to clean up adequately. Since this was a topic that clearly raised their blood pressure, it seems important to share a few of the lessons they have learned.

Being a Good Roommate

During our discussion, Donnie shared an anecdote that illustrates the kinds of problems that can occur when teachers have to share rooms.

> I share the room with a long-term substitute who's supposed to monitor a study hall in my room during second period. He thinks he doesn't really have to watch the kids, so they sit there and write all over the desks. Finally, I couldn't stand it any more; I took a sponge and cleanser and cleaned all the tables before school began. I taught first period and then turned the room over to him. When I came back third period, the desks were covered with writing again! I was furious!

Given the other teacher's status as a long-term substitute coming in the middle of the year, Donnie's situation was particularly difficult. In general, however, it is helpful to work out an explicit agreement at the very beginning of the year about how the room is to be left. You and your roommate might agree that desks are to be returned to their standard places, boards are to be erased, the floor is to be cleaned, no food is to be in the room, and (of course) no writing is to be on the desks. You also need to agree on a procedure to follow if the agreement is violated, so you don't have to suffer in silence. As Sandy tells us, "It's not enough to have an agreement; you have to follow through. My roommate and I have agreed to hold the kids accountable for the condition of the room. If I come in and find a problem, I tell her about it, and she deals with it the next time she sees those students."

FINAL COMMENTS

Despite the constraints imposed by sharing rooms, all four teachers agreed on the importance of thinking about the physical environment. As Fred commented:

> Some of the ideas—like the action zone, for example—are important for teachers to know about even if they move from room to room and have little control over the classroom. On the other hand, some of the ideas—like psychological security—are hard to put into practice if you're a nomad like I was. But that's okay; thinking about these issues is important anyway. We need to say to new teachers, "Listen, folks, you're going to have to be clever in dealing with this. If you can't add soft, warm fuzzies to your room, then you're going to have to compensate. You're going to have to find other ways of providing psychological security, like making sure your kids feel safe in your classroom because they know they're not going to get hammered."

As Fred's comments suggest, it is not easy for secondary teachers to create their ideal classroom settings. Nonetheless, I hope this chapter has given you a greater awareness of the physical environment and its impact, along with a realistic sense of how you can use the environment to meet your goals.

SUMMARY

This chapter discussed how the physical environment of the classroom influences the way teachers and students feel, think, and behave. It stressed the need for teachers to be aware of the *direct* and *indirect* effects of the physical environment. This awareness is the first step to developing *environmental competence*. The chapter suggested ways to design a classroom that will support your instructional goals, using *Steele's six functions of the environment* as a framework for discussion.

Security and Shelter

• Be aware of and implement safety guidelines for dangerous supplies and equipment.
  • Add elements of softness.
  • Arrange space for freedom from interference.
• Create opportunities for privacy by adding cubicles or folding cardboard dividers.

Social Contact

- Consider how much interaction among students you want there to be.
- Think about whether you are making contact with *all* of your students; avoid a small action zone.

Symbolic Identification

- Personalize your classroom space so that it communicates information about you, your students, and your subject matter.

Task Instrumentality

- Make sure frequently used materials are accessible to students.
- Make it clear where things belong.
- Plan pathways to avoid congestion and distraction.
- Arrange seats for a clear view of presentations.
- Locate your desk in an appropriate place (off to the side helps to ensure that you will circulate).

Pleasure

- Create an aesthetically pleasing environment through the use of plants, color, bulletin board displays.

Growth

- Stock your room with a variety of materials relevant to your content area.
- Create relevant bulletin board displays.

Careful planning of the physical environment is an integral part of good classroom management. When you begin to design your room, think about the activities it will accommodate; if possible, invite your students to participate in the design process. Try your arrangement, evaluate it, and redesign as necessary. If you are sharing your room with other teachers, be sure to work out an explicit agreement about how the room is to be left at the end of the period.

ACTIVITIES

The following activities are intended to help you think about classroom physical environments. The activities are appropriate for inservice teachers with their own classrooms, as well as preservice teachers engaged in pre-student-teaching field experiences or student teaching.

1. Visit a junior- or senior-high classroom, draw a classroom map, and evaluate the physical layout in terms of Steele's six functions of the environment. The following questions, adapted from Bruther (1991), may be helpful.

Security and Shelter

- Does the classroom feel like a safe, comfortable place to be?
- Does it contain furnishings and materials that are soft or inviting?
- Do students have freedom from intrusion and interference?
- Is there any opportunity for privacy?

Social Contact

- Does the desk arrangement facilitate or hinder social contact among students? Is this compatible with the explicit objectives?

Symbolic Identification

- Are there displays of students' work in the room?
- Does the room communicate information about the teacher, students, or the subject matter? What is communicated?

Task Instrumentality

- Are frequently used classroom materials accessible to students?
- Are shelves and cabinets well organized so that it is clear where materials/equipment are stored?
- Are pathways clearly visible?
- Does the seating arrangement allow students to see instructional presentations without difficulty?

Pleasure

- Are there any amenities present (e.g., plants, bulletin board displays, etc.)?
- Is the classroom colorful and brightly decorated?

Growth

- Does the classroom contain a wide variety of materials relevant to the subject matter?
- Does the classroom contain any computers?

2. Imagine for a moment that you have a classroom of your own: You don't have to change rooms, and you don't even have to share it with any other teacher! Furthermore, you have an unlimited budget to purchase furniture, equipment, and supplies. Using the symbols shown in Figure 3-8, draw a floor plan of this ideal classroom. Be prepared to explain why you are designing the room this way.

3. Consider the following seating arrangements. For each one, think about the types of instructional strategies for which it is appropriate or inappropriate. The first one has been done as an example.

Arrangement	Instructional strategies for which this arrangement is appropriate	Instructional strategies for which this arrangement is inappropriate
Rows	teacher or student presentations; audio visual presentations; testing	student-centered discussions; small-group work
Horizontal Rows		
Horseshoe		
Small clusters		
Circle		

REFERENCES

Adams, R. S., and Biddle, B. J. (1970). *Realities of teaching: Explorations with video tape.* New York: Holt, Rinehart, & Winston.

Axelrod, D., Hall, R. V., and Tams, A. (1979). Comparison of two common classroom seating arrangements. *Academic Therapy, 15,* 29–36.

Bennett, N., and Blundell, D. (1983). Quantity and quality of work in rows and classroom groups. *Educational Psychology, 3,* 93–105.

Bruther, M. (1991). Factors influencing teachers' decisions about their classroom physical environments. Unpublished doctoral dissertation, Rutgers Graduate School of Education

Coles, R. (1969). Those places they call schools. *Harvard Educational Review: Architecture and Education, 39*(4), 46–57.

Genishi, C. (1988). Kindergartners and computers: A case study of six children. *Elementary School Journal, 89,* 185–201.

Hill, W. (1968). Using students as school design consultants. *School Management,* November, 81–86.

Horowitz, P., and Otto, D. (1973). *The teaching effectiveness of an alternate teaching facility.* Alberta, Canada: University of Alberta (ERIC Document Reproduction Service No. ED 083 242).

Krantz, P. J., and Risley, T. R. (September, 1972). The organization of group care environments: Behavioral ecology in the classroom. Paper presented at the Annual Convention of the American Psychological Association, Honolulu. ERIC No. ED 078 915.

Maslow, A. H., and Mintz, N. L. (1956). The effects of esthetic surroundings: I. *Journal of Psychology, 41,* 247–254.

Proshansky, E., and Wolfe, M. (1974). The physical setting and open education. *School Review, 82,* 557–574.

Sommer, R. (1974). *Tight spaces: Hard architecture and how to humanize it.* Englewood Cliffs, NJ: Prentice-Hall.

Sommer, R., and Olsen, H. (1980). The soft classroom. *Environment & Behavior, 12*(1), 3–16.

Steele, F. I. (1973). *Physical settings and organization development.* Reading, MA: Addison-Wesley.

Weinstein, C. S. (1982). Privacy-seeking behavior in an elementary classroom. *Journal of Environmental Psychology, 2,* 23–35.

Weinstein, C. S. (1991). The classroom as a social context for learning. *Annual Review, 42,* 493–525.

Wheldall, K., Morris, M., Vaughn, P., and Ng, Y. (1981). Rows versus tables: An example of the use of behavioral ecology in two classes of eleven-year-old children. *Educational Psychology, 1*(2), 171–184.

FOR FURTHER READING

Hannah, G. G. (1982). *Classroom spaces and places. 65 projects for improving your classroom.* Belmont, CA: Fearon Teacher Aids, a division of Pitman Learning, Inc.

Loughlin, C., and Suina, J. H. (1982). *The learning environment: An instructional strategy.* New York: Teachers College Press.

Weinstein, C. S. (1981). Classroom design as an external condition for learning. *Educational Technology, 21*(8), 12–19.

Chapter Four

Developing and Teaching Rules and Routines

Secondary teachers sometimes contend that their students know how to behave, since they've been in school for many years. The argument goes like this:

> My kids aren't babies. By junior- or senior-high school, students know the importance of coming to class on time, doing homework, respecting other people's property, and raising their hands to make a comment. Besides, there's so much material to cover, I can't waste time teaching rules to kids who should already know all this stuff.

This reasoning has a certain appeal, particularly for teachers who are enthusiastic about their content area and eager to get started. Yet it's important to recognize that although your students have general notions about appropriate school behavior, they do not know *your specific expectations*. Furthermore, your students probably see five different teachers each day, and specific expectations vary from class to class. A student's first-period teacher may not mind if everyone is milling around the room when the bell rings, while the second-period teacher insists that students be in their seats. In third period, the teacher wants students to put homework in the upper right-hand corner of their desks, but the fourth-period teacher has students drop homework in a basket at the front of the room.

What will *you* expect with regard to basic classroom routines like these—and how will your students know what to do if you don't tell them? It is *unfair* to keep students guessing about the behaviors you expect. Not knowing the norms for appropriate behavior causes insecurity and misunderstandings, even among "school smart" adolescents. In contrast, *clearly defined classroom rules and routines help to create an environment that is predictable and comprehensible.*

Rules and routines have another major benefit. As Chapter One emphasized, classes are crowded, public, unpredictable places in which individuals engage in a variety of activities, often within the time constraints of a 42- or 45-minute period. *Clear rules and routines minimize confusion and prevent the loss of instructional time.* They enable you to carry out "housekeeping" tasks, like taking attendance, distributing materials, and cleaning up, smoothly and efficiently—almost automatically. They free you and your students to concentrate on the real tasks of teaching and learning.

This chapter describes research that demonstrates the importance of rules and routines. We then consider some principles to guide you in establishing rules for your own classrooms. We'll also learn how Donnie, Carmen, Sandy, and Fred introduce rules and routines to their students and what they think about this central task of classroom management.

RESEARCH ON EFFECTIVE CLASSROOM MANAGEMENT

Prior to 1970, teacher-preparation programs could offer only limited advice about classroom management to beginning teachers. Teacher educators shared useful "tricks of the trade" (e.g., flick the lights on and off for quiet), stressed the importance of firmness and consistency, and warned prospective teachers not to smile until Christmas. But research identifying the behaviors of effective managers was unavailable, and it was simply not clear why some classrooms function smoothly and others are chaotic.

That situation began to change in 1970, with the publication of Jacob Kounin's study of orderly and disorderly classrooms. You may recall from Chapter One that Kounin (1970) set out to compare teachers' methods of responding to misbehavior. To his surprise, he found that the reactions of good classroom managers were not substantially different from the reactions of poor classroom managers. What *did* differ were the strategies that teachers used to *prevent* misbehavior. Effective classroom managers constantly monitored students' behavior. They displayed what Kounin called "withitness": they were aware of what was happening in all parts of the room, and they communicated this awareness to students. They also exhibited an ability to "overlap"—to do more than one thing at a time—certainly a desirable skill in a setting where so many events occur simultaneously! Furthermore, effective managers kept lessons moving at a brisk pace, so that there was little opportunity for students to become inattentive and disruptive.

Kounin's work led researchers to wonder how effective managers began the school year. In the late 1970s, a series of studies was launched at the Research and Development Center for Teacher Education, located at the University of Texas at Austin. One project (Evertson and Emmer, 1982) involved observations of 26 mathematics teachers and 25 English teachers in junior high schools in an urban district. Each teacher was observed teaching two different classes. During the first three weeks of school, researchers observed extensively in each classroom and kept detailed records of what occurred. During the rest of the academic year, each teacher was observed once every three to four weeks (in both of his or her classrooms). On the basis of these latter data, the researchers identified six more- and six less-effective managers in mathematics and seven more- and seven less-effective managers in English. They then went back to the information collected at the beginning of the year and compared what the teachers had done during the first three weeks of school. Striking differences were apparent—even on the very first day of school!

Among the major differences documented by Evertson and Emmer was the way teachers handled rules and procedures. Although all of the teachers had expectations for behavior, and they all took time to present or discuss these with students, the more-effective managers were more successful in *teaching* the rules and procedures. For example, the more-effective teachers were more likely to distribute handouts stating their behavioral expectations or to have students copy them into their notebooks. They were also clearer and much more explicit about behaviors that are likely to cause problems—namely, those that occur frequently and that may vary from teacher to teacher (e.g., call-outs, movement through the room, student-student interaction, hand-raising). Interestingly, for behaviors that occur infrequently per period (e.g., tardiness, bringing materials) and are fairly straightforward, no differences between the two groups of teachers were apparent.

Subsequent research has confirmed the importance of explicitly teaching students your expectations for their behavior. Douglas Brooks (1985), for example, videotaped two experienced and two inexperienced junior high school teachers (two in math and two in science) as they met with their classes for the very first time. The contrast between the experienced and inexperienced math teachers is especially vivid.

The experienced math teacher, perceived by students and administrators as exceptionally clear and organized, began her presentation of behavioral expectations by distributing a copy of class rules that students were to keep in their folders. She first discussed schoolwide policies, but spent most of the time on classroom standards—how to enter the class, how to use materials, how to interact with the teacher and other students, what to do in the case of an emergency, and how to exit the class. In general, *she stated a rule, explained the rationale, provided an example* of an appropriate behavior, and concluded with the *consequences for noncompliance*. Interestingly, she rarely smiled during her presentation of rules and procedures (although she smiled a lot during her later introduction to the course). She spoke in a businesslike tone and continually scanned the classroom; no instances of disruption were observed during her presentation.

In contrast, the inexperienced math teacher was rambling and disorganized. Students were not given a copy of the rules, nor were they encouraged to write them down. Even as the teacher presented rules and procedures about talking in class, she tolerated students' talking to each other. In addition, she repeatedly smiled during her presentation of the consequences for misbehavior, a nonverbal behavior that seems incompatible with a discussion of detention and calling home (and might have sent the message that she was not serious about imposing these consequences).

As the following excerpt from the transcript illustrates, the inexperienced math teacher provided few examples or rationales. In fact, she *never* used the experienced teacher's sequence of rule–rationale–example–consequence. Although many of the rules resembled those of the experienced math teacher, she presented rules she could not enforce (wanting students to respect all teachers), and she omitted discussion of some fundamental rules (listening while the teacher is talking). Furthermore, the rules did not appear to be prioritized or organized in any way:

OK. I'm just going to tell you a few of my classroom rules. And, ah, so that you'll know these. The first thing I want you to know is I want, that I expect every student will obey any school policies that there are. . . . OK, all the school policies, if you haven't gotten it as of yet you will get it, this yellow sheet. It's got all the school policies on it. It explains everything to you. These apply in school and around school. . . . OK, another thing when you come in that door I expect you to walk through that door being prepared to start class. When you come in don't plan on going back out to get something out of your locker. . . . OK, when you come in you'll have a pencil, your paper, your folders, and a book. . . . OK, if you're fast at working you might bring something extra to do after you finish your work so that you can have something to keep you busy because I don't want any talking. . . . OK, and all times we'll use pencil . . . I don't want any ink on your homework papers or test papers. It should all be done in pencil. . . . OK, we'll also have a folder that we'll do and I'll tell you about it later. . . . OK, another thing is I expect you to be respectful. First, I want you to respect yourself, at all times respect yourself and then your classmates and also the teachers. Any teacher in the building should be respected by you and each student and if you see one anything they say goes. . . . (pp. 67–68)

Reading this transcript, it's impossible not to feel sympathy for this inexperienced teacher. After all, most beginning teachers, particularly those being observed, are nervous on the first day of school. But it is precisely *because* of this nervousness that you must (1) think about your expectations ahead of time and (2) plan the way you will present them to your students. Let's look at each of these steps separately.

DEFINING YOUR EXPECTATIONS FOR BEHAVIOR

Before the first student enters your classroom, you need to think about your expectations for behavior. Not only do you need to decide on *rules for students' general conduct,* you also need to identify the *behavioral routines or procedures* you and your students will follow in specific situations. For example, when students arrive at your classroom door, are they to go immediately to their seats, or may they congregate in small groups and socialize until you tell them to be seated? May they go to the storage cabinet and get the projects they've been working on, or should they wait for you to give out the projects one by one? When students need paper or rulers or protractors for an assignment, will they get them by themselves, will you have students distribute the materials, or will you distribute them yourself? If students have to leave your classroom to go to their lockers or to the library, must they have a pass? When students are working at their seats, may they help one another or must they work individually?

Because these seem like such trivial, mundane issues, it is easy to underestimate their contribution to classroom order. But lessons can fall apart while you try to decide how to distribute paper, and students feel anxious if they're unsure whether answering a classmate's question during an in-class assignment is helping or cheating. As we will see, rules and routines may vary from class to class, but no class can function smoothly without them.

Planning Rules for General Conduct

Rules describe the behaviors that are necessary if your classroom is to be a good place in which to live and work—for example, "bring all needed materials to class," "follow directions," "respect others," and "be in your seat and ready to work when the bell rings." In Carmen's class, the norms for general conduct are posted on a large wall chart entitled "Art Room Rules." Here are some of her basic rules:

- Pay attention to directions.
- Be polite!
- Work at your seat.
- Share supplies.
- Talk quietly.
- Clean up when told.
- Work hard, think, and have fun!

As you reflect on these rules for your own classroom, there are four principles to keep in mind. (These are summarized in Table 4-1.) First, *rules should be reasonable and necessary.* Think about the age and characteristics of the students you are teaching, and ask yourself: What rules are appropriate for them? For example, it would be unreasonable for Carmen to expect her students to carry out their art projects without talking to one another. Given adolescents' irresistible need to socialize, creating such a rule would only result in resentment, frustration, and subterfuge. It's far more sensible to establish a rule like "talk quietly," which specifies *how* the talk is to occur.

Also ask yourself whether each rule is necessary. Is there a compelling reason for it? Will it make the classroom a more pleasant place to be? Will it increase students' opportunity to learn? Can you explain the rationale to students, and will they accept it? Sandy stresses the importance of this principle when she comments:

> Rules have to have reasons. For example, one of my rules is about coming to class on time. Students know they'll get detention if they're late—even once. At the beginning of

TABLE 4-1
FOUR PRINCIPLES FOR PLANNING CLASSROOM RULES

Principle	Questions to Think About
1. Rules should be reasonable and necessary.	What rules are appropriate for this grade level? Is there a good reason for this rule?
2. Rules need to be clear and understandable.	Is the rule too abstract for students to comprehend? To what extent do I want my students to participate in the decision-making process?
3. Rules should be consistent with instructional goals and with what we know about how people learn.	Will this rule facilitate or hinder my students' learning?
4. Classroom rules need to be consistent with school rules.	What are the school rules? Are particular behaviors required in the halls, during assemblies, in the cafeteria, etc.?

the year, students think I'm unnecessarily strict about that. But I'm not trying to be mean. I want students there on time because I always start class when the bell rings, and if they're not there, they miss important material. After awhile, they begin to realize there's a real reason for the rule. I hear them say to their friends, "I have to get to class on time because they'll have started."

Contrast this situation with that of a biology teacher I know who insists that students take notes in black pen only. Although the teacher is able to enforce the rule, she's unable to explain it with any conviction, and her classes perceive it as arbitrary and ridiculous. Similarly, an English teacher insists that students use cursive writing during spelling and vocabulary tests. Even to her student teacher, this seems like an unreasonable rule:

> Being a printer myself whose cursive has not improved beyond the third grade, I am not a fan of mandated cursive writing. In the real world whenever I have filled out a form, I have been required to print so the words are legible to the reader. The only time cursive is required is when I sign my name and for vocabulary tests in my cooperating teacher's class. I can see why students are sometimes annoyed with our rules.

It's easier to demonstrate that a rule is reasonable and necessary if it applies to *you* as well as your students. Although some rules may be intended only for students (e.g., raise your hand to speak), others are relevant for everyone (e.g., show respect for other people and their property). Sandy tells us, "If a rule is important for kids, it's important for you too. For example, I make sure that I get to class on time, and if I'm late, I owe them an explanation." Fred echoes this idea when he observes, "I try to make it clear to my students that we *all* have to follow the rules. After all, rules are not about power; they're what make civilized life possible."

Second, *rules need to be clear and understandable.* Because rules are often stated in very general terms ("be polite"), they may be too abstract to have much meaning. When planning your rules, you need to think of specific examples to discuss with students. For example, one of Donnie's basic ground rules is "Be prepared." She makes sure that "preparation" is spelled out in precise, concrete behaviors: "Class preparation consists of having your homework, notebook, pen or pencil, and a covered textbook with you each day."

Some teachers believe that rules are more understandable and more meaningful when students are allowed to participate in the decision-making process. Participation, especially at higher grade levels, may increase students' willingness to "buy into" the rules, may make them more invested in seeing that rules are followed, and may help to prepare students for adult life (Solomon, Watson, Delucchi, Schaps, and Battistich, 1988). On the other hand, allowing students to decide on class rules may result in a different set of rules for each class you teach, surely a confusing situation!

If you decide to include students in the process of deciding on rules, be prepared to receive some suggestions that are silly, sarcastic, or overly harsh ("students who forget homework have to copy 100 pages from the dictionary"). Don't be afraid to veto inappropriate rules, but make sure your reason for rejecting a seriously made suggestion is clear to students.

As a beginning teacher, you may feel more comfortable presenting rules you have developed yourself. In fact, despite their years of experience, neither Donnie, Carmen, Sandy, nor Fred allows students to create classroom rules. Research by Evertson, Emmer, and their colleagues (e.g., Emmer, Evertson, and Anderson, 1980) has demonstrated that these four teachers are not alone: many effective teachers do not allow students to participate in the decision-making process. They do, however, discuss the rationales for the rules they have established, and they solicit examples from students.

A third principle to keep in mind is that *rules should be consistent with instructional goals and with what we know about how people learn.* Chapter One discussed the assumptions underlying this book. One assumption was that the need for order should not supersede the need for meaningful instruction. As you develop rules for your classroom, think about whether they will *facilitate or hinder the learning process.* For example, in the pursuit of order, some teachers prohibit talking during in-class assignments, and others refrain from using cooperative learning activities for fear that students will be too rowdy. Obviously, such restrictions are necessary at times (e.g., you may want students to work alone on a particular assignment so you can assess each student's comprehension of the material). It would be sad, however, if restrictions like this became the status quo. Educational psychologists who study the ways children learn stress the importance of children's interaction. Much of this thinking is based on the work of the Soviet psychologist, Lev Vygotsky, who believed that children's intellectual growth is fostered through collaboration with adults who serve as coaches and tutors and with more capable peers (Wertsch, 1985). Interestingly, recent research on the use of small groups indicates that these interactions benefit the *tutor* as well as the person being tutored. Noreen Webb (1985), for example, found that junior high school students who provided explanations for their peers showed increased achievement themselves. Given the important role that interaction plays in young people's learning and cognitive development, it seems sensible not to eliminate interaction, but to spend time teaching students how to interact in ways that are appropriate. (This topic will be addressed more fully in Chapter Nine.)

Finally, *classroom rules need to be consistent with school rules.* The importance of this principle can be illustrated by an excerpt from a student teacher's recent journal entry:

> The first week of school I ejected a student from the room and told him he couldn't come back into the class until he had a note from his parents. Not only was the student back in class the next day without a note, but I was informed that (1) I was in violation of the school code when I ejected the student, and (2) only homeroom teachers communicate directly with the parents.

Your school may hold an orientation meeting for new teachers where school rules, policies, and procedures are explained. In particular, find out about behaviors that are expected during assemblies, in the cafeteria and library, and in the hallways. You should also learn about the administrative tasks for which you are responsible (e.g., taking attendance, collecting field trip money, supervising fire drills, recording tardiness). If there is a school handbook, be sure to get a copy and use it as a guide for establishing your own rules and routines.

You also need to know if you are supposed to review the handbook with students. For example, Fred's students receive a booklet explaining "South Brunswick High School's Rules, Regulations, and Policies," and teachers go over it with their first-period class (their homeroom class) on the first day of school. The handbook covers policies and procedures with respect to lateness, absenteeism, school detention, smoking, substance abuse, leaving school grounds, bias incidents, and appropriate language. After reviewing the handbook, students sign a statement indicating they agree to abide by the rules. The statement is then returned to the main office.

Reviewing the handbook with his students allows Fred to explain how his classroom rules and routines jibe with those of the school:

> Okay, as you can see, the school rule is that you have to bring a note when you return to school after an absence. Let's talk about this a little more. When you're absent, it's *your* responsibility to call someone in class and make up the activity. So before you leave school today, get someone's phone number. [He smiles.] Try to get someone who is as smart or smarter than you. [The students laugh. He continues.] Now the school rule is that if you're out for three days, you have that many days to make up the work. I tend to be a little more lenient than that, but you need to come see me and ask for additional time. Any questions? [There are none.] Okay. With respect to lateness, the school rule is "Don't be late." If you're late three times, there's a penalty. I watch the lates pretty carefully, so I'll warn you if I think you're getting in trouble. Now, about cutting. You cut, I'll ask for you to leave my class. Jason, what did I say? [Jason repeats the comment.] Right! I can't teach you if you're not in my class. [He speaks slowly and with emphasis.] *If you cut my class, I take it personally.* Now I'm a human being. I realize there are times when you need to not be here; you have to go to the bathroom or the library. But you need to come and ask and get a pass. If you don't, that's a cut. And I'm *death on that one.* So don't cut.

Planning Routines for Specific Situations

So many different activities occur in classrooms that trying to define behavior for specific situations can be daunting. Researchers at the Learning Research and Development Center at the University of Pittsburgh have observed the behavior of effective classroom managers and have categorized the routines they use (Leinhardt, Weidman, and Hammond, 1987). I have adapted their three-category system to provide you with a way of thinking about routines for your own classroom.

Class-Running Routines These are *nonacademic routines that enable you to keep the classroom running smoothly.* This category of routines includes *administrative duties* (taking attendance; recording tardiness; distributing school notices), *procedures for student movement* (entering the room at the beginning of the period; leaving the room at the end of the period; leaving the room to go to the nurse, the library, or lockers; fire drills; moving around the room to sharpen pencils or get materials), and *housekeeping routines* (cleaning lab tables; watering plants; maintaining storage for materials used by everyone).

Without clear, specific class-running routines, these activities can consume a significant part of the school day. Research on the way time is used in fifth-grade classrooms has indicated that, on the average, these activities (transition, waiting, housekeeping) consume almost 20 percent of the time spent in the classroom—more than the amount of time spent in mathematics instruction (Rosenshine, 1980). This figure is undoubtedly higher in classrooms that are not well managed.

By defining how students are to behave in these specific situations, you can save precious minutes for instruction. You also enable students to carry out many of these routines without your direct supervision, freeing you to concentrate on instruction. For example, before the school day begins, Carmen assembles all the supplies her students will need to carry out their art projects and makes sure everything is readily accessible and carefully organized. During art period, students can take what they need when they need it; this not only saves Carmen innumerable interruptions, it also eliminates the "down time" that occurs when students have to wait for the teacher to deliver a needed item. Reflecting on this practice, Carmen tells us:

> I really want my students to be able to do things for themselves. I want them to be able to walk around, to make choices about colors, papers, paint, and string. If they can do it themselves, then I can just be the facilitator.

Lesson-Running Routines These routines directly support instruction *by specifying the behaviors that are necessary for teaching and learning to take place.* They allow lessons to proceed briskly and eliminate the need for students to ask questions like "Do I have to use a pen?" "Should we number from 1 to 20?" and "What do I do if I'm finished?"

Lesson-running routines describe what items students are to have on hand when a lesson begins, how materials and equipment are to be distributed and collected, what kind of paper or writing instrument is to be used, and what should be done with the paper (e.g., folded into eight boxes; numbered from 1 to 10 along the left margin; headed with name, date, and subject). In addition, lesson-running routines specify the behaviors that students are to engage in at the beginning of the lesson (e.g., have books open to the relevant page, silently sit and wait for instructions from the teacher) and what they are to do if they finish early or if they are unable to finish the assignment by the end of the time period.

Clear lesson-running routines are especially important in classroom situations that are potentially dangerous, such as woodworking, auto mechanics, and cooking. When Sandy introduces chemistry labs, for example, she is very careful to specify the special safety procedures:

> There are some special safety procedures for this lab. First, before working with the bunsen burners, make certain your hair is tied back. Second, make certain your goggles are on. Third, I'll have a beaker on my desk where you can discard the metals. Everything else you can throw away in the sink. Finally, after you're finished, go to your seat and write the equations. There are reference books up here to help you. You may find that you have to go back and redo part of the lab. That's okay.

Homework procedures can also be included among lesson-running routines, since the pace and content of a lesson often depend on whether students have done their homework assignments. You need to establish routines for determining quickly which students have their homework and which do not, as well as routines for checking and collecting assignments. You also need to have routines for providing assignments for students who have been absent.

Interaction Routines   These routines refer to the *rules for talk*—talk between teachers and students and talk among students themselves. Interaction routines specify *when talk is permitted and how it is to occur.* For example, during whole-class discussions, students need to know what to do if they want to respond to a question or contribute a comment. All four of our teachers, like many others, usually require students to raise their hands and wait to be called on, rather than simply calling out. In this way, the teachers can distribute opportunities to participate throughout the class and can ensure that the conversation is not dominated by a few overly eager individuals. The teachers can also check on how well the class understands the lesson by calling on students who do not raise their hands.

Often it's hard to keep track of which students have had an opportunity to speak. In order to avoid this problem, Donnie sometimes creates a pattern for calling on students, one that is more subtle than simply going up and down rows:

> I may start at the back corner of the room and call on students in a diagonal line. Or I might use the alphabetical list of students in my grade book, and alternate between students at the beginning of the list and those at the end. I try not to be obvious, but sometimes students figure out the pattern, and they'll say to me, "You missed so-and-so," or "I didn't get a question," so we'll go back and make sure that person has a turn.

Another way to keep track of which individuals have had a turn is to use the "cup system"—a coffee mug or a box containing slips of papers with students' names. Shake the cup, pull out a name, and then place the slip of paper on the side until you've worked your way through the whole class.

During some lessons, you may want students to respond chorally rather than individually (e.g., during a foreign language drill on verb conjugations). A simple signal can be used to indicate that the rules for talk have changed. For example, Donnie nods and extends her hands, palms up, in a gesture of invitation. Fred, with a background in music, literally conducts the group as if it were a chorus.

Sandy also suspends the normal rules for talk at times, but she adds words of caution for beginning teachers:

> If I'm at the board, with my back turned to the class, and a student wants to ask a question, I don't mind if he or she just calls out, "Mrs. K, I don't understand . . ." Or sometimes, during a whole-class discussion, someone will ask a question, and I'll ask other kids to help out. They'll turn to one another and start asking and answering questions as if I weren't even there. I can just stand aside and watch. It's great to see this kind of student-student interaction. But beginning teachers need to be careful about this. If things start to get unruly, I can just say, "Hey, guys, use hands," and things settle right down, but I've seen situations like this get out of hand for beginning teachers.

Interaction routines also include *procedures that students and teachers use to gain each other's attention.* For example, if students are busy working, and you need to give additional instructions, how will you signal that you want their attention? Will you say, "Excuse me," the way Donnie does, or will you flick the lights or hold up your arm? Conversely, if you are busy working with a small group or an individual, and students need your assistance, how will they communicate that to you? Will they be allowed to call out your name or leave their seats and approach you?

Finally, you need to think about the rules that will govern *talk among students.* When 20 to 30 students sit so close to one another, it's only natural for them to talk. You must decide when it's all right for students to talk about the television show they saw last night (e.g., before the bell rings) and when their talk must be about academic work (e.g., during cooperative learning activities). You also need to think about times when students may talk quietly (e.g., during in-class assignments), and when you need to have absolute silence (e.g., when you are giving instruction or during a test).

Table 4-2 summarizes the three types of routines we have just discussed.

THE FIRST FEW DAYS OF SCHOOL: TEACHING STUDENTS HOW TO BEHAVE

Learning how to behave in school is not always easy. Too often, students have to guess the rules for appropriate behavior from teachers' indirect statements like "I see someone whose hands are not folded" [*translation:* students' hands should be folded now] (Shuy, 1988) or "I don't see any hands" [*translation:* students should raise their hands if they wish to speak] (Gumperz, 1981). Students must also be sensitive to cues provided by nonverbal behavior, like voice tone and pitch, posture, tempo and rhythm of speech, and facial expression. Sometimes students "misbehave" simply because they have interpreted these subtle cues incorrectly!

In order to minimize confusion, you need to *teach the rules for general conduct,* defining terms clearly, providing examples, and discussing rationales. As I indicated earlier in this chapter, Evertson and Emmer's (1982) research indicates this is crucial for behaviors that are likely to occur frequently and where the appropriate behavior may be ambiguous (e.g., talking during a seatwork assignment). You also need to *teach the routines* you want students to follow for specific situations. Such thoroughness is particularly important in new situations, like chemistry laboratories, wood shop, keyboarding, or ceramics studios, where students have had little prior experience.

Let's see what this looks like in action. On the morning of the first day of school, Donnie began by introducing herself to her students and asking them to introduce themselves. Afterwards, she introduced the topic of "ground rules." Note that she also provided information on topics that are sure to be on students' minds—homework, notebooks, grading, and extra help:

> Today our main concern is to talk about how we're going to operate in here, what I expect of you in terms of behavior and what the consequences might be for some kinds of behavior. I want to discuss my ground rules or codes of behavior. I'll pass these out, and

TABLE 4-2
SUMMARY OF CLASSROOM ROUTINES

CLASS-RUNNING ROUTINES: Nonacademic routines that enable the classroom to run smoothly

Administrative routines
  Taking attendance
  Recording tardiness
  Distributing school notices

Routines for student movement
  Entering the room at the beginning of the period
  Leaving the room at the end of the period
  Going to the restroom
  Going to the nurse
  Going to the library
  Fire drills
  Sharpening pencils
  Using computers or other equipment
  Getting materials

Housekeeping routines
  Cleaning chalkboards
  Watering plants
  Storing personal items (book bags)
  Maintaining common storage areas

LESSON-RUNNING ROUTINES: Routines that directly support instruction by specifying the behaviors that are necessary for teaching and learning to take place

  What to bring to class
  Collecting homework
  Recording who has done homework
  Returning homework
  Distributing materials
  Preparing paper for assignment (heading, margins, type of writing instrument)
  Collecting in-class assignments
  What to do when assignments have been completed

INTERACTION ROUTINES: Routines that specify when talk is permitted and how it is to occur

Talk between teacher and students
  During whole-class lessons
  When the teacher is working with a small group
  When the teacher needs the class's attention
  When students need the teacher's attention

Talk among students
  During seatwork assignment
  Before the bell rings
  During transitions
  During loudspeaker announcements
  When a visitor comes to speak with the teacher

---

we'll discuss them. If you have any questions or problems, let me know. [She distributes a packet of handouts.] It looks like an awful lot, but it's not really. A lot will be familiar; I'm sure it will be similar to other teachers'.

Okay, let's look at the first page. Here we have my ground rules. The first item on the page deals with general class procedures. *I expect you to be in your seat when the bell rings.* [She says this slowly and firmly. Her tone is serious but pleasant.] Today several people were tardy. I can understand that. I recognize that today is the first day and you're running around, maybe lost. [She smiles.] But I anticipate that *there will be no late arrivals after this.* I'll talk about what happens for tardiness in a few minutes. [She continues to elaborate on the printed statements, answering questions, inviting comments. She reviews the ground rules for notebooks, homework, extra help, paper headings, and participation, and goes on to explain the grading system. She then goes over an assignment sheet that students may use to record assignments and due dates, and elaborates on a checklist she will use to evaluate notebooks.]

As this example illustrates, teaching students the rules for conduct doesn't have to be unpleasant or oppressive. In fact, some teachers don't even use the word "rules." Sandy, for example, prefers to talk about "chemistry classroom guidelines" (see Figure 4-1), but, like Donnie, she makes sure her expectations for behavior are explicit. She defines terms ("Late means not being in the room when the bell rings"), provides examples wherever necessary, and stresses the reasons for each guideline. She explains why it's important for textbooks to be covered ("so they don't get chemicals on them"); why she has a "disclaimer" in her guidelines reserving the right to give unannounced quizzes ("That's there in case I see you're not doing the reading. But I really don't like to do this; I want kids to do well on tests"); why hats cannot be worn in class (for safety reasons); why she insists on promptness ("I start when the bell rings"); and why she lets them leave when the bell rings—even if she's in the middle of a sentence ("I will not keep you, because you'd be late to the next class and that's not fair to you or to the next teacher. But don't pack up books before the bell rings"). Sandy also discusses course requirements. In particular, she explains how grades are calculated and how homework is assigned and evaluated:

Okay, people, let's talk about homework. Homework is assigned a point value of 10. I always write the homework assignments in this corner of the chalkboard and they're always given as block assignments with stated due dates. For example, your very first assignment is to do pages 3–29, with all the problem numbers. This averages out to five pages plus five problems a night. It's in your best interest to do some every night, instead of waiting until the very end. Please keep in mind that I will not accept late homework. It doesn't all have to be in the same pen; it doesn't all have to be in the same color. I don't care if you start in blue and finish in black. But it does have to be in at the beginning of the period on the day it's due. Part of the assignment is to get it in on time. I'll give you a reminder when you come in that homework is due, but if you don't hear and then you remember halfway through I don't want it. It's also important for you to understand that homework is not graded based on how correct it is. It's graded on the basis of your effort. Homework is not useless in my class. We go over every single item.

1 Always be prepared for class. You MUST bring the following items with you each class period.
   a. notebook
   b. pen or pencil
   c. your COVERED textbook
   d. a scientific calculator

2 Be prompt to class. Tardiness will not be tolerated. You are considered late to class if you enter the room after the bell rings.
   a. 1st late 10 minutes after school (with me)
   b. 2nd late 20 minutes after school (with me)
   c. 3rd late 30 minutes after school (with me)
   d. 4th late 7:15 A.M. detention

3 Grades are calculated according to a point system. Every assignment (labs, homework, classwork) and exams (tests and quizzes) are assigned points. Your grade is the number of points received compared with the total number of possible points.

4 Tests and quizzes are based on the information received through class discussions, textbook readings, and lab work. It is imperative that you take notes during class discussions. All tests (with the exception of the midterm and final) are assigned a value of 100 points. Quizzes range in point value from 25–50. A quiz does not have to be announced.

5 Homework is assigned a point value of 10. Homework is always given as a block assignment with a stated due date. Any written work that is assigned will be collected on the stated due date. NO LATE HOMEWORK WILL BE ACCEPTED.

6 If you are absent, it is YOUR responsibility to find out what was missed. Any lab missed due to an absence must be made up within one week of the absence. EXCEPTIONS: (a) If you are absent 3 days or more, more time will be allowed for make-up; (b) If you are absent the day of a test or quiz and you were in class the day before, you will be required to make up that test the day you return to school.

7 THERE WILL BE NO CUTTING!!!!

8 Hats may not be worn in class.

9 NO EXTRA CREDIT POINTS ARE GIVEN IN THIS CLASS!!!

FIGURE 4-1
Chemistry Classroom Guidelines
Mrs. Krupinski

Finally, Sandy stresses the need to come to class (in terms that are amazingly similar to Fred's):

> Okay, Number 7 is pretty clear ("There will be no cutting"); I don't really think this needs to be discussed. I want you here. I expect you to be here. *And I take it personally if you're not.*

Different Approaches to Teaching Rules and Procedures

As we have seen, Donnie and Sandy are relatively formal when introducing rules and routines. Both teachers spend a considerable amount of time explaining their expectations and both provide students with a handout for their notebooks. In contrast, Carmen spends only a few minutes reviewing rules and routines since she's taught her seventh- and eighth-graders for many years, and they are familiar with her expectations for behavior:

> [It's the first Friday of the school year. Carmen stands by the door and greets her eighth-grade class.] Ladies and gentlemen, go in and sit anywhere you want for the moment. [Students enter the room and sit down very quietly. Carmen quickly checks attendance.] Okay, before we begin, let's just review a few things. First, if you have to go to the bathroom or get a drink, try to do that before art class, because we have so little time. Understand? Now, can you think of any problems we had here last year? [Silence.] What about cleaning up? [A student comments that sometimes they didn't clean up well enough.] Right. And remember when Marcus [a 200-pound student] almost fell on me? He was walking around with a tray of water and tripped, and the water got all over. This year let's work on those two things. I'll give you warning when it's time to start cleaning up, and you're going to make sure all the supplies are put away and the tables are cleared off. And you're going to stay at your seats unless you need to get something for your project, like scissors or paint. Okay? By the way, what do you do with your chair before you leave the room? [Students answer chorally: Push it in.] Okay, good. Also, don't wear anything good to school on the day you have art. That's just a reminder. We're going to be working with Paris Craft and all kinds of messy materials. Any questions? Okay, now let's talk about what we're going to do this year . . .

With the bilingual eighth-grade class that comes in immediately afterwards, Carmen takes a somewhat different tack; once again, however, she spends only a brief time discussing the rules for behavior. Speaking in both English and Spanish, she begins by taking attendance; she checks to see if a new student from Puerto Rico understands any English. Then she gathers students in the instructional area at the back of the room, where all the students can see the wall chart listing the Art Room Rules:

CARMEN: Pick out a rule you think is important. [Students raise their hands. She calls on a girl.]
STUDENT: "Pay attention to directions."
CARMEN: Yes, that's especially important, because if you pay attention then you'll be doing all the other things on the list, too.
STUDENT: "Clean up when told."
CARMEN: Yes, it's important to clean up quickly because we have so little time. And the room needs to be ready for the next class that comes in. You know, if you did just those two things ["pay attention" and "clean up when told"], then you'd be doing the last one! ["Work hard, think, and have fun!"] Okay, now does anyone remember what we did in here last year?

Like Carmen, Fred also introduces rules and routines in a relatively informal way. As we saw earlier, when he reviews the school handbook with his first-period class of sophomores, he uses the school rules as a jumping-off point for a presentation of his class rules. Even here, however, he distributes no handouts, nor does he post rules, and he interjects a degree of humor:

> [Fred finishes reviewing the handbook and has students sign the page acknowledging receipt and agreement. He then continues with his own rules for the class.] Do you

know what an acronym is? It's letters that form a word and each letter stands for a word. PITA is an acronym. And it's the main rule we have in here: *Don't be a PITA.* What's a PITA, Suzanne? [She shakes her head.] You don't know? [He looks around to see if anyone else knows. There's silence.] A PITA is a . . . pain . . . in . . . the . . . neck! [There's some laughter as the class catches on.] I want you to inscribe PITA across your forehead. Don't forget: Don't be a PITA. Now, I have one rule for me, too: I must make you laugh once every day. If I don't, I go home in a suicidal mood. [Students laugh.] Okay, let's talk about what you'll be learning in U.S. History I . . .

With his seniors, Fred prefers an even less systematic approach. On the first day of class, he introduces himself, takes attendance, and immediately launches into a description of the course. During the period, he explicitly teaches his students routines for specific situations that arise (e.g., how to pass in papers), but he does not teach rules for general conduct. Instead, he monitors the class carefully and immediately informs students about behavior he finds unacceptable. His interactions with individual students are watched carefully by the rest—and they quickly learn what he expects. When Fred asks one student to take off his baseball cap, for example, another hears and takes off his own hat. To a student wearing sunglasses, Fred asks, "Is there a medical reason for those glasses?" and the student immediately removes them. Later on, when the same student yawns loudly and conspicuously, Fred turns to him and speaks firmly:

FRED: James, please don't do that.
STUDENT: I was just yawning.
FRED: If you have to do that, please transfer to a different class. Okay?
STUDENT: Okay. [Fred moves closer to James and continues the discussion.]

At the end of the period, Fred asks James to stay for a minute, a request that is obviously noted by the other students. They speak privately, and then James leaves for his next class. Afterwards, Fred shares what happened:

That was clearly a test, but I think I passed it. I told him that yawning like that was clearly inappropriate and that if he couldn't demonstrate the same respect for me that I showed him, then he'd have to find another place to be. I can't operate in an atmosphere of "me against you." He said it was because he hadn't had a cup of coffee. I told him there are no excuses, that it just won't happen in here, that he can't be here if he acts inappropriately. He said okay, and we agreed to chalk it up to a mistake and forget about it. But I'll have to watch him.

As this incident illustrates, Fred communicates expectations for conduct to older students primarily by providing clear, immediate feedback when behavior is unacceptable. He recognizes that one reason this approach works for him is the reputation he has established during his years at the high school. Reflecting on this reputation, Barry Bachenheimer, Fred's student teacher, observes:

Everyone knows that he plays the "dumb old man," but that he's not. He has this incredible relationship with the kids; he knew everyone's name within two days. He works them hard, but he projects warmth, and the kids know he really cares. I've never seen a kid give him lip. One look is enough.

CONCLUDING COMMENTS

Donnie, Carmen, Sandy, and Fred all have well-defined expectations for student behavior, and they make these expectations absolutely clear. Nonetheless, the four teachers introduce rules and routines in different ways. These differences reflect their beliefs about what works best for their own particular students in their own particular contexts. Donnie and Sandy teach rules and routines in a systematic, explicit fashion; they both spend considerable time explaining what they expect, and they both distribute written copies of the rules for students to keep in their notebooks. Carmen posts a large chart listing the rules for the art room, but she reviews them only briefly with her seventh- and eigth-graders since she knows that students are well acquainted with her expectations. With his sophomores, Fred explicitly teaches rules, but he neither posts them nor distributes copies. With his seniors, he teaches specific routines, but relies primarily on monitoring and feedback to communicate what he expects in terms of general conduct.

As a beginning teacher, you would be wise to adopt a deliberate, thorough approach to teaching rules and routines. Once you've gained experience—and a reputation—you might try a less formal approach with your older students. But remember, whatever approach you choose, "one look is enough" only if students already understand what you expect them to do.

SUMMARY

This chapter discussed two important functions of rules and routines in the classroom: (1) to provide a structure and predictability that help students to feel more comfortable; and (2) to reduce the complexity of classroom life, allowing you and your students to concentrate on teaching and learning. I outlined two broad categories of behavioral expectations—*rules for general conduct* and *routines for specific situations*—and emphasized the need to teach these explicitly.

When deciding on rules for general conduct, make sure they are:

- reasonable and necessary
- clear and understandable
- consistent with instructional goals and with what we know about how people learn
- consistent with school rules

Plan routines for specific situations:

- class-running routines
    administrative duties
    procedures for student movement
    housekeeping responsibilities
- lesson-running routines
    routines governing use and distribution of materials

routines for paper headings, homework procedures, what to do if you finish early
- interaction routines
    routines specifying when talk is permitted and how it is to occur
    routines for students and teachers to use to get each other's attention

Teach rules and routines explicitly:

- define terms
- discuss rationales
- provide examples

Remember, developing good rules and routines is only the first step. For rules and routines to be effective, you must actively teach them to your students. Time spent on rules and routines at the beginning of school will pay off in increased instructional time throughout the year.

ACTIVITIES

1. Thinking about rules

   a. Obtain a copy of the school handbook, or talk to the principal or another teacher, to determine the school rules.

   b. Develop a set of rules for your classroom. About five rules should be sufficient. For each rule, list a rationale and examples that you will discuss with students to make the rules more meaningful. Check your rules against the school rules to ensure there is no conflict.

   c. Think about which rules are most important to you and why.

2. Below is a list of areas for which you will need specific behavioral routines. Use this list to help you think through the ways you expect your students to behave.

Class-running routines:

Entering the room at the beginning of the period
Going to the lavatories
Going to lockers
Taking attendance
Recording tardiness
Fire drills
Sharpening pencils
Keeping track of work for absent students
Cleaning up
Leaving the room at the end of the period

Lesson-ru70nning routines:

Distributing materials and equipment
Paper heading

Homework distribution
Homework collection
What to do when assignment has been completed

Interaction routines:

Talking during seatwork assignment
Hand-raising during whole-class discussion
Behavior during interruptions (e.g., a visitor comes to the door; an announce-
ment comes over the loudspeaker)
Signalling the teacher for help during an in-class assignment

3. Not all of the routines you thought about in Activity 2 can be taught that first
day. You need to decide on priorities and teach routines when it is most appropriate
(and most likely to be remembered). Decide which ones are necessary for the first
day.

REFERENCES

Brooks, D. M. (1985). The teacher's communicative competence: The first day of school.
Theory into Practice, 24(1), 63–70.
Emmer, E. T., Evertson, C. M., and Anderson, L. M. (1980). Effective classroom manage-
ment at the beginning of the school year. *The Elementary School Journal, 80*(5),
219–231.
Evertson, C. M., and Emmer, E. T. (1982). Effective management at the beginning of the
school year in junior high classes. *Journal of Educational Psychology, 74*(4),
485–498.
Gumperz, J. J. (1981). Conversational inference and classroom learning. In J. Green and C.
Wallat (Eds.), *Ethnography and language in educational settings.* Norwood, NJ: Ablex.
Kounin, J. S. (1970). Discipline and group management in classrooms. New York: Holt,
Rinehart & Winston.
Leinhardt, G., Weidman, C., and Hammond, K. M. (1987). Introduction and integration of
classroom routines by expert teachers. *Curriculum Inquiry, 17*(2), 135–175.
Rosenshine, B. (1980). How time is spent in elementary classrooms. In C. Denham
and A. Lieberman (Eds.), *Time to learn.* Washington, D.C.: U.S. Department of
Education.
Shuy, R. (1988). Identifying dimensions of classroom language. In J. L. Green and J. O.
Harker (Eds.), *Multiple perspective analyses of classroom discourse.* Norwood, NJ:
Ablex.
Solomon, D., Watson, M. S., Delucchi, K. L., Schaps, E., and Battistich, V. (1988). Enhanc-
ing children's prosocial behavior in the classroom. *American Educational Research
Journal, 25*(4), 527–554.
Webb, N. M. (1985). Student interaction and learning in small groups: A research summary.
In R. E. Slavin, S. Sharan, S. Kagan, R. Hertz-Lazarowitz, C. Webb, and R. Schmuck
(Eds.), *Learning to cooperate, cooperating to learn.* New York: Plenum.
Wertsch, J. V. (1985). *Vygotsky and the social formation of mind.* Cambridge, MA: Harvard
University Press.

FOR FURTHER READING

Canter, L., and Canter, M. (1992). *Assertive discipline: Positive behavior management for today's classroom.* Santa Monica, CA: Lee Canter & Associates.

Emmer, E. T. (1988). Classroom management and discipline. In V. Richardson-Koehler (Ed.), *Educator's handbook: A research perspective.* New York: Longman.

Emmer, E. T. and Evertson, C. M. (1981). Synthesis of research on classroom management. *Educational Leadership, 38,* 342–347.

Emmer, E. T., Evertson, C. M., Clements, B. S., Sanford, J. P., and Worsham, M. E. (1994). *Classroom management for secondary teachers* (3rd edition). Boston: Allyn and Bacon.

Chapter Five

Gaining Students' Cooperation

Not too long ago, I read an entry in the journal of a student teacher whose fourth- and fifth-period English classes were giving her a hard time. It was the middle of November, and Sharon was feeling frustrated by the disrespectful and disruptive behavior of her students. "They just won't sit still long enough to hear directions," she wrote. "I am spending more and more time on telling people to 'Shhh.' I don't understand why they are so rude, and I just don't know what to do."

As I read more, it became clear that this student teacher's problem was not due to an absence of clear rules and routines:

> On the first day that I took over, we reviewed the rules my cooperating teacher had established (just like you suggested): come to class on time, don't call out, treat each other with respect, etc. They were really cooperative; I thought this was going to be great, but I guess they were just "psyching me out." Now they argue with me all the time. I say "quiet" and they say, "But I was just telling him . . . " I say, "Put the newspaper/comic book/photo album away," and they say "Just let me look, I have to see . . ." There doesn't seem much else to do except repeat myself. Sometimes it works, sometimes it doesn't. . . . I'm really at my wit's end. If I can't gain some control, there's obviously no way I can teach anything. Sometimes I think I'd be better off if I just forgot about trying to have interesting discussions, projects, small groups, etc., and just gave out worksheets every day, lectured, and didn't allow *any* talking. That's a far cry from the kind of classroom I wanted to have. I wanted to respect my students, to treat them like adults, but I found I can't. I've always gotten along great with kids, but not now. All these kids seem to understand is discipline referrals and detention.

This student teacher had learned a sad fact of classroom life: having clear, reasonable rules and routines doesn't automatically mean that everyone will follow them. To achieve order, you must find ways to *gain students' cooperation*. As Walter Doyle (1986) has observed, classroom order is like conversation: it can only be achieved if both parties agree to participate. Indeed, if students are resistant, classroom events turn into a series of hostile showdowns, and teaching becomes "a contest of wills" (Clark, 1989, p. 22). (Figure 5-1 illustrates the difficulty Calvin's teacher has in gaining his cooperation.)

What can you do to prevent this situation from occurring? How can you get students to comply willingly with classroom rules and to become productively involved in learning activities? As you reflect on these questions, keep in mind the characteristics of classroom groups that were discussed in Chapter One. Recall that, unlike most other social groups, students do not come together voluntarily. They are a captive audience, required to work on tasks they have not selected and in which they may have little interest. Remember, too, that classroom groups are formed somewhat arbitrarily; students do not usually choose their peers *or* their teachers, yet they are expected to cooperate with both. Recalling these special characteristics makes it easier to see why teachers must work to gain students' cooperation. These characteristics also help to explain why "getting along great with kids" *outside* school may not be the same as "getting along great with kids" *inside* school.

This chapter examines four approaches to gaining cooperation. The first approach focuses on *establishing a positive relationship with students.* It is based on the assumption that teachers who have their students' respect and affection are more likely to gain their cooperation (Good and Brophy, 1994). The second approach emphasizes the importance of *fostering students' motivation to learn* (Brophy, 1987). As Kounin's (1970) work has shown, students who are interested and involved in the academic work at hand are less likely to misbehave. The third approach involves *sharing responsibility with students.* The assumption here is that students who are allowed to exercise some autonomy and to make decisions about their own behavior will be more committed to acting responsibly. Finally, I discuss the *use of rewards to encourage and reinforce appropriate behavior.* The rationale for this approach is the psychological principle that behavior followed by a reward tends to be repeated.

ESTABLISHING A POSITIVE RELATIONSHIP WITH STUDENTS

Like Sharon, many beginning teachers assume they will have few behavior problems because they have always "gotten along great with kids." They plan to respect their students and anticipate that the respect will be returned. They envision a classroom characterized by harmony and good will, and they are disappointed and disillusioned when students test the limits and begin to misbehave. But what does it really mean to "respect" students? What kind of teacher-student relationship is most helpful in creating an environment where students are actively and productively involved in learning tasks?

Not surprisingly, observers of classroom life suggest that the most resistance occurs in classes where students dislike the teacher (Cusick, 1994). Robert Everhart (1983), who spent two years conducting fieldwork in a junior high school, found that students "bug" teachers who "are not nice to us," who "talk down to us," or who "treat us like babies":

> Most teachers who were bugged seemed, to the students, to be distant from them and to
> have a sense of superiority. Additionally, they were "mean" because they had lots of
> "stupid rules" which did not make any sense: rules like having to print instead of write

Calvin and Hobbes

by Bill Watterson

FIGURE 5-1
Calvin's teacher has difficulty gaining his cooperation. *(Calvin and Hobbes © Watterson. Dist. by Universal Press Syndicate. Reprinted with permission. All rights reserved.)*

your names and if you didn't you had to do your paper again, or rules like writing your name in the right-hand corner of your paper rather than in the left-hand corner, or rules like doing "stupid exercises" in grammar books. When this existed, . . . a teacher "deserves" to get bugged. (p. 183)

Mr. Richards, one of the most disliked teachers in the school, was a special target of students' bugging. Not only was he boring, he was also perceived to be unfair and authoritarian ("He'll give you detention if you pick your nose"). So students engaged in subtle forms of resistance, "just to piss him off" (p. 184)—smiling at him at inappropriate times, piling books the wrong way on the counter, and tapping their feet.

In an effort to avoid being like Mr. Richards (and all the other authoritarian teachers they have known), beginning teachers sometimes try to be "friends" with their students, aiming for the kinds of relationships they have had with adolescents outside of school. Unfortunately, this can lead to another whole set of problems. Consider the following scenario provided by Grant (1988). Here we can see that students like their teacher, Mr. Carnova, yet they do not feel compelled to behave appropriately:

Students enter after the bell and constantly interrupt roll call with comments and questions. "Are you telling us our grades yet?" He answers patiently, "Your grades will be on your report cards," to which a student replies, "Report cards are for parents." He completes the roll call and reminds the class that the words on the board are for a spelling test Friday. A student shouts. "Right on! Why don't you give us those work sheets on the words?" Another student, obviously mocking one of the teacher's frequent comments, chimes in: "Take your time on that vocabulary, Mr. Carnova," and a chorus of others join the fun: "Take your time on that spelling, Mr. Carnova . . . take your time on that teaching, Mr. Carnova." He absorbs this good naturedly, apparently enjoying the ruckus as much as they and calling it to a halt just short of pandemonium. (Grant, 1988, p. 69)

Mr. Carnova is good natured, and students obviously enjoy the informality and easy give-and-take. Nonetheless, it seems unlikely that Mr. Carnova can obtain the cooperation that is needed for students to become involved in productive academic work (Cusick, 1994). Clearly, neither Mr. Richards' authoritarianism nor Mr. Carnova's affability is a good model for beginning teachers. We need to find a middle ground between the "witch" and the "wimp."

The results of a study conducted by Brekelmans, Wubbels, and Creton (1990) in the Netherlands provide some clues about what it means to have a good relationship with students. Gathering questionnaire data from 65 ninth-grade physics classes, these investigators explored the relationship between students' perceptions of their teachers' interpersonal behavior and students' attitudes towards physics (e.g., whether they liked going to physics lessons, their motivation for physics, whether they thought they were learning a lot).

To appreciate the results of the study, we need to understand the model of teachers' interpersonal behavior that the researchers used as the basis for their questionnaire. Brekelmans, Wubbels, and Creton characterized teachers' behaviors in terms of two dimensions. The first dimension, *dominance/submission,* refers to the degree to which teachers influence student behavior (i.e., do they lead, organize, set tasks, establish and enforce rules *or* do they give in, give latitude, and "keep a low profile"?). The second dimension, *cooperation/opposition,* refers to the degree to which teachers demonstrate helping, supportive, friendly behavior *or* adversarial, irritated, negative behavior.

These two dimensions serve as the vertical and horizontal axes of the model shown in Figure 5-2. Behavior placed in the upper half of the model is characterized as dominant behavior (e.g., giving instructions), while teacher behavior in the lower half is submissive (e.g., giving in to students). Teacher behavior that is cooperative (e.g., helping students) is on the right side of the vertical axis, while behavior that is oppositional (e.g., punishing) is on the left. Thus, the four quadrants represent behaviors that are combinations of these four characteristics.

By drawing two more lines, the model is further subdivided into eight sections, each of which represents a type of interpersonal behavior. For example, in the section labeled in DC, teacher behavior is both dominant and cooperative, but the dominant aspect is stronger than the cooperative aspect (e.g., the teacher provides leadership); in the section labeled CD, the behavior is also dominant and cooperative, but the cooperative aspect is more salient than the dominant (e.g., the teacher behaves in a friendly, supportive manner). On the left side of the model, behavior labeled OS would indicate that the teacher's behavior is both oppositional and submissive, but the oppositional aspect is stronger than the submissive (e.g., the teacher shows dissatisfaction and looks glum). Before going any further, read the descriptions in each of the eight sections. Think about where you might fall or where teachers you have liked might fall.

The results of this study suggest that teachers who show more behavior on the right side of the D-S axis have students who think more positively about their physics classes. This can be seen in Figures 5-3 and 5-4. The shaded areas indicate the behavior that is characteristic of teachers with relatively positive (Figure 5-3) and relatively negative (Figure 5-4) student attitudes. As we can see, students feel more positively about their classes when teachers show more helping, friendly, and

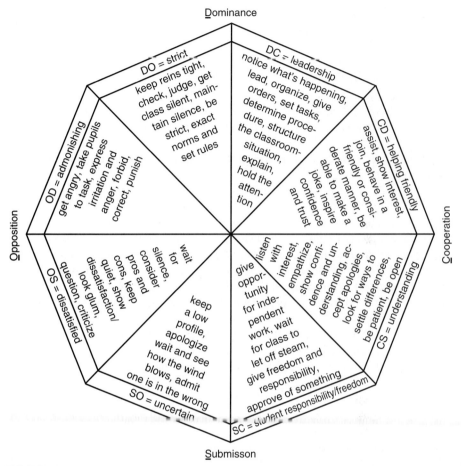

FIGURE 5-2
A model of teacher behavior (from Wubbels, and Levy, 1993)

understanding behavior (sections CD and CS)—*but they also like teachers to show leadership* (section DC).

From this portrait, we can see that having a good relationship with students is more than being congenial and good natured. A positive relationship is created through the planning and the behavior of effective managers—the way they structure classroom situations, the way they show interest in students, the way they communicate. Furthermore, this portrait describes a teacher who is *in charge*—not a teacher who keeps a low profile, who waits and hopes that students will cooperate; in sum, a teacher who can create a *classroom that is not only relaxed and comfortable, but also orderly and productive.*

It is obvious that the four teachers with whom we are working are able to create this kind of classroom. As we saw in the last chapter, these teachers provide leader-

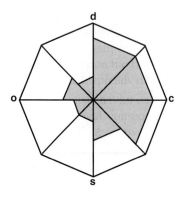

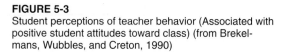

FIGURE 5-3
Student perceptions of teacher behavior (Associated with positive student attitudes toward class) (from Brekelmans, Wubbles, and Creton, 1990)

ship by establishing the rules and routines that will guide classroom behavior; they clearly communicate to students that they are in charge, that students cannot "run all over them." Nonetheless, their efforts to build good relationships with their students are striking. They learn students' names quickly, so they can avoid saying, "Hey, you, with the green sweater." They talk about their families, hobbies, and experiences; they exhibit a sense of humor; they reveal their feelings and encourage students to reveal theirs. Furthermore, they work hard to establish an environment where students feel safe, where it's okay to make mistakes, and where they know they won't be humiliated—by the teacher or by other students.

On the first day of school, Fred introduces himself to students: "Good morning, ladies and gentlemen, my name is Fred Cerequas, and I'm your homeroom teacher and your first period teacher. Many students in the past have called me Mr. C because they've had trouble with my name. You're welcome to call me Mr. C too. . . . Now let's find out who *you* are. When I call your name, please indicate your presence here. If I mispronounce your name, please tell me." As Fred calls students' names, he checks if they have any nicknames they would prefer him to use; occasionally he asks about ethnic origin ("And what kind of a name is that?") and chats about siblings he has taught. He asks one student if she is the youngest of the children in her family, and she replies that she is. He turns to the whole class: "Do you think birth order is related to school achievement?" Chorally, they respond "No. . . ." Fred asks, "How many first children

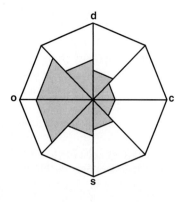

FIGURE 5-4
Student perceptions of teacher behavior (Associated with negative student attitudes toward class) (from Brekelmans, Wubbles, and Creton, 1990)

are in this class?" [It is an honors class, and a lot of students raise their hands.] Fred indicates the large number of hands that are up, and smiles, "Yes, it *is* related!" [Students nod and laugh.] After the attendance is taken and school rules have been reviewed, Fred gives the first homework assignment. [Students groan until they hear what it is.] "I want to know what *your* expectations are for *me.* Write down a few notes and come in tomorrow prepared to tell me what you want from me. Also, what are the expectations you have for yourself?

It's the first day of school. Donnie begins class by telling students about herself. She explains how she got the name Donnie, that her husband is a supervisor in the New Brunswick schools, and that they have one daughter who "is one year short of a quarter of a century." When students look at her questioningly, she laughs and tells them, "Do your math!" Then she selects an adjective to describe herself: caring. She tells students, "I care about my students and my work. If you see me in the hallway, say hello, feel free to talk to me. Please understand that I care about you; I am dedicated to your success. I want you to be the best you can be. If you had some bad habits last year, like not doing your homework or cutting class, I hope you'll change those habits this year and be determined to be the best you can be." After introducing herself, Donnie asks the students to tell her about themselves in the same way: "Tell me your name, where you got it from or what it means, if you have a nickname you want me to use, and then choose an adjective to describe yourself. I'm going to write these down so I can learn your names as quickly as possible. But please be patient; it might take a little while."

Sandy is meeting with her class after a long, unexpected "vacation" due to a severe blizzard. Students are about to resume doing a lab they had begun before the blizzard; it requires them to use pipettes, a new piece of equipment. Several students express concern about having forgotten how to use the pipettes. Sandy acknowledges their concerns: "I know that some of you are worried that you don't remember how to use the equipment. That's a valid concern, since it's been such a long time since you practiced. But don't worry. See if you remember, and if not, just call me over and I'll help you out." Later, when two students express confusion over the lab procedure, she comments: "Your confusion is understandable, because this is the first time we're doing this procedure. Next time we do it you'll know what to do. Remember when we were learning to use the balance, and you were so confused? The first time is always a challenge." At the end of the period, the students express anxiety over an upcoming test: "What if it snows again tomorrow and we don't have a chance to finish the lab, and we're supposed to have the test the next day?" Sandy is reassuring: "If we are in school tomorrow [a Wednesday], then the test will be on Thursday as scheduled. But if we have a delayed opening or no school tomorrow, the test will be on Friday. You've got to see my face for a whole period before the test! However, that doesn't mean you don't have to prepare, so this is what I'm asking you to do . . .

Carmen's class is working on Venetian masks, the first project of the year. Students are cutting, wetting, and applying strips of Paris Craft to the cardboard models they created the week before. Carmen is circulating, helping, supervising, reminding students of the next steps. She sees one boy having difficulty cutting the Paris Craft. "Tommy, maybe you should try another scissor. This looks too dull." She gets him one, which works much better. She continues to circulate and notices Ebony not working. To Carmen's query, Ebony points to the eyes of her cardboard model: "I just can't do this." Carmen speaks in a reassuring voice: "You want to cut those out? Here, keep it flat like this and stab them out. If it's a little off, it's okay. You'll never notice." She gets Ebony back on track and moves on. A girl sitting nearby comments on Carmen's new short haircut. Carmen laughs: "Yeah, I was going to cut it even shorter, but I chickened out. But when I retire, I'm going to shave my head and get an earring in my nose. What do you think, Shanika?" The girl laughs and tells her she likes her better this way.

These examples of relationship-building echo the results of a study by Chris Clark (1989). In an effort to define "good teaching," Clark spoke with about 60 elementary and secondary teachers and their students. His conversations revealed that, for teachers, the essence of good teaching is in the arena of human relationships: "Teaching is good when a class becomes a community of honest, nurturant, and mutually respectful people" (p. 16). Students' views of good teaching also stress relationships: teachers are good when they take the time to learn who their students are and what they like, when they tell stories of life outside school, when they laugh with students, when they make sure students don't feel lost or humiliated, and when they are *both a friend and a responsible adult.*

FOSTERING STUDENT MOTIVATION TO LEARN

We sometimes speak about students' motivation as if it were a stable, unchangeable characteristic, like gender or eye color. From this perspective, some individuals are motivated, and some aren't. Some youngsters come to school wanting to learn, and some don't. This can be a comforting point of view: if motivation is an innate characteristic, then we don't have to spend time and energy figuring out ways to motivate students.

On the other hand, some educators argue that motivation is an acquired disposition that is developed through experience and is amenable to change. It can also be situation-specific, varying with the nature of the particular activity. Thus, students in foreign language classes can be enthusiastic about role playing a visit to a restaurant, but can appear bored and uninterested when it's time to conjugate verbs.

According to this latter view, teachers are responsible for stimulating student motivation and involvement in learning activities. This is easier said than done, of course, especially when dealing with adolescents. The downturn in motivation during the transition years from elementary to secondary school is well-documented (Anderman and Maehr, 1994), but it is often dismaying to beginning teachers—especially those who are passionate about their subject fields. Consider this entry taken from the journal of a student teacher in English:

> I began my student teaching with all of these grand ideas about how I was going to enlighten students to the beauty of literature and unlock all the insight and talent that had been buried. . . . I gave serious, complicated lectures and multitudes of homework assignments, sure that my students would all be grateful when they witnessed the emergence of their intellectual prowess. Somewhere in the middle of the third week, however, the truth came rearing its ugly head: Most of my students did not, and probably never would, approach literature with the enthusiasm equalling that of a new Sega game.

To assist teachers in the challenging task of stimulating student motivation to learn, Jere Brophy (1987) reviewed relevant theory and research and derived a set of motivational principles that teachers can apply in their classrooms. These principles are based on the idea that motivation to perform a task depends on *students' expectation of success* and *the value they place on the task* (Feather, 1982). The two factors work together like a multiplication equation (expectancy × value): if either one is missing (i.e., zero), there will be no motivation.

A number of the principles that Brophy has developed focus on ways of increasing students' expectation of success. Let's look at some of these principles, along with examples of how they are used by our four teachers:

Provide opportunities for success.   If tasks appear too difficult, students may be afraid to tackle them. You may have to modify assignments for different students, make assignments open-ended so that a variety of responses can be acceptable, provide additional instruction, or allow extra time. When Sandy's classes begin learning the symbols for chemical ions, for example, she doesn't insist that they immediately commit them to memory—a task they would find extremely daunting. Instead, she has them work with the ions and their symbols over a six- to eight-week period; they use them in writing equations, they see them on the chalkboard, and they look them up in their textbook. When it's finally time to have the symbols memorized, students find the task much less formidable.

Sometimes it's necessary to go back and re-teach material, rather than simply plowing ahead. For example, during one class period when Donnie was explaining how to construct and bisect congruent angles, it became apparent that most youngsters were lost. As students labored over their papers, frustrated comments began to be heard from all corners of the room: "I can't do it; you told me not to change the compass, but I had to"; "I need an eraser"; "Huh?", "How you do this?"; "I don't get this." Circulating around the room, Donnie tried to help individuals who were having trouble. Finally, she moved to the front and center of the room and addressed the class: "Okay, let's start again. I see a lot of people are out in left field." She began to explain the procedure again, very slowly. After every step, she asked, "Does everyone have this?" before moving on to the next step. Students began to respond more positively: "Yeah," "Uh-huh," "Okay, we got it." One girl, who had been having particular difficulty, called out, "C'mere, Miss Collins, I wanna show you what I got." Donnie checked her work; it was correct. The girl turned to her neighbor and announced loudly, "You see, all I needed was a little help. Sometimes I gotta work step by step. I got it. I got it."

During one class session with a particularly unmotivated group of seniors, Fred told them to construct a four-sentence paragraph on the following topic: "What do you think about [pause] CELERY?" There was surprised laughter, and then, one by one, students began to write. (Fred sat at his desk and wrote a response too.) After a few moments, Fred asked individual students to read what they had written. The first student rose and read from his paper: "Celery is disgusting. The strings get in your teeth. The only way I like it is with peanut butter. It comes with buffalo wings." After several others had read their responses, Fred moved on to a new topic: Revenge. Once again, students wrote paragraphs and then read them to the class. Afterwards, Fred reflected on the purpose of the lesson: "I'm going to *force* these kids to succeed—in spite of themselves—because success is a better motivator than anything else I know. This lesson was designed to have them be successful.

Anybody can think about celery; it would be hard *not* to have something to say. And the same with revenge. If a kid writes a good paragraph and can say, 'Hey, this is pretty good,' they begin to get hooked. I've never met a kid who wanted to grow up to be a bum. If I can get them to feel success, if I can create situations where they *have* to make the effort and they *have* to succeed, then maybe I'll be able to get through to them."

Teach students to set reasonable goals and to assess their performance. Some students think anything less than 100 on a test is a failure, while others are content with a barely passing grade. You may have to help students set goals that are reasonable and obtainable. At the very beginning of the year, for example, one of Fred's eleventh-grade students turned in an appalling essay; not only was it short, superficial, and vague, but both the handwriting and spelling were atrocious. When Fred investigated, he found out that the student had a learning disability; nonetheless, he told the student in no uncertain terms that his performance was inadequate: "Look, you can't write, you can't even print, and you can't spell. But you're not stupid. So what are you going to do to get better? Let's set some goals." With the assistance of the resource room teacher, they devised a plan for the student to learn keyboarding—and to use a spellchecker. When the next writing assignment was due, the student came to Fred complaining that it was too hard. Fred was sympathetic and supportive—but adamant that the student complete it. He did, and although it was far from adequate, it was a definite improvement over the first assignment. Reflecting on the student's problems, Fred comments: "We can all feel sorry for him, but he can't go around like this; he has to be pushed to overcome his deficits. People have allowed him to stay a baby, but it's time for him to grow up. There are ways he can improve. My job is to teach him to set some reasonable goals and then work to achieve them."

Help students to recognize the relationship between effort and outcome. Some youngsters proclaim defeat before they've even attempted a task. When they don't do well on an assignment, they attribute their failure to lack of ability, not realizing that achievement is often a function of effort. Other students may be overconfident—even cocky—and think they can do well without exerting much effort. In either situation, you have to make the relationship between effort and outcome explicit. Whenever possible, point out students' improvement and help them to see the role of effort: "See, you did all your math homework this week, and it really paid off. Look at how well you did on the quiz!"

The relationship between effort and outcome became painfully clear to a student in Sandy's class who refused to take notes during class. When Sandy first noticed that he wasn't taking notes, she told him to take out his notebook and open it. He did, murmuring, "I'll open my notebook, but you can't force me to take notes." Later, he told Sandy he didn't need to take notes like the other kids, because he had a good memory. She explained that her years of experience had shown her that taking notes in chemistry was absolutely necessary; she suggested he keep his notebook out and open "just in case." When the first test was given, the boy's grade was 40. Sandy told him: "I know it's not because you're unable to do the work. So what do you think? What conclusion do you draw from this?" The boy responded, "I guess I gotta take notes."

SHOE   By JEFF MACNELLY

FIGURE 5-5
It's important to point out the relevance of learning activities. *(Reprinted with permission © 93 Tribune Media Service, Inc. All rights reserved.)*

Some of Brophy's other motivational strategies address the *value* portion of the expectancy × value equation:

Relate lessons to students' own lives so that the content is more meaningful and relevant. A study of motivational strategies (Newby, 1991) demonstrated that on-task behavior is higher in classrooms where teachers provide students with reasons for doing tasks and relate lessons to students' personal experiences. Unfortunately, Newby found that first-year teachers use these "relevance strategies" only occasionally. (See Figure 5-5.)

Observations of our teachers provide numerous examples of attempts to link academic tasks to youngsters' lives. When Carmen's students create Renaissance banners, they decorate them with their own names or initials. When Carmen introduces a portrait activity, she shows portraits done by Diego Rivera, a famous Mexican muralist. A student whose surname is also Rivera jokes, "No relation," and they talk about popular names in Hispanic culture. When Fred's students study the Bill of Rights, they debate whether wearing a t-shirt with an obscene slogan is protected free speech. When Sandy's students do a lab in which they create silver, she jokes with them about getting rich from their labor: "Okay, your last task today is to determine how much silver we made here and to decide if I'm going to get rich. Look up the price of silver on the open market. Was this procedure cost effective?"

Model an interest in learning and express enthusiasm for the material. When Carmen shows her students paintings by various artists, she shares her enthusiasm for the work of Frida Kahlo. She tells students: "I really love Kahlo's paintings. . . . Let me tell you a story about her. It's a really interesting story. You'll like this. It explains why a lot of her paintings show people in agony." When Fred is about to introduce a difficult concept, he announces: "Now please listen to this. Most Americans don't understand this at all; they don't have a clue. But it's really important, and I want you to understand it."

Include novelty/variety elements. Donnie's class is about to do the "challenge problem of the day." She distributes a reproduced copy of the dollar bill and tells students to figure out how many $1 bills would be needed to make one mile if they were lined up end to end. Fred also uses money to make a point about choosing a more difficult, but more ethical course of action. He moves up an aisle and drops a

$5.00 bill on an empty chair. Turning to the girl sitting in the next seat, he says, "You could just stick that in your pocket, walk out the door and go to McDonald's, right? Take the money and run. That would certainly be possible, but would it be right?"

Provide opportunities for students to respond actively. So often the teacher talks and moves, while students sit passively and listen. In contrast, when Donnie reviews a problem involving supplementary and complementary angles, she asks students to suggest a strategy for solving the problem. After each suggestion, she asks, "Okay, what do I do next? What's the next step?" When students give the answers, she asks, "How did you get that? Explain your reasoning." Fred also structures lessons so that students must be actively involved. When students in his IPLE class study the judicial system, they engage in a mock trial. When his Contemporary World Issues class discusses extending "most favored nation" status to China, Fred tells his students: "Okay, you're one of our state representatives. How are you going to vote? Take out a piece of paper, write down yes or no, and your reasons." After a few minutes, he announces that the House of Representatives is now in session. He asks a few students to share their opinions and then calls the question.

Allow students to create finished products. Unlike Carmen's art classes, where students' efforts always result in finished products, too much school time is devoted to exercises, drills, and practice. Students practice writing, but rarely write. They practice reading skills, but rarely read. They practice mathematical procedures, but rarely do real mathematics. Yet, creating a finished product gives meaning and purpose to assignments and increases students' motivation to learn.

After a fierce winter blizzard that closed school for seven days and left administrators trying to figure out how to make up the lost time, Fred's students wrote letters to state legislators offering various proposals. Since the task was *real,* the letters had to be suitable for mailing; motivation was far greater than it would have been if the task had been a workbook exercise on writing business letters. Similarly, Sandy's labs are not simply exercises in following a prescribed set of steps leading to a foregone conclusion. They are real investigations into real problems.

Provide opportunities for students to interact with peers during academic activities. All four teachers firmly believe that motivation (and learning) are enhanced if students are allowed to work with one another. They provide numerous opportunities for peer interaction (a topic that will be explored further in Chapter Nine).

Sometimes, groups are carefully planned; at other times, they are formed more casually. For example, one day I saw Donnie shuffle a deck of cards (admitting that she never learned how to do this really well) and then walk around the room, asking each student to pick a card. She then told students to get up and find the person or persons with the same number or face card that they had. Once students had found their partners, she proceeded to explain the group task.

As I said earlier, recognizing that teachers have a responsibility to stimulate students' motivation to learn doesn't mean that the task is easy. This year, for example, one of Fred's Contemporary World Issues classes has a large proportion of students who, according to Fred, are "just marking time." During one conversation, Fred shared both his frustration and his determination:

Providing opportunities for students to respond actively: Fred consults with students planning a mock trial.

These kids are a constant struggle—the toughest kind of kids to work with. They're not dumb; they're not bad; they're just not intrinsically motivated. And they're used to taking it easy; for the last three years of high school, they've found that passive resistance works. They're so passive that teachers just leave them alone. But I refuse to give up on them. I look them in the face and say, "Tell me you want to stay home and be a slug and I'll leave you alone." And nobody's told me that. Actually, I think they're finally getting resigned to the fact that they can't coast in my class. And they can't even be mad at me, because they know that I'm on their side.

SHARING RESPONSIBILITY WITH STUDENTS

A third approach to gaining students' cooperation is to provide opportunities for them to exercise some autonomy and to make decisions about their own behavior. None of us like to feel controlled or manipulated, and it seems clear that students who feel empowered will be more likely to share the responsibility for seeing that classroom norms are enforced.

We already touched on this topic in the last chapter, when we discussed the idea of allowing students to participate in rule-setting. But providing opportunities for students to make decisions about behavior doesn't end on the first day of school; it is an ongoing process. For example, Sandy usually gives students a "block homework assignment"—perhaps 25 to 30 problems and a certain amount of reading—that is due in a week or so. She recommends that students do four or five problems a night, but she does not require them to show her their work on a daily basis. She realizes that this means some students will wait until the last night to do all the problems:

> High school teachers have to remember that students want to be treated like young adults, not like babies. It's important to give them some responsibility for their own behavior. They might make the wrong decisions and "fall and scrape their knees," but then they can see the consequences. I think they're more likely to take responsibility for their mistakes if teachers don't dictate everything.

In a similar way, Fred suggests that his students take notes, but he doesn't specify a particular format:

> I tell my students that it's helpful to take notes, but they should decide how and when. I tell them, "Just make sure they work. If you bomb out on a test because you couldn't read your notes or remember what a particular scribble meant, then your notes didn't work." I show them my notes—my notes look terrible, but they work for me. That's what's really important. I tell them, "They're your notes, make sure they work for you. If you want me to help you develop a better way to take notes, then I will."

Carmen also emphasizes the importance of providing students with the opportunity to make choices:

> I really want my students to be able to walk around and get their materials and decide how they want to do their projects. If they can do it themselves, then I can be the facilitator. I hate seeing everyone do the same thing in the same way. Often, it doesn't matter if they approach the project backwards or forwards; they'll get there anyway. Some teachers only give kids three colors and say "This is how you are to proceed." But I want to give my students choices; I want to treat them like human beings.

Sharing decision-making can be difficult for teachers (Schmuck and Schmuck, 1988). When you're feeling pressured to "cover the curriculum" and to maximize learning time, it's easier to make the decisions by yourself. For example, assigning topics for a term paper is faster than allowing students to decide on their own topic; giving students a particular kind of paper and three paint colors is simpler than helping them to decide on the paper and colors they want to use. Involving students can be "messy" and time-consuming, and allowing students to make decisions about their own behavior means that they'll sometimes make the wrong decisions. Nonetheless, the opportunity to exercise judgment and to make decisions not only increases students' willingness to cooperate, but also enhances their independence, self-control, and socially responsible behavior (Solomon, Watson, Delucchi, Schaps, and Battistich, 1988).

REWARDING APPROPRIATE BEHAVIOR

Many effective managers find it useful to provide students with rewards for appropriate behavior and for involvement in academic work. The use of rewards in classrooms is based on the psychological principle of *positive reinforcement:* behavior that is rewarded is strengthened and is therefore likely to be repeated. One advantage of this approach is that it forces us to focus on the positive. Instead of vigilantly watching students for instances of misbehavior, we must be alert to instances of appropriate behavior. We must "catch 'em being good."

This section of the chapter discusses the kinds of rewards that are available to teachers, examines some problems that may diminish their effectiveness, and presents some guidelines for their use.

Kinds of Rewards

Rewards can be divided into three categories: social rewards, activity rewards, and tangible rewards. *Social rewards* are verbal and nonverbal indications that you recognize and appreciate the way students are behaving. A pat on the back, a smile, a thumbs-up signal—these are commonly used social rewards that are low in cost and readily available.

Praise can also function as a social reward. Interestingly, however, research has shown that teachers use very little praise in classrooms. Jere Brophy (1981) reports that praise of good conduct appears only once every two to ten hours in the early grades and essentially disappears after that! Furthermore, praise can be misused, applied in ways that diminish its positive impact. For example, if public praise is given to only a few students, they may become known as "teacher's pets"—hardly a rewarding label. Another problem arises when teachers praise students they don't particularly like, and inadvertently contradict the praise with frowns or other nonverbal indicators of disapproval. When that happens, the verbal praise is likely to be perceived as insincere (Brophy, Evertson, Anderson, Baum, and Crawford, 1981).

Despite the problems, Brophy (1981) concludes that "effective praise can be informative as well as reinforcing, can provide encouragement and support, and can help teachers establish friendly relationships with students" (p. 274). In order to be effective, however, praise must be *specific and sincere.* Instead of "you were great this morning," try "I really like the way you came into the room, took off your baseball caps, and immediately got out your notebooks." Being specific will make your praise more informative; it will also help you to avoid using the same tired, old phrases week after week, phrases that quickly lose any impact (e.g., "good job"). If praise is to serve as a reinforcer, it also needs to be *contingent on the behavior you are trying to strengthen.* In other words, it should be given only when that behavior occurs, so that students understand exactly what evoked the praise.

> Donnie distributes a lab worksheet that asks students to draw a parallelogram and then work through five activities to "discover" the figure's properties. She stresses that students should write down their observations after each activity and then draw some final conclusions. As students work on the problems, she circulates through the room, helping, correcting, encouraging, and commenting. When she sees Shaneika's paper, she tells her: "Shaneika, you are really following directions. You're writing the answers as you go along."

In addition to pats on the back and verbal praise, some teachers institute more formal ways of recognizing accomplishment, improvement, or cooperation. For example, they may display student work, provide award certificates, nominate students for school awards given at the end of the year, or select "Students of the Week." Whichever approach you use, be careful that this strategy of public recognition doesn't backfire by causing students embarrassment. As Sandy reminded us in Chapter Three, secondary students generally do not want to stand out from their peers.

In addition to social rewards, teacher sometimes use *special activities* as rewards for good behavior. In junior and senior high, watching a video (with popcorn!), listening to music, having free time, or having a night of no homework can be very reinforcing. Carmen finds that allowing students to help make decorations for the hallway or for special events is also a very attractive reward.

One way of determining which activities should be used as rewards is to listen carefully to students' requests. If they ask you for the opportunity to listen to music or have a popcorn party, you can be confident that those activities will be reinforcing (at least for those particular students). It's also helpful to observe what activities students engage in when they have free time (e.g., do they read *Sassy* or *Sports Illustrated* magazines? talk with friends? draw?).

Finally, teachers can use *tangible, material rewards* for good behavior—cookies, candy, key chains, pencils—although such rewards are used less in high school than in elementary school. For example, Donnie goes to a discount supermarket and buys a big supply of candy that she keeps in a back closet; when students have been especially cooperative, she'll break out the Twizzlers™ for an unexpected treat. Similarly, Fred sometimes gives prizes when students have to review factual information for tests, a task they usually find boring. He may have students play vocabulary bingo, telling them: "I have two prizes in my pocket for the winner—two tickets for an all-expense-paid trip to Hawaii or a piece of candy. You get whichever one I pull out of my pocket first." Every now and then, Fred also uses candy to show his appreciation for good behavior. In his words,

> If someone has never given me grief, I may be moved to a spontaneous act of generosity. I'll say, "Here take this," and give them a Sugar Daddy™ or package of Sweet Tarts™. It's amazing; kids go crazy over a little piece of candy.

Problems with Rewards

The practice of rewarding appropriate behavior has been the focus of considerable controversy. In particular, educators have debated the legitimacy and ultimate value of *tangible* rewards. Even among our four teachers, there is disagreement. While Fred and Donnie occasionally use tangible rewards, Sandy and Carmen do not.

One objection is that giving students tangible rewards in exchange for good behavior or performance is tantamount to bribery. Proponents of this position argue that students should engage in appropriate behavior and activities for their own sake: they should be quiet during in-class assignments because that is the socially responsible thing to do; they should do their homework so that they can practice skills taught during class; they should learn verb conjugations in Spanish because they need to know them. Other educators acknowledge the desirability of such intrinsic motivation, but believe that the use of rewards is inevitable in situations where people are not completely free to follow their own inclinations. They ask: How many of us would go to work each day if we weren't going to collect a pay check at the end of the week?

Another major concern is that rewarding students for behaving in certain ways actually undermines their intrinsic motivation to engage in those behaviors. This concern requires us to distinguish between the use of rewards for teaching and reinforcing *appropriate classroom behaviors* and rewarding students for successful *academic performance* (e.g., getting an A on a vocabulary test). A long history of research on behavior modification has demonstrated that when students have difficulty behaving appropriately, rewards can be used to increase acceptable behaviors (e.g., following directions) and to reduce unacceptable behaviors (e.g., making distracting comments during discussions). (We will return to this topic in Chapter Six.) But what happens when you reward students, not for the behaviors required for an orderly environment, but for engaging in academic activities they already know how to do—and even enjoy? Is it possible that providing rewards in a case like this can actually decrease students' intrinsic motivation?

This question was explored in an influential study conducted by Lepper, Greene, and Nisbett (1973). First, the researchers identified preschoolers who showed interest in a particular drawing activity during free play. Then they met with the children individually. Some children were simply invited to draw with the materials (the "no-reward" subjects). Others were told they could receive a "good-player" award, which they received for drawing (the "expected-reward" subjects). Still others were invited to draw and were then given an unexpected reward at the end (the "unexpected-reward" subjects). Subsequent observations during free play revealed that the children who had been promised a reward ahead of time engaged in the art activity half as much as they had initially. Children in the other two groups showed no change.

The study by Lepper, Greene, and Nisbett stimulated a great deal of research on the potentially detrimental effects of external rewards. Although the results were not always consistent, this research led educators to conclude that *rewarding people for doing something they already like to do decreases their interest in continuing that behavior.* Recently, however, the debate over external rewards has heated up once again. Judy Cameron and W. David Pierce (1994) conducted an extensive analysis of 96 previous studies and concluded that teachers can use rewards without worrying that their students will lose their intrinsic motivation. In fact, Cameron and Pierce found that verbal praise significantly *increased* intrinsic motivation, while unexpected tangible rewards had no effect. Even expected, tangible rewards did no harm, unless they were given simply for doing a task, rather than meeting a specified level of performance or completing a task. According to Cameron and Pierce's findings, this means that it's all right to say, "If you complete the assignment accurately, you'll get some free time at the end of the period" (reward contingent on completion and level of performance), but it's not all right to say, "Work on the assignment, and you'll get some free time at the end of the period."

Despite the persuasiveness of Cameron and Pierce's arguments, the debate is far from over. Already other researchers have challenged both their methods and their findings (*Harvard Education Letter,* 1995). At the present time, caution in the use of external rewards is clearly in order. Nonetheless, it still appears that the judicious use of rewards can help in the task of gaining students' cooperation and increasing their involvement in learning activities (Cohen, 1985).

Using Rewards Effectively

As you contemplate a system of rewards for your classroom, keep in mind the following suggestions:

• *Distinguish between rewarding appropriate behaviors and rewarding performance on academic activities.* Rewards (verbal, social, and tangible) can be helpful to teach students the behaviors needed for order and learning, such as speaking quietly, sitting still, focusing on schoolwork, and remembering to bring their homework. But don't wait for perfect performance; instead, shape youngsters' behavior by rewarding improvement.

• *Use verbal rewards to increase intrinsic motivation for academic tasks.* It seems clear that praise can have a positive impact on students' intrinsic motivation. But remember that teenagers may be embarrassed by public praise, and they are good at detecting phoniness. In order to be reinforcing, praise should be specific, sincere, and contingent on the behavior you are trying to strengthen.

• *Save tangible rewards for activities that students find unattractive.* When students already enjoy doing a task, there's no need to provide tangible rewards. Save tangible rewards for activities that students tend to find boring and aversive.

• *If you're using tangible rewards, try to provide them unexpectedly, after the task performance.* In this way, students are more likely to view the rewards as information about their performance and as an expression of the teacher's pleasure, rather than as an attempt to control their behavior.

• *Be cautious about using expected tangible rewards. Be sure to make them contingent upon completion of a task or achieving a specific level of performance.* If you reward students simply for engaging in a task, regardless of their performance, they are likely to spend less time on the task once the reward is removed.

• *Make sure you select rewards that students like.* You may think that animal stickers are really neat, but if your high school students do not find them rewarding, their behavior will not be reinforced.

• *Keep your program of rewards simple.* An elaborate system of rewards is impossible to maintain in the complex world of the classroom. The fancier your system, the more likely you will abandon it. Moreover, if rewards become too salient, they overshadow more intrinsic reasons for behaving in certain ways. Students become so preoccupied with collecting, counting, and comparing that they lose sight of why the behavior is necessary or valuable.

WHAT DO THE STUDENTS SAY?

While working on this chapter, I became curious about the perceptions of students in the classrooms of our four teachers. In particular, I was interested in why they thought junior- and senior-high students behaved in some classes and misbehaved in others, as well as their views of the particular classes I was observing. In each class, the teacher left the room so that the students and I could talk more comfortably. I explained that I wanted the "student perspective" on classroom management and asked them to explain in writing "why kids behave in some classes," "why kids misbehave in some classes," and "how kids generally behave in this class and why." After students had a chance to write down their thoughts, they shared their responses.

Across classes, students demonstrated extraordinary consistency. Whether students were eighth graders or twelfth graders, their responses reflected three main themes. First, students stressed the importance of teachers' *relating to students with caring and respect.* They talked about teachers who "can relate to our teenage lifestyle," who "try to understand us," "who create trust," who "help you and explain what they want," and "who have a sense of humor." One student in Fred's class put it this way: "When a teacher takes some time to get to know students and shows some humor or shares a bit of their personal life, students may relate to them better." In Sandy's class, someone wrote, "The teacher must relate to the students. Understand when there is a problem and try to solve it. When the students see a teacher doing his/her best to make them feel comfortable with what they're learning, they behave well."

Clearly, not all teachers relate to students in this way. Students wrote about teachers "who put students down" and treat them like "little kids," about teachers who "don't care," and about teachers who are "beyond strict and just don't want to hear what we have to say." As one student wrote:

> Sometimes, if a teacher really demands the respect from day one, instead of earning it, a disliking developes [sic]. If a teacher doesn't think about what the students are feeling, they won't like him/her. Students can always detect those sort of things. Dislike = misbehave.

Many students used the word "respect" in both their written and oral comments, and I pressed them to tell me what "respecting students" looks like. They didn't have difficulty: teachers respect students when they give them their grades privately, when they don't put them down, when they don't tell students a question is dumb, when they "scold a child quietly instead of in class in front of others," when they take time to help kids who are confused, when they allow students to give their own opinions, when they make sure students treat each other well (e.g., they don't allow kids to talk when another kid is talking), and when they show students they *care.*

A second theme to emerge from students' comments was the importance of *teaching in a way that is motivating and interesting.* One of Donnie's students captured this widely shared perspective:

> Teachers have to make the class fun, but organized. Have a lot of interaction between students and challenge them. . . . Sometimes teachers are boring. The class drags on and the students lose attention span towards the teacher and the class. If the teacher teaches in an old-fashion style, the kids become frustrated.

These ideas were expressed in a number of ways: teachers need to be knowledgeable and to *love* what they do ("kids can tell"); teachers need to teach in creative ways—not just out of the book; they need to get the whole class involved; they need to relate the material to students' lives. Although a lot of people used the word "fun," one student wrote, "Not everything can be fun; it doesn't have to be fun, but there are ways teachers can make it more interesting and more challenging."

The final major theme that students discussed was the need for teachers to *set the rules and follow them.* This was expressed in a number of different ways: "teachers need to be a strong authority figure"; "teachers need to tell kids what they expect and give no second tries"; "teachers need to show strength"; "teachers need to be strict (but not mean)"; "teachers need to come off as someone who has control." What is clearly conveyed by these responses is students' lack of respect for teachers who are too permissive, who are "too cowardly to take charge," and who "let kids run all over them." One student wrote: "Kids misbehave when the teacher lets them pretty much do whatever they want. If they're disrupting class the teacher will try to go on with her class by maybe trying to speak above the person disrupting the class or ignoring it." This view was reiterated in another student's response: "Usually misbehavior happens in classes when teachers are too lenient. Every class needs to have some time to relax and fool around, but the teacher should know the limit." Still another summed it up this way:

> Some teachers seem very insecure about misbehaving students. They tend to say "stop or I'll send you to the office" too much. When a teacher first meets his/her class they need to set down guidelines and go over them confidently and be sure of what he/she is doing.

In sum, the first two themes to emerge from students' comments—treating students with respect and teaching in a motivating way—reflect two of the approaches discussed in this chapter (establishing a positive relationship and motivating students to learn). The third theme—setting limits—is pursued in the next chapter, "When Prevention Is Not Enough: Protecting and Restoring Order."

SUMMARY

This chapter discussed the fact that having clear, reasonable rules and routines doesn't automatically mean that everyone will follow them. I reiterated the fact that students are a "captive" audience, stressed the need to gain students' cooperation, and suggested four approaches to this task.

Establishing a Positive Relationship

- Provide leadership (structure situations, organize, set tasks)
- Behave in a friendly, considerate manner; listen, help

- Create a safe environment, where individuals treat each other respectfully
- Show a sense of humor

Fostering Students' Motivation to Learn

- Keep in mind Feather's theory of motivation: expectation of success × value = motivation
- Provide opportunities for success
- Teach students to set reasonable goals and to evaluate their own performance
- Emphasize the relationship between effort and outcome
- Relate lessons to students' own lives
- Model interest and enthusiasm
- Include novelty/variety elements
- Provide opportunities for students to respond actively
- Allow students to create finished products
- Provide opportunities to interact with peers

Sharing Responsibility

- Share decision making
- Provide opportunities for students to monitor their own behavior

Using Rewards

- Keep in mind the different types of rewards:
  social rewards
  special activities
  tangible rewards
- Be aware that rewarding people for doing something they already like to do may decrease their interest in continuing that behavior
- Think carefully about when and how to use rewards:
  Distinguish between rewarding appropriate behavior and rewarding performance on academic activities
  Use verbal rewards to increase intrinsic motivation for academic tasks
  Save tangible rewards for activities that students find unattractive (not for ones they already like)
  If you're using tangible rewards, provide them unexpectedly, after the task performance
  Provide expected tangible rewards only for completion of a task or for achieving a specific level of performance
  Select rewards that your students like
  Keep your reward program simple

Strive to create an environment that is relaxed and comfortable, but orderly and productive. Remember, classroom order is like conversation: it can only be achieved if both parties agree to participate.

ACTIVITIES

1. Think about the teachers you had in junior and senior high school. Select one teacher who had a positive effect on you as a student and one teacher who had a negative effect. Write a paragraph on each teacher, focusing on one of the approaches described in this chapter for gaining students' cooperation (fostering positive relationships with students; motivating students to learn; sharing responsibility with students; using rewards to encourage and reinforce appropriate behavior). Provide details and examples to illustrate each teacher's use of the approach (or lack thereof).

2. Plan three activities for the first week of school: (1) an introductory, get-acquainted activity; (2) an introductory activity in your content area; and (3) a "hands-on" activity.

Select any topic you like. Describe each of your activities in narrative form. As you plan, keep in mind the ways of gaining students' cooperation described in this chapter. Code your activity descriptions with the following letters, indicating the ways in which the activities are designed to motivate your students and build positive relationships.

a. Provides opportunities for success.

b. Content is meaningful and relevant; connects with their lives.

c. Allows for peer interaction.

d. Requires active participation by all.

e. Creates a relaxed and pleasant atmosphere.

As an example, here is an activity I observed in Donnie's class:

Activity	Code
Students work in groups of three to solve the following problem: The names of eight colors (blue, brown, green, maroon, orange, red, white, and yellow) can be placed in eight sections of the wheel at the bottom of the page. Use the following clues to fill each section. 1. No two words next to each other are the same length. 2. No two words with double letters are next to each other. 3. The word in Section 1 has no letters in common with the words in either section next to it. 4. The word in section 3 has the same number of letters as the word in section 7. The same is true for sections 4 and 8. 5. The words red, yellow, and blue do not all appear in the same half of the wheel.	a, c, d, e

3. In addition to rule setting, how might you involve your students in decision making to develop a feeling of shared responsibility? In the following two vignettes, the teachers have directed the activity. Think about ways they could have involved students in the planning, directing, creating, or evaluating. Rewrite each vignette to show this more student-centered approach.

a. Mrs. Peters felt that the unit her seventh-grade class completed on folk tales would lend itself to a class play. She chose Paul Bunyan and Pecos Bill as the stories to dramatize. The students were excited and Mrs. Peters gave out parts and assigned students to paint scenery. Mrs. Peters wrote a script and sent it home for the students to memorize. She asked parents to help make the costumes. After three weeks of practice, the play was performed for the elementary classes and the parents.

b. Mr. Wilkins wanted his tenth-grade World Civilization class to develop an understanding about ancient civilizations. He assigned a five-part project. Students had to research four civilizations (Egyptian, Mesopotamian, Indus Valley, and Shang); write a biography of Howard Carter, a famous archaeologist; describe three pyramids (step, Great Pyramid, Pyramid of Sesostris II); outline the reigns of five kings (Hammurabi, Thutmose III, Ramses II, David, and Nebuchadnezzar); and make a model of a pyramid. He gave the class four weeks to complete the projects and then collected them, graded them, and displayed them in the school library.

REFERENCES

Anderman, E. M., and Maehr, M. L. (1994). Motivation and schooling in the middle grades. *Review of Educational Research, 64*(2), 287–309.

Brekelmans, M., Wubbels, T., and Creton, H. (1990). A study of student perceptions of physics teacher behavior. *Journal of Research in Science Teaching, 27*(4), 335–350.

Brophy, J. (1981). On praising effectively. *The Elementary School Journal, 81*(5), 269–277.

Brophy, J. (1987). Synthesis of research on strategies for motivating students to learn. *Educational Leadership, 45* 40–48.

Brophy, J., and Evertson, C., with Anderson, L., Baum, M., and Crawford, J. (1981). *Student characteristics and teaching.* New York: Longman.

Cameron, J., and Pierce, W. D. (1994). Reinforcement, reward, and intrinsic motivation: A meta-analysis. *Review of Educational Research, 64,* 363–423.

Clark, C. (October 1989). The good teacher. Plenary lecture presented to The Norwegian Research Council for Science and the Humanities Conference: "Education from Cradle to Doctorate." Trondheim, Norway.

Cohen, M. W. (1985). Extrinsic reinforcers and intrinsic motivation. In M. K. Alderman and M. W. Cohen (Eds.), *Motivation theory and practice for preservice teachers* (Teacher Education Monograph No. 4). Washington, D.C.: ERIC Clearinghouse on Teacher Education, 6–15.

Cusick, P. A. (1994). *The educational system: Its nature and logic.* New York: McGraw-Hill.

Doyle, W. (1986). Classroom organization and management. In M. C. Wittrock (Ed.), *Handbook of research on teaching.* New York: Macmillan.

Everhart, R. B. (1983). *Reading, writing and resistance: Adolescence and labor in a junior high school.* Boston: Routledge & Kegan Paul.

Feather, N. (Ed.) (1982). *Expectations and actions.* Hillsdale, NJ: Erlbaum.

Good, T. L., and Brophy, J. E. (1994). *Looking in classrooms* (6th edition). New York: HarperCollins.

Grant, G. (1988). *The world we created at Hamilton High.* Cambridge, MA: Harvard University Press.

The Harvard Education Letter (January/February 1995). The debate over incentives heats up. *The Harvard Education Letter, 11*(1), 6.

Kounin, J. (1970). *Discipline and group management in classrooms.* New York: Holt, Rinehart & Winston.

Lepper, M., Greene, D., and Nisbett, R. E. (1973). Undermining children's intrinsic interest with extrinsic rewards: A test of the "overjustification" hypothesis. *Journal of Personality and Social Psychology, 28,* 129–137.

Newby, T. (1991). Classroom motivation: Strategies of first-year teachers. *Journal of Educational Psychology, 83,* 195–200.

Schmuck, R. A. and Schmuck, P. A. (1988). *Group processes in the classroom* (5th edition). Dubuque, Iowa: Wm. C. Brown.

Solomon, D., Watson, M. S., Delucchi, K. L., Schaps, E., and Battistich, V. (1988). Enhancing children's prosocial behavior in the classroom. *American Educational Research Journal, 25*(4), 527–554.

Wubbels, T., and Levy J. (Eds.). (1993). Do you know what you look like? *Interpersonal relationships in education.* Washington, DC: The Falmer Press.

FOR FURTHER READING

Jones, V. F., and Jones, L. S. (1986). *Comprehensive classroom management: Creating positive learning environments* (2nd edition). Boston: Allyn and Bacon. (Chapter 4 discusses positive teacher-student relationships).

Purkey, W. W., and Novak, J. M. (1984). *Inviting school success—A self-concept approach to teaching and learning* (2nd edition). Belmont, CA: Wadsworth.

Schaps, E., and Solomon, D. (1990). Schools and classrooms as caring communities. *Educational Leadership, 48*(3), 38–42.

Schmuck, R. A. and Schmuck, P. A. (1988). *Group processes in the classroom* (5th edition). Dubuque, Iowa: Wm. C. Brown.

Wlodkowski, R. J. (1986). *Motivation and teaching: A practical guide.* Washington, D.C.: National Education Association.

Chapter Six

When Prevention Is Not Enough: Protecting and Restoring Order

In the early 1980's, James Allen, a 30-year-old doctoral student in education, went undercover as a student in a southern California high school (Allen, 1986). He enrolled in a set of ninth-grade classes—agriculture, Spanish, health education, and English. Despite his beard, Allen was accepted by students, who "were neither overly curious or friendly" (p. 441), and teachers were asked to treat him as just another member of the class. Allen took tests, did homework, and participated in all classroom activities. But he also watched, listened, took notes, and, later, interviewed students and teachers. His goal: to learn what students think about life in school—especially, their views of classroom management.

From his massive pile of field notes, Allen eventually constructed a model of the students' "classroom agenda." According to his model, students had two major goals: *to socialize* and *to pass the course*. Six general strategies were used to achieve these goals—figuring out the teacher, having fun, giving teachers what they want, minimizing work, reducing boredom, and staying out of trouble—but students' use of these strategies varied from class to class. Allen noted that students "would wait for the teacher to set the initial classroom management structure (or lack of it)" (p. 450). Then they would use those strategies that were relevant and helpful in achieving their two goals. From the students' perspective, the best of all classes was a class that allowed them "to socialize while learning something interesting as they pass the course" (p. 456).

What can we learn from Allen's study? First, it reminds us (once again!) that teachers and students have different agendas for what happens in class. Although these agendas overlap (presumably both parties want students to pass the course), students are more concerned about socializing, while teachers are more concerned about instruction, learning, and order. Of course, the more we can accommodate students' need to socialize (e.g., by allowing them to work together and to engage in cooperative learning activities), the more we can merge the two agendas. Nonetheless, no matter how hard teachers work to establish positive relationships with students and to involve them in meaningful learning activities, conflicts are bound to occur when people have different agendas.

Second, Allen's study reveals the fact that, at the beginning of the school year, students work hard at "figuring out the teacher"—determining teachers' expectations and requirements, the amount of socializing they will tolerate, and how far they can be pushed. Most students will pursue their agendas within the limits the teacher sets, but *they need to know those limits.* This underscores the importance of communicating your behavioral expectations to students (the topic of Chapter Four)—and then enforcing those expectations. In other words, just as it's part of the students' role to push, it's part of the teacher's role to communicate that students can't push too far. Listen to Sandy:

> It's crucial to hold high school students to the expectations you set. In the beginning of the year, they'll try different things to see how much they can get away with. They're constantly testing you. Knowing that, I don't overlook *anything* in the first few weeks of school; I try to be on top of *everything.* That way students learn that they can't pull one over on you.

Donnie also recognizes that students are busy figuring her out during the first few days of school. She comments:

> New teachers should not be fooled by the good behavior that students exhibit at the very beginning of school. I usually find that on the first day of school, everyone is really subdued. They're checking you out. It isn't until the second week that they really start testing. That's when the problems start!

In this chapter, we consider ways of responding to the problems that you may encounter—from minor, disruptive infractions to chronic, more serious misbehaviors. Before going any further, however, let's consider what these problems are likely to be.

WHAT'S IN STORE

Newspaper headlines about drugs, guns, and violence sometimes convey the image of secondary classrooms as "blackboard jungles." (We will consider these difficult issues in Chapter Twelve, "Helping Students with Serious Problems.") But apathy and resistance can often be more problematic than overt rebellion and actual disruption. Consider the following scene, witnessed by Alpert (1991) in an English class composed of juniors and seniors:

TEACHER: . . . now, ah, the first four stanzas certainly do create a mood for the reader. Now, what adjectives would you use to describe that mood?

STUDENTS: (Silence)

TEACHER: Think about it a little bit and then try to run it through your mind. How do we describe moods? Cheerful? Light headed? Sympathetic?

STUDENTS: (Silence)

TEACHER: What adjectives would you use to describe this one?

STUDENTS: (Silence, then a student mumbles) Mellow.

TEACHER: Mellow? OK, I can buy that to a certain extent. What [else]?
A STUDENT: (Mumbles) Solemn.
TEACHER: OK. Sarah suggests the word "solemn." Does that sound good?
SOME STUDENTS: (Mumble) No. (p. 354)

In addition to resistance, teachers commonly encounter a host of other mundane problems (Doyle, 1986, 1990)—socializing at inappropriate times, coming late, not having homework done, calling out, daydreaming, forgetting to bring supplies and books, teasing, and name-calling. A national survey of teachers (Center for Education Statistics, 1987) indicates that problems such as these are widespread; more than half of the senior-high teachers reported that in just the previous week a student had talked back to them (54 percent), whispered or passed a note (86 percent), or come late to class (91 percent).

Even if behaviors like these are not seriously disruptive, they can be aggravating, discouraging, and wearing. Furthermore, inappropriate behavior *threatens classroom order by interrupting the flow of instructional activity.* Lessons cannot proceed smoothly and efficiently if students haven't done their homework; class discussions fall apart if individuals refuse to participate; and giving instructions is a waste of time if no one is listening.

PRINCIPLES FOR DEALING WITH INAPPROPRIATE BEHAVIOR

There is little research on the relative effectiveness of disciplinary strategies (see Emmer and Aussiker, 1990), but four principles guide our discussion. First, when dealing with misbehavior, *the overriding goal should be to keep the instructional program going with a minimum of disruption.* Achieving this goal requires a delicate balancing act. On one hand, you cannot allow inappropriate behavior to interrupt the teaching-learning process. On the other hand, you must realize that disciplinary strategies themselves can be disruptive. As Doyle comments, interventions are "inherently risky" because they call attention to misbehavior and can actually pull students away from a lesson (1986, p. 421). In order to avoid this situation, you must try to anticipate potential problems and head them off; if you decide that a disciplinary intervention *is* necessary, you need to be as unobtrusive as possible.

Watching the four teachers in action, it is clear that they recognize the importance of protecting the instructional program. In the following incident, Carmen sizes up a potentially disruptive situation and is able to maintain the flow of her lesson:

After a short introduction on figure drawing, Carmen's eighth-grade students gather up the materials they will need—paper, pencils, cloth, reference books—and move to their tables. They are obviously excited about the day's activity. As Tommy nears his table, he purposely collides with a girl and takes her pencil. The girl tries to get her pencil back, and a minor scuffle begins. Swiftly, Carmen intercedes. Without raising her voice, she moves toward Tommy and points to a free table in the back of the room. "Tommy, you want to sit over here today?" She moves close to him and shepherds him back to the table. "You sit over here, where I can help you better." He sits down, and she makes sure he has pencil and paper. She moves away momentarily to see that the other students have started working, but comes back to Tommy: "Tommy, have you decided what you're going to do? Is your person going to have a hat?" He nods. "Okay, then choose a piece of colored paper or a piece of cloth." He does, and sets to work.

Later, she reflected on the importance of maintaining the flow of the lesson:

> Sometimes I have to "ride with them." Someone comes in all riled up, and I know that things could fall apart. But I try to overlook the little things, instead of making a big deal about them, and get the activity going. If I can do that, then they settle down and they're fine.

The second principle is that *whether or not a particular action constitutes misbehavior depends on the context in which it occurs* (Doyle, 1986). There are obvious exceptions to this notion—punching another person and stealing property are obvious violations that always require a teacher response. But other behaviors are not so clear cut. For example, in some classes, wearing a hat, sitting on your desk, chewing gum, and talking to neighbors are all misbehaviors, while in other classes these are perfectly acceptable. What constitutes misbehavior is often a function of a particular teacher's tolerance level or the standards set by a particular school (Cairns, 1987). Even within a class, the definition of misbehavior is dependent upon the context. A teacher may decide that talking out of turn is acceptable during a class discussion, as long as students' comments contribute to the lesson and the situation doesn't turn into a free-for-all; at other times, this same teacher may feel that a more structured lesson is needed.

When determining a course of action, you need to ask yourself, "Is this behavior disrupting or benefiting the ongoing instructional activity? Is it hurtful to other students? Does it violate established rules?" If the answer to these questions is no, disciplinary interventions may not be necessary.

> "I've got no control today," Fred announces with a grin. A glance around the room seems to confirm his assessment. Some students are sitting on their desks; others are standing in the aisles, leaning over other students who are writing. In the back of the room, four students are turned around in their seats and are having an animated discussion. One girl is standing by Fred's desk, loudly debating with a girl seated nearby. Just about everyone is talking. After a few moments, the topic of all this heated conversations becomes clear. Because of severe winter storms, the South Brunswick school district has exceeded the normal allotment of snow days. In order to meet the state mandate for 180 days of school, the board of education must now decide whether to eliminate spring break or extend the school year. Fred has seized the opportunity to teach a lesson on political activism. His students are to think about the issue, consider whether there should be a waiver from the 180-day mandate, and write to their state legislators. Today's assignment is to construct the first draft of the letter. After class, Fred thinks about the atmosphere in the class: "I know I could have exerted a lot more control over the situation. I could have told them to sit quiet, to jot down ideas, and then silently write a first draft. But what would I have gained?"

Third, this discussion is based on the principle that *disciplinary strategies must preserve students' dignity.* Richard Curwin and Allen Mendler (1988), authors of

Discipline with Dignity, put it this way:

> Students will protect their dignity at all costs, even with their lives if pushed hard enough. In the game of chicken, with two cars racing at top speed toward a cliff, the loser is the one who steps on the brake. Nothing explains this bizarre reasoning better than the need for peer approval and dignity. (p. 27)

In order to protect students' dignity, it is important to avoid power struggles that may cause students to lose face with their peers. Consider this incident, recently related by a student teacher in an English class:

> In our remedial writing lab, a student left to get a drink of water and was gone too long. Upset that the student took too long to get a drink, and upset that the student had failed to write his name on an in-class essay, the teacher proceeded to write the student's essay on the board for all to see. A few moments later, class was interrupted by a fire alarm. Again the student returned later than he was expected to return—between 30 seconds and a minute—and my teacher proceeded to yell and yell loudly right up in the kid's face. The student asked to speak but his request was denied. After the exchange, my teacher went to the board and proceeded to rip apart the student's essay. The student reminded him that he was not done and that the class was told that they could work on their essays today. The teacher said that this essay was going nowhere, even if given an extra day. I watched the student's face while his essay was being critiqued, and I realized first-hand how vulnerable and powerless students can be. Here is a group of students who lack confidence in writing, who do not dare to take risks with their writing—and this is how we treat them.

In contrast to this teacher, all four teachers make a real effort to speak with misbehaving students calmly and quietly. They don't bring up past sins. They take care to separate the youngster's *character* from the specific *misbehavior;* instead of attacking the student as a person ("You're lazy"), they talk about what the student has done ("You have not handed in the last two homework assignments"). When more than a brief intervention is necessary, they try to meet with students privately.

During the first week of school, I witnessed a good example of disciplining with dignity in Sandy's classroom. Even though it was so early in the school year, some students had already begun to test Sandy's adherence to the rules she had distributed a few days earlier:

> Sandy stands by the door, greeting students as they come in. The bell rings; Sandy begins to close the door, when William breathlessly rushes up. "You're late," she tells him quietly. "Does that mean I have to come after school?" he asks. "I'll talk to you later," she replies and moves to the front of the room to begin the lesson.
>
> Later in the period, students are working in small groups on a lab experiment. Sandy circulates through the room, helping students with the procedure. She goes over to William and pulls him aside. She speaks softly: "You owe me 10 minutes. Today or tomorrow?"
>
> "What's today?"
>
> "Tuesday."
>
> "Uh-oh." William looks worried.
>
> "Is it better for you to come tomorrow?" Sandy asks.
>
> "Yeah—but will you remind me?"

"I certainly will," she says with a rueful smile. Sandy goes over to her desk, makes a note in her grade book, and then continues circulating. A few minutes later, she stands beside William again, helping him with a problem and encouraging his progress.

In this vignette, we see how Sandy tried to avoid embarrassing William by speaking with him privately; how she demonstrated concern for William by offering him a choice about when to come for detention; how she avoided accusations, blame, and character-assassination; and how she showed William that she held no grudge by helping him with the lab a few minutes later. In short, the vignette demonstrates the way a teacher can communicate clear expectations for appropriate behavior while preserving a student's dignity.

Another way of disciplining with dignity is to structure opportunities for students to assume some responsibility for regulating their own behavior. In Chapter Five, I talked about gaining students' cooperation by sharing responsibility and decision-making authority. This chapter continues that theme by discussing strategies that involve students in solving the problems that arise in classrooms.

Finally, the fourth principle emphasizes the importance of *making sure a disciplinary strategy matches the misbehavior you are trying to eliminate.* Research (e.g., Pittman, 1985) has indicated that some teachers think about misbehavior in terms of three categories: *minor* misbehaviors (noisiness, socializing, daydreaming); *more serious* misbehaviors (arguing, failing to respond to a group directive); and *never tolerated* misbehaviors (stealing, intentionally hurting someone, destroying property). They also consider whether the misbehavior is part of a pattern or an isolated event.

When deciding how to respond to a problem, it is useful to think in terms of these categories and to select a response that is congruent with the seriousness of the misbehavior. This is easier said than done, of course. When misbehavior occurs, teachers have little time to assess its seriousness, decide if it's part of a pattern, and select an appropriate response. And too often, the situation is ambiguous: since misbehavior often occurs when the teacher is looking somewhere else, it may not be absolutely clear who is doing what to whom. Nonetheless, you don't want to ignore or react mildly to misbehavior that warrants a more severe response; nor do you want to overreact to misbehavior that is relatively minor.

With these four principles in mind—protecting the instructional program, considering the context, disciplining with dignity, and selecting a disciplinary strategy that matches the misbehavior—we turn now to specific ways of responding to inappropriate behavior.

DEALING WITH MINOR MISBEHAVIOR

As I mentioned in Chapter Four, Jacob Kounin's (1970) classic study of orderly and disorderly classrooms gave research support to the belief that successful classroom managers have eyes in the back of their heads. Kounin found that effective managers knew what was going on all over the room; moreover, *their students knew they knew,* because the teachers were able to spot minor problems and "nip them in the bud." Kounin called this ability "withitness," a term that has since become widely used in discussions of classroom management.

How do "with it" teachers deal with minor misbehavior? How do they succeed in nipping problems in the bud? This section discusses both nonverbal and verbal interventions and then considers the times when it may be better to do nothing at all. (Suggestions are summarized in Table 6-1.)

Nonverbal Interventions

A while back, an 11-year-old I know announced that she could be a successful teacher. When I asked why she was so confident, she replied: "I know how to make *the look*." She proceeded to demonstrate: her eyebrows slanted downward, her forehead creased, and her lips flattened into a straight line. She definitely had "the look" down pat.

The "teacher look" is a good example of an unobtrusive, nonverbal intervention. Sandy points out one benefit of this strategy when she comments: "In a science

TABLE 6-1
DEALING WITH MINOR MISBEHAVIOR

Strategy	Advantages

1. Nonverbal interventions:
    Facial expressions
    Eye contact
    Hand signals
    Proximity
	Allow you to prompt appropriate behavior without disrupting lesson
	Encourage students to assume responsibility for changing behavior

2. Verbal interventions: Direct commands	Straightforward
Stating student's name	Brief, unobtrusive
Rule reminders	Reinforce desired behavior
Calling on student to participate Incorporating student's name into lesson	Gets student back on task without even citing misbehavior; maintains flow of lesson
Use of gentle humor	Prompts a smile along with appropriate behavior
I-messages	Minimize negative evaluations and preserve relationships Point out consequences of behavior Promote student's autonomy and responsibility for actions
3. Ignoring the misbehavior	Unobtrusive; protects the flow of the lesson

class, it's really important not to raise your voice a lot. If my students get used to yelling, in an emergency lab situation I won't be able to get their attention. So I give *looks* instead." Making eye contact, using hand signals (e.g., thumbs down; pointing to what the individual should be doing), moving closer to the misbehaving student, and lightly touching a shoulder are other nonverbal ways of communicating withitness. All of these convey the message "I see what you're doing, and I don't like it," but since they are less directive than verbal commands, they encourage students to assume responsibility for getting back on task.

Nonverbal strategies are most appropriate for behaviors that are minor but persistent—frequent or sustained whispering, staring into space, calling out or walking around the room, putting on makeup, and passing notes. The obvious advantage of using nonverbal cues is that you can deal with misbehaviors like these without distracting other students. In short, nonverbal interventions enable you to protect and continue your lesson with minimum disruption.

> Donnie is at the board demonstrating how to construct congruent segments and congruent angles. Students are supposed to be following along, constructing congruent segments with rulers and compasses. Instead of working, two boys sit twirling their rulers on their pencils. Donnie notices what they are doing, but continues with her explanation. While she's talking, she gives the two boys a long, hard stare. They put down the rulers and get to work.

In the following incident, Carmen is able to nudge a student to begin working without any verbal reference to what is happening:

> Students are working on their drawings while Carmen circulates throughout the room providing encouragement and help. She spots Diego who's just sitting and staring into space. She moves over to him; without a word, she points to his paper, looks at him, and raises her eyebrows, as if to say, "Well, are you going to start?" He picks up his pencil and begins to draw.

As these anecdotes illustrate, a nonverbal cue is sometimes all that's needed to stop a misbehavior and get a student back "on task." In fact, a study of six middle school teachers (Lasley, Lasley and Ward, 1989) found that the *most successful responses to misbehavior were nonverbal.* These strategies stopped misbehavior 79 percent of the time; among the three "more effective managers," the success rate was even higher—an amazing 95 percent.

Verbal Interventions

Sometimes you find yourself in situations where it's just not possible to use a nonverbal cue. Perhaps you can't catch the student's eye, or you're working with a small group, and it would be too disruptive to get up and walk across the room to the misbehaving individual. Other times, you're able to use a nonverbal cue, but it's unsuccessful in stopping the misbehavior.

In cases like this, you might use a *nondirective verbal intervention.* These allow you to prompt the appropriate behavior, while leaving the responsibility for figuring out what to do with the misbehaving student. For example, *simply saying the student's name* might be enough to get the student back on task. Sometimes it's possible to *incorporate the student's name into the ongoing instruction:*

> Donnie's algebra class is reviewing homework. In the front row, a girl leans over and starts playing with the hand of the girl seated across the aisle from her. Without breaking stride, Donnie says, "So added together, that would be 4y, right, Ismara?" The girl straightens up and turns to her homework.

> Shaheed is slouching down in his seat and appears inattentive. As Fred talks about respect for the elderly in China, he moves closer to him. "Let's say Shaheed was my son, and I beat him up because he was getting a failing grade in class. What happens to me?" Shaheed sits up and "tunes in."

If the misbehavior occurs while a group discussion or recitation is going on, *you can call on the student to answer a question.* Consider the following example:

> The fifth-period geometry class is going over homework on isosceles triangles. As Donnie calls on students to do the problems, she walks through the room. "Okay, we need someone to do #14." Hands begin to go up. Donnie notices a girl in the back of the room who is gazing off into space. "Dominica, please do #14." Dominica "comes back" from wherever she was, looks at the book, and answers correctly. Donnie smiles, "Good!"

Calling on a student allows you to communicate that you know what's going on and to capture the student's attention—without even citing the misbehavior. But keep in mind what we said earlier about preserving students' dignity. If you are obviously trying to "catch" students and to embarrass them, the strategy may well backfire by creating resentment (Good and Brophy, 1994).

The *use of humor* can provide another "gentle" way of reminding children to correct their behavior. Used well, humor can show students that you are able to understand the funny sides of classroom life. But you must be careful that the humor is not tinged with sarcasm that can hurt students' feelings.

> Carmen's students are mixing paint, trying to achieve a color that matches their own skin tone. Carmen has warned them not to "make a gallon," since they only need the paint for one portrait, but one boy has gotten carried away. Carmen notices that he has three cups of paint spread before him and is still making more. She moves over, points to the cups of paint, and exclaims, "Jerome, you're making enough skin tone to paint a *nude,* and you're only doing a face!"

> It's near the end of the year, and Fred's students obviously have a case of "senioritis." They have just entered the room, and Fred is trying to get them to settle down. "Ladies and gentlemen, I know it's almost the end of the year, but could we make believe we're students now?"

> Donnie's class is about to do the challenge problem of the day. She tells the students that they may work together, but then announces with a smile that Zelia, a very talented math student, is getting a "handicap." She won't be allowed to talk, although she may work with other students. Zelia moans, but there's a big smile on her face. As the stu-

dents work, it is clear that Zelia finds it hard to restrain herself. She quickly works the problem, and she wants to tell her groupmates how to do it. When Donnie begins to question students about their thinking, Zelia jumps up and calls out, "I know, Ms. Collins." Then she catches herself, laughs, and sits back down. Later, Donnie explains that Zelia often dominates class discussion by calling out the (correct) answers and telling her peers what to do. In an effort to give other students a chance to think for themselves, Donnie occasionally gives Zelia a "handicap." This helps to remind Zelia that other students need a chance to work the problems, but it's more fun than constantly saying things like, "Zelia, other people need a chance too. Please, Zelia, don't call out."

An *"I-message"* is another way of verbally prompting appropriate behavior without giving a direct command. This strategy was developed by Thomas Gordon, a clinical psychologist and author of *T.E.T.—Teacher Effectiveness Training* (1974). Gordon recommends that I-messages contain three components. First, the teacher *describes the unacceptable behavior* in a nonblaming, nonjudgmental way. This phrase often begins with "when": "When people talk while I'm giving directions . . ." The second component describes the *tangible effect* on the teacher: "I have to repeat the directions and that wastes time . . ." Finally, the third part of the message states the *teacher's feelings* about the tangible effect: "and I get frustrated." Consider these examples of I-messages:

> "When you come to class without your supplies, I can't start the lesson on time, and I get really irritated."

> "When you leave your book bag in the middle of the aisle, I can trip over it, and I'm afraid I'll break a leg."

Although I-messages ideally contain all three components in the recommended sequence, I-messages in any order, or even with one part missing, can still be effective (Gordon, 1974). I've witnessed the four teachers use "abbreviated" I-messages. For example, Fred communicates how strongly he feels about paying attention when he tells his class: "If you pass notes while I'm lecturing, I'll become suicidal." To a student who called him by his first name, he says, "I really feel uncomfortable when you call me by my first name in school."

There are several benefits to using Gordon's approach. In contrast to typical "you-messages" (e.g., "You are being rude," "You ought to know better," "You're acting like a baby"), I-messages minimize negative evaluations of the student. They make it easier to avoid using extreme (and usually inaccurate) words like "always" and "never" (as in "You *always* forget to do your homework" or "You're *never* prepared for class"). For these reasons, they foster and preserve a positive relationship between people. Since I-messages leave decisions about changing behavior up to students, this approach is also likely to promote a sense of responsibility and autonomy. In addition, I-messages show students that their behavior has consequences and that teachers are people with genuine feelings. Unlike you-messages, I-messages don't make students defensive and stubborn; thus, they may be more willing to change their behavior.

Most of us are not used to speaking this way, so I-messages can seem awkward and artificial. With practice, however, using I-messages can become natural. I recently heard a four-year-old girl (whose parents had consistently used I-messages at home) tell her nursery school peer: "When you poke me with that pencil, it really hurts, and I feel bad 'cause I think you don't want to be my friend."

In addition to these nondirective approaches, there are also *more directive strategies* you can try. The most straightforward approach is to *direct students to the task at hand* ("Get to work on that math problem"; "Your group should be discussing the first three pages"). You can also *remind the student about the rule or behavioral expectation that is being violated* (e.g., "When someone is talking, everyone else is supposed to be listening"). Sometimes, if inappropriate behavior is fairly widespread, it's useful to review rules with the entire group. This is often true after a holiday, a weekend, or a vacation. Carmen used this strategy one Friday morning in February, after school had been closed off and on for several weeks because of snow:

> The eighth-grade bilingual class enters the room in a very rowdy fashion. Carmen tells students to sit at their tables, rather than gathering together in the instructional area at the back of the room. She speaks in a serious tone: "I know we haven't been in school much lately, with all the snow, and you've missed a lot of art. From the way you came in today, I think you've forgotten our rules. I think we need to review." She points to the chart on the wall and reminds students about how they are supposed to enter the art room.

Another strategy is to *give students a choice between behaving appropriately or receiving a penalty for continued inappropriate behavior* (e.g., "If you can't handle working in your group, you'll have to return to your seats"; "You either choose to raise your hand instead of calling out, or you will be choosing not to participate in our discussion"). Statements like these not only warn students that a penalty will be invoked if the inappropriate behavior continues, they also emphasize that students have real choices about how to behave and that penalties are not imposed without reason.

> Donnie's class is having difficulty settling down and paying attention. She looks at her watch and then comments quietly, "We can either do this now, or we can do this at 2:00 [after school]. I know that I'm in no rush to go home."

> One of Sandy's male students comes in wearing a t-shirt (over another shirt) that promotes the use of marijuana. She quickly moves over to him and calmly tells him the shirt is inappropriate for school. She gives him a choice: "If you really feel you must wear it, go to the office. Your other option is to turn it inside out or to take it off." He takes it off.

And in the following example, we see how Fred embellishes this strategy with a little humor:

> The bell rings; Fred moves to a podium in the front of the room and tries to get his students' attention. They continue talking. "Ladies and gentlemen, if you want a zero for life, talk now. If you don't, listen." Students laugh and settle down.

Deliberately Ignoring the Misbehavior

If misbehavior is extremely brief and unobtrusive, the best course of action may be *in*action. For example, during a discussion a student may be so eager to comment that she forgets to raise her hand; or someone becomes momentarily distracted and inattentive; or two boys quietly exchange a comment while you're giving directions. In cases like these, an intervention can be more disruptive than the students' behavior.

One risk of ignoring minor misbehavior is that students may conclude you're unaware of what's going on. Suspecting that you're not "with it," they may decide to see how much they can get away with, and then problems are sure to escalate. You need to monitor your class carefully to make sure this doesn't happen.

Another problem is that occasional ignoring can turn into full-fledged "blindness." This was vividly demonstrated in a study of a student teacher named Heleen (Creton, Wubbels, and Hooymayer, 1989). When Heleen was lecturing, her students frequently became noisy and inattentive. In response, Heleen talked more loudly and looked more at the chalkboard, turning her back on her students. She did not allow herself to see or hear the disorder—perhaps because it was too threatening and she didn't know how to handle it. Unfortunately, Heleen's students seemed to interpret her "blindness" as an indication that noise was allowed, and they became even more disorderly. Heleen eventually recognized the importance of "seeing" and responding to slight disturbances, in order to prevent them from escalating.

DEALING WITH MORE SERIOUS MISBEHAVIOR: USING PENALTIES

Sometimes, nonverbal cues or verbal reminders are not enough to convince students that you're serious about the behavioral expectations you've established. And sometimes misbehavior is just too serious to use these kinds of low-level responses. In cases like these, it may be necessary to impose a penalty in order to enforce your expectations for appropriate behavior.

In some cases, teachers discuss penalties when they teach rules and procedures, so students understand the consequences of violating a rule from the very beginning. We saw Sandy do this with her students in Chapter Four, when she laid out the penalties for coming late to class. This practice prevents unpleasant "surprises," and hopefully minimizes protests of blissful ignorance—"But you didn't *tell* me that would happen!"

Selecting Penalties

It's often difficult for beginning teachers to decide on appropriate penalties. One student teacher in social studies recently vented his frustration in this way:

> These two kids come to class every day and sit and do absolutely nothing. They don't create a big disturbance, and they're not really nasty or belligerent; they just won't do any work. They prefer to sit there and talk, and draw cartoons, and goof off. I keep

telling them they're getting a zero for each day they just sit, and that they're going to fail for the marking period, but they just don't care. I've told them I'm going to call their parents, but they just laugh. I don't want to send them to the disciplinarian's office, because my cooperating teacher says I could get a reputation as a teacher who can't control the class, and I'd really like to get a job in this district. So I'm really at a loss. These kids are really smart, and I hate to see them fail. But what can I do?

During one meeting, I posed this question to all four teachers and learned about the types of penalties they typically use. The question brought a variety of responses, but one theme emerged clearly. In Fred's words:

It's important to remember that the goal of a penalty is not to hurt kids, but to help them change their behavior. It's not to put kids down; it's to bring them up. If kids see that, then they'll accept the penalty. But if the behavior doesn't change, it's not a good penalty, no matter what it is.

With this idea in mind, let's consider the seven categories into which these teachers' penalties generally fall.

Mandatory private conferences   When students do not respond to nonverbal cues or verbal reminders, our teachers generally call a private conference, often after school or during a free period. During these conferences, they express their disappointment in the student's behavior. We normally don't think of this as a penalty, but since students in these classes really like their teachers, they feel bad when their teachers are upset. In serious, almost sorrowful tones, our teachers express their disappointment and surprise at the inappropriate behavior and direct students to think about the consequences of their actions. Sometimes, they will negotiate a plan for change, trying to get the students to take responsibility for their behavior. For example, when a student in Sandy's class failed a test, she held a private conference with him after school. Sandy shares this account of their meeting: "We talked about how he had been doing in class, and what had happened in this particular exam. It turned out that he had gone clubbing until 11:30 the night before the test. I told him, 'Well, that was your choice, and this was the outcome. What do you think? Do you like this outcome?' Obviously he didn't. We agreed that the next time there was a test, he wouldn't stay out late the night before and see if it makes a difference. I really think it's important to approach teenagers this way—to put the responsibility back on them whenever possible."

Loss of privileges   Sometimes students in the four teachers' classes may lose the right to sit wherever they like, particularly if their behavior is having a negative impact upon other students. Other privileges that can be taken away include working with a friend, free time, chewing gum, freely moving around the room, and joining in a class popcorn party.

Isolation from the group   All four teachers will move a student to an isolated or secluded area of the room if they are unable to work productively, but they try to be positive rather than negative about the move. (Recall that Carmen did this with Tommy when he became involved in a scuffle.) Fred will signal a student to move to a place that's "less distracting." When Sandy covered a seventh-grade class, she sometimes had to tell a student, "Come with me. Let's go to the back of the class and see what you can do back here where you can concentrate better. This will be your own private office."

Exclusion from class   All four teachers believe that "kicking kids out" is a strategy that should be reserved for major disruption. As Donnie points out, "Some students *want* to get out; they'll provoke a teacher just so they can leave the room. I know teachers who throw kids out all the time, but what's the point? Kids can't learn if they're in the office."

Despite their preference for handling problems within the room, the teachers recognize that there are times when this is just not possible. Sandy remembers how she sent a student to the "time-out" room when his behavior was so infuriating that she couldn't discuss it calmly: "I was so mad, I knew I was losing it. I was yelling, and the kid was yelling. So it was better for him to be out of the room. But ten minutes later, I called and told him to come back. By then we had both cooled down and we were able to talk." Similarly, Fred will send students to the office if their behavior is really out of control. He recalls one student who was severely disturbed: "I had it worked out with the office, so they knew what to do with him when he showed up. In the beginning, I had to kick him out three times a week, but slowly he got better about controlling his behavior, and we got it down to once every two weeks. But this only worked because class was a good place to be. He had friends there, we laughed every day, he got to do good stuff. If he hadn't liked it—and me—getting to leave would have been a reward."

Detention   For routine violations of rules (e.g., coming late to class), Donnie, Sandy, and Fred use regular school detention as a penalty. However, they are cautious about using this for "big" problems. As Sandy puts it, "If students are disrespectful, or really having problems controlling themselves, I prefer to talk privately with them. What's going to be learned from 45 minutes of detention?"

Written reflections on the problem   Sometimes, a situation is so complex that it warrants serious reflection in writing. Fred recalls this incident: "My senior honors class was supposed to do a short research paper on China. When I began to grade the papers, it seemed to me that a lot of the citations were suspicious. I did some checking at the library, and found that some students had simply taken material from an encyclopedia and made up the references. I went into class and told them how serious this was, and how they would all get zeros for their papers if they couldn't validate their references. But I gave them a way out: they could write a letter to me explaining what they had done and why, and they had to make 'reparation' by doing two additional research papers with valid citations. The letters were really revealing. A lot of these kids were absolutely clueless about why it's important to reference accurately. One kid came in and thanked me for making a big deal about this. He said he really didn't know that what he was doing was dishonest."

Contacting parents   Donnie, Sandy, and Fred all contact parents or guardians if a student shows a pattern of consistent misbehavior. For example, when a student in Sandy's class repeatedly "forgot" to do his homework, Sandy told him she would be calling his parents to discuss the problem. She tried to make it clear that she was calling, not in anger, but out of serious concern. She also wanted to convey the idea that "between all of us, maybe we can help you get it together." In contrast to the other three teachers, Carmen generally goes to the homeroom teacher when there is a consistent problem; since she sees students only 40 minutes a week, she is cautious about going to parents until she has learned about the family situation and has tried to work out a solution with the youngster's regular teacher. She also remembers (all too vividly) the time she called parents about a student's misbehavior—and her call resulted in the child's being beaten. "(Working with parents is discussed further in Chapter Eleven.)"

These penalties illustrate the ways Carmen, Donnie, Fred, and Sandy choose to deal with problems when they have a degree of flexibility. In addition, there are times when they are required to follow school policies mandating particular responses to specific misbehaviors. In Carmen's school, for example, the vice-principal (who serves as the school disciplinarian) requires that teachers send students to his office in cases of continual defiance, use of profanity, threats, physical assaults, fighting, and possession of weapons. In Sandy's school, teachers must confront a student on the first cut, write up the incident, call the parent, and assign detention. (Figure 6-1 shows the consequences that Highland Park High School mandates for cutting.) In all the schools, incidents of fighting result in automatic suspension. Be sure to find out what your school policies are with respect to serious problem behaviors.

Selecting Penalties That Are Logical Consequences   Whenever possible, penalties should be *logically related to the misbehavior* (e.g., Curwin and Mendler, 1988; Dreikurs, Grunwald, and Pepper, 1982). For example, when a boy in Carmen's

FIGURE 6-1
Highland Park High School's Consequences for Cutting
Highland Park High School, *Student Handbook*

Cutting		
Cut #1	Two 3:05 p.m. detentions.	Teacher Call to Parent(s)/guardian(s)
Cut #2	Loss of open campus privileges for 5 days and 4 days 3:05 p.m. detention.	Conference with Teacher/Parent(s)/guardian(s)/ Counselor/Administrator
Cut #3	Exclusion from school, loss of open campus privileges for 10 days. Review of eligibility for extracurricular activities and possible referral to PAC.	Conference with Teacher/Parent(s)/guardian(s)/ Counselor/Administrator
Cut #4	Saturday Detention *(Pending Board of Education Approval.)*	Conference with Teacher/Parent(s)/guardian(s)/ Counselor/Administrator

Teachers are not required to provide makeup work for you if you cut. Additionally, teachers may give you a zero for a test or assignment that was missed because of a confirmed cut.

class got paint on a girl's shirt because he was fooling around, he and Carmen agreed that he would wash the shirt. Similarly, if students make a mess in the home economics kitchen, a logical penalty would be to make them clean it up. If an individual forgets his book and can't do the assignment, he must borrow someone else's book and do the assignment during free period. A student who cannot work cooperatively in a group must leave the group until she decides she can cooperate. A student who hands in a carelessly done paper has to rewrite it.

Dreikurs, Grunwald, and Pepper (1982) distinguish logical consequences like these from traditional punishments, which bear no relationship to the misbehavior involved. An example of punishment would be to have students write "I will not come late to class" 50 times. Here are some other examples of punishments that are unrelated to the offense:

> A student continually whispers to her neighbor. Instead of isolating the student (a logi-cal consequence), the teacher makes her do an additional homework assignment.

> A student forgets to get his parent's permission to go on a field trip. Instead of having the student write a letter home to parents about the need to sign the permission slip (a logi-cal consequence), the teacher gives him detention.

> A student continually calls out during a whole-class discussion. Instead of having him make a cue-card to post on his desk ("I won't call out") or not allowing him to partici-pate in the discussion, the teacher gives him an F for the day.

According to Dreikurs and his colleagues, punishment is likely to be seen as an arbitrary exercise of power by a dictatorial teacher. Sometimes, youngsters do not even associate the punishment with the misbehavior, but rather with the punisher. Instead of teaching students about the unpleasant results of their inappropriate be-havior, unrelated punishments teach students only to make certain they don't get caught the next time around!

Imposing Penalties

It's frustrating when students misbehave, and sometimes we let our frustration color the way we impose penalties. I've seen teachers scream at students from across the room, lecture students on their history of misbehavior, insinuate that they come from terrible homes, and attack their personalities. Clearly, behavior like this destroys students' dignity and ruins the possibility of a good relationship with them. How can you avoid creating a situation like this?

First, if you're feeling really angry at a student, it's a good idea to *delay the dis-cussion.* You can simply say to the individual, "Sit there and think about what hap-pened. I'll talk to you in a few minutes." During one observation in Fred's room, it was clear that he was becoming really annoyed at two students who were talking while he was introducing a film the class was about to watch. Twice during his comments he turned and told them to stop talking, but their conversation would be-gin again. I watched with curiosity to see if he would do anything further, but he continued the lesson. At the end of the period, however, he promptly went over and quietly spoke with the two offending students. Later, he reflected on their conversation:

> I told them I couldn't talk while they were talking, that it distracted me and made me really mad—especially since I was talking about Gandhi, who's one of my favorite guys. They apologized; they said they had been talking about some of the ideas that had come up in class. I told them I was really glad they were so excited, but they had to share their thoughts with the whole class, or wait until after class to talk. I think they got the message. Talking with them after class had three advantages: It allowed me to continue with my lesson, it gave me a chance to calm down, and it made it possible to talk to them privately.

As Fred's comments point out, by delaying discussion, you have a chance to calm down and to think about what you want to say. You'll also be more able to separate the student's character from the student's behavior. Your message must be: *"You're okay, but your behavior is unacceptable."*

Second, it's a good idea to *impose penalties privately, calmly, and quietly.* Despite the temptation to yell and scream, Richard Curwin and Allen Mendler (1988) contend that the more *closely* you stand to the student and the *softer* your voice, the more effective you tend to be. Remember, students are very concerned about saving face in front of their peers. Public sanction may have the advantage of "making an example" out of one student's misbehavior, but it has the disadvantage of creating resentment and embarrassment. In fact, a study by Turco and Elliott (1986) found that fifth, seventh, and ninth graders viewed public reprimand as the *least acceptable method* of dealing with problems. Our four teachers agree. Sandy observes:

> Let's say you've just given back some paper you graded. A student looks at his or her paper, crumples it up, and throws it on the floor. If you yell, "Pick that paper up," you've created a confrontational situation. It's a lot better to go over and talk privately and calmly. If you say something like, "If you have a problem with your grade, we can talk about it," then the kid doesn't lose face. It's really important not to back students into a corner; if you do, they'll come out fighting and create an even bigger problem than before."

Finally, after imposing a penalty, it's a good idea to get back to the student and *reestablish a positive relationship.* At the very beginning of this chapter, we saw how Sandy made a point of helping William with his lab experiment after giving him detention. Similarly, complimenting a student's work or patting a back communicates that there are no hard feelings.

The Issue of Consistency

As Emmer, Evertson, and their colleagues (1994) note, "The dictum 'be consistent' has been repeated more frequently than the pledge of allegiance" (p. 116). Beginning teachers are taught that if they do not consistently enforce the rules, students will become confused, will begin to test the limits, and misbehavior will escalate.

There is research evidence to support this emphasis on consistency. Recall

Evertson and Emmer's (1982) study of effective classroom management on the junior-high level (discussed in Chapter Four). This study showed that more successful managers responded in a consistent, predictable fashion, often invoking the rules or procedures in order to stop the disruptive behavior. In contrast, the ineffective managers were more likely to act inconsistently: sometimes they ignored the behavior; sometimes they invoked a prestated consequence (e.g., detention); sometimes they warned students of penalties, but then didn't act on their warnings. Inevitably, behavior problems increased in frequency and severity.

Although the importance of being consistent is obvious, teachers sometimes feel trapped by the need for consistency. When a normally conscientious student forgets a homework assignment, it seems unreasonable to send the same note home to parents that you would send if a student repeatedly missed assignments. Furthermore, what is an effective consequence for one person may not be effective for another (Dreikers, Grunwald, and Pepper, 1982). Having detention might be a negative experience for an individual who is eager to get to soccer practice; for an individual who has nothing special waiting at home, detention (particularly if it's in the classroom with the teacher) could actually be a positive, rewarding experience.

In order to get out of this bind, it's desirable to develop a *range of alternative consequences* that can be invoked if rules are violated. Some teachers develop a graduated list of generic consequences that can be applied to all misbehaviors. For example, Lee and Marlene Canter, authors of *Assertive Discipline* (1992), suggest the following discipline hierarchy for grades seven through twelve:

First time a student breaks a rule:	Warning
Second time:	Stay in class 1 minute after the bell
Third time:	Stay in class 2 minutes after the bell plus write in behavior journal
Fourth time:	Call parents
Fifth time:	Send to principal

Another approach is to develop a graduated list of consequences for individual classroom rules. Richard Curwin and Allen Mendler (1988) suggest the following consequences for not bringing in homework:

1 Reminder.
2 Warning.
3 Student must hand homework in before close of school that day.
4 Stay after school to finish homework.
5 A conference among teacher, student, and parent to develop an action plan for completing homework on time.

Sandy used this approach when she developed her graduated list of consequences for coming late (see Chapter Four), and she makes sure to enforce the consequences no matter who is involved. She tells us:

> Kids have got to see that you're fair. If my best student walks through that door late, I have to give the same detention that I'd give to my worst student. If I don't give deten-

tion, the kids will see that and think to themselves, "She's playing favorites. She's letting him get away with coming late." That's the end of my relationship with them.

Although all four teachers are absolutely consistent with dealing with straight-forward behaviors like coming late, they consider these the "little problems." With the "big things," they prefer to talk privately with students and to develop a plan of action that is tailored to the individual student. By holding "mandatory private con-ferences," the four teachers can show students they are consistent in terms of en-forcing class rules and dealing with problem behavior, but they can remain flexible with respect to the solution.

Penalizing the Group for Individual Misbehavior

Sometimes teachers impose a consequence on the whole class even if only one or two individuals have been misbehaving. The hope is that other students will be an-gry at receiving a penalty when they weren't misbehaving and will exert pressure on their peers to behave.

I decided to ask our four teachers what they think about this practice. They were unanimous in their negative response. Donnie observed, "If you even attempt to do this, students will be furious. You'll alienate the whole class." And Fred put it this way: "I do this when I'm teaching about the causes of revolutions. It's a great way to foment a rebellion!"

DEALING WITH CHRONIC MISBEHAVIOR

Some students with persistent behavior problems fail to respond to the routine strategies we have described so far—nonverbal cues, verbal reminders, and penal-ties. What additional strategies are available? In this section, we consider two basic approaches. Both require the active participation of students and provide them with opportunities to assume some responsibility for controlling their own behavior.

The first approach was developed by Thomas Gordon (1974), the psychologist whose "I-messages" were discussed earlier in this chapter. Gordon's approach sees classroom problems as conflicts that can be solved through a "no-lose method" of problem solving. Next, we examine four self-management approaches based on principles of behavior modification—namely, self-monitoring, self-evaluation, self-instruction, and contingency contracting.

Gordon's No-Lose Method of Resolving Conflicts

For Thomas Gordon, the relationship between the teacher and the student is para-mount, and the way to maintain a positive relationship is to avoid the use of power when trying to solve problems. Most teachers, according to Gordon, think in terms of winning or losing when they think about classroom conflicts:

> This win-lose orientation seems to be at the core of the knotty issue of discipline in schools. Teachers feel that they have only two approaches to choose from: They can be

strict or lenient, tough or soft, authoritarian or permissive. They see the teacher-student relationship as a power struggle, a contest, a fight. . . . When conflicts arise, as they always do, most teachers try to resolve them so that they win, or at least don't lose. This obviously means that students end up losing, or at least not winning. . . . (p. 183).

Gordon offers a third alternative: a no-lose problem-solving method of conflict resolution. Appropriate for use with an individual child or with a group, Gordon's method has six steps. In Step 1, the teacher and the student (or students) *define the problem.* In Step 2, everyone *brainstorms possible solutions.* As in all brainstorming activities, suggestions are not evaluated at this stage. In Step 3, the *solutions are evaluated*: "Now let's take a look at all the solutions that have been proposed and decide which we like and which we don't like. Do you have some preferences?" It is important that you state your own opinions and preferences. Do not permit a solution to stand if it is not really acceptable to you. In Step 4, you and the students involved *decide on the solution you will try.* If more than one student is involved, it is tempting to vote on the solution, but Gordon warns against doing this. Voting always produces winners and losers unless the vote is unanimous, so some people leave the discussion feeling dissatisfied. Instead, Gordon urges you to work for consensus.

Once you have decided which solution to try, you move to Step 5 and *determine how to implement the decision:* Who will do what by when? Finally, in Step 6, *the solution is evaluated.* Sometimes the teacher may want to call everybody together again and ask, "Are you still satisfied with our solution?" It is important for everyone to realize that decisions are not chiseled in granite and that they can be discarded in search of a better solution to the problem.

During one meeting, Donnie explained how she used this approach when some of her students were not sitting in their assigned places during assemblies:

Whenever there's an assembly program, we're supposed to walk together to the auditorium and sit together. But it's crowded in the halls on the way to the auditorium, and everyone "loses" kids; someone has darted here or there, joined another class, faded into the crowd. By the time we get to the auditorium, the kids are scattered all over. They sit with other classes, and they act up. The teachers don't really know who they are, and sometimes the kids even give wrong names when the teachers ask. The behavior in assembly programs can be really bad. I decided this was a problem we had to deal with before another assembly program was held.

I told the class I felt this was a problem, and they agreed. Then I explained we were going to brainstorm solutions. Boy, these kids can really be hard on each other! They came up with about eight different solutions:

Kick the offenders out of the assemblies.
Don't let past offenders go to assemblies at all.
Suspension.
Kids have to get permission to sit with another class.
Bring your friend to sit with you and your class (your friend would have to have special permission from his/her teacher).
Invite parents to assemblies (kids would act better).

Take attendance once you get to the assembly.
Have a buddy system.

The next day, we talked about each of these possible solutions, focusing on how they would affect everyone. I told them I didn't like the one about kicking people out of the assemblies because assembly programs were part of their education. I also explained that teachers don't have the right to suspend students, and if we chose that one, we'd have to get the disciplinarian involved. The kids said they could live with getting permission, and they also liked the buddy system. They said buddies should also have the responsibility of telling the person next to them to stop if he or she was disruptive. So we agreed to try those two. We also agreed that I would use the "teacher look" technique if I saw kids acting up and then write up a referral to the disciplinarian if they didn't stop.

We haven't had an assembly program yet, so I don't know how this is going to work, but I think it was good to get the kids involved in trying to solve the problem. Maybe they'll be more interested in trying to improve the situation.

Approaches Based on Principles of Behavior Modification

Behavior modification programs involve the systematic use of reinforcement to strengthen desired behavior. Probably more research has focused on the effectiveness of behavior modification than any other classroom management approach, and dozens of books on behavior modification techniques are available for teachers (e.g., Epanchim, Townsend, and Stoddard, 1994; Evans, Evans, and Schmid, 1989; Sparzo and Poteet, 1989).

In recent years, however, educators have come to view full-blown behavior modification approaches as ill-suited for most regular classroom teachers (Evertson, 1989). First of all, a single teacher working with a class of 30 students cannot possibly keep track of—let alone systematically reinforce—all the desirable behaviors each student exhibits (Brophy, 1983). Second, in order to extinguish inappropriate behavior that is maintained by teacher attention, behavior modification calls for teachers to ignore the behavior. Although this is effective in one-to-one situations, ignoring misbehavior in the crowded, public environment of the classroom can cause problems to escalate (an issue that was discussed earlier). This is even more likely to occur if teachers forget that ignoring is not a behavior management strategy by itself, but must be paired with attention for positive and appropriate behaviors. Finally, traditional behavior modification techniques emphasize external control by the teacher, rather than trying to foster internal control by the student (Kneedler and Hallahan, 1981).

For all of these reasons, educators have recently begun to recommend behavioral approaches that involve the student in *self-management:* self-monitoring, self-evaluation, self-instruction, and contingency contracting. The goal of these self-management strategies is to help students learn to regulate their own behavior. The perception of control is crucial in this process. As Anderson and Prawat (1983) observe, "Individuals who feel in control are much more willing to accept responsibility for their own behavior" (p. 62).

Self-monitoring

The object of self-monitoring is to help individuals gain an accurate picture of their own behavior. Some students may not realize how often they're out of their seats or how frequently they sit daydreaming instead of focusing on their work. Others may be unaware of how often they call out during class discussions or how many times they make nasty comments to other members of their small group. Youngsters like this may benefit from a self-monitoring program, in which they learn to observe and record a targeted behavior during a designated period of time. Interestingly, self-monitoring can have positive effects even when youngsters are *inaccurate* (Graziano and Mooney, 1984).

Recording can be done in two ways. The first approach has individuals tally each time they engage in the targeted behavior. For example, students can learn to chart the number of math problems they complete during an in-class assignment, the number of times they blurt out irrelevant comments during a discussion, or the number of times they raise their hand to speak. In the second approach, individuals observe and record the targeted behavior at regular intervals. At the designated time, the student marks the recording sheet with a "+" or a "–," depending on whether she or he is engaged in the appropriate or inappropriate behavior.

These two approaches are well illustrated in an early study conducted by Broden, Hall, and Mitts (1971). In the first part of the study, Liza, an eighth-grade girl who had difficulty paying attention in history class, was directed to record her "study" or "on-task" behavior on the sheet shown in Figure 6-2. Before Liza began recording her behavior, she was on task only about 30 percent of the time. During the self-recording phases, Liza averaged on-task rates of 76 percent to 89 percent.

The second part of the study involved Stu, an eighth-grade boy whose math

FIGURE 6-2
The recording sheet used by Liza

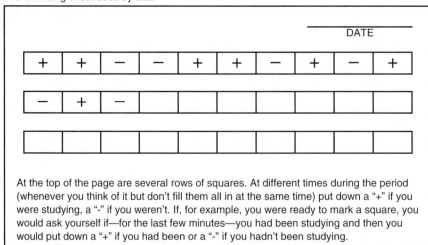

At the top of the page are several rows of squares. At different times during the period (whenever you think of it but don't fill them all in at the same time) put down a "+" if you were studying, a "-" if you weren't. If, for example, you were ready to mark a square, you would ask yourself if—for the last few minutes—you had been studying and then you would put down a "+" if you had been or a "-" if you hadn't been studying.

teacher wanted to find a way "to shut Stu up" (p. 195). According to the teacher, Stu continually talked out in class, disturbing both the teacher and the other students. Having Stu record his talking-out behavior on the simple form shown in Figure 6-3 led to a decrease in his calling out, although the self-monitoring seemed to lose its effectiveness after a while (possibly because the teacher never acknowledged Stu's improved behavior).

Self-evaluation   This second self-management approach goes beyond simple self-monitoring by requiring individuals to judge the quality or acceptability of their behavior (Hughes, Ruhl, and Misra, 1989). Sometimes self-evaluation is linked with reinforcement, so that an improvement in behavior brings points or rewards.

A study by Smith, Young, West, Morgan, and Rhode (1988) provides a good example of how these strategies can be used to reduce off-task, disruptive behavior. The study involved four students (ages 13–15) who spent half of each day in a special education resource room; three students were classified as behaviorally disordered, and one was classified as learning disabled. All four students were taught to rate how well they followed the resource room rules, using a simple scale that went from zero ("unacceptable") to five ("excellent"). Ratings were converted to points that could be exchanged for snacks, school supplies, or magazines at the end of each class period. Since bonus points were earned when students' ratings closely matched their teacher's ratings, the students were rewarded not only for behaving well, but also for rating themselves accurately.

By tracking students' behavior over time, the investigators were able to show that the self-evaluation procedures were extremely effective in decreasing students' inappropriate behavior in the resource room. Darren, for example, went from an av-

FIGURE 6-3
The recording sheet used by Stu

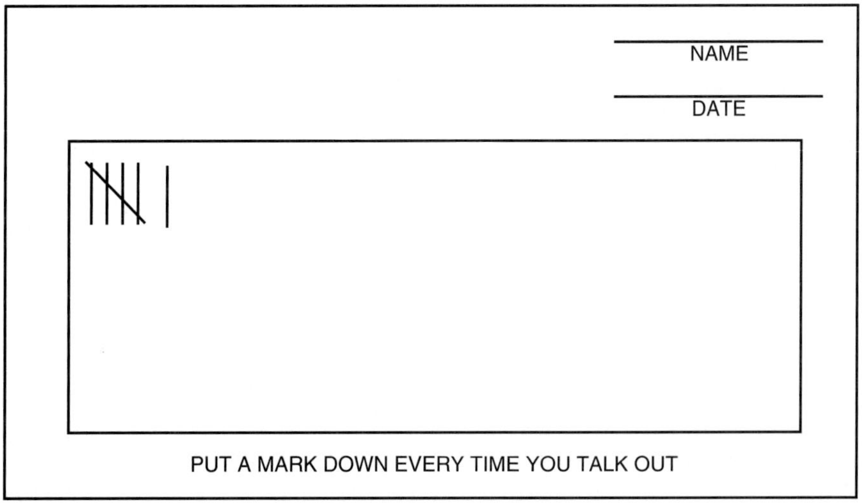

erage of 71 percent off-task, disruptive behavior to 17 percent. Sadly, the results weren't as impressive when self-evaluation was tried in the regular education classes, where the teachers were less consistent in doing the ratings.

Recently, Fred decided to try a self-evaluation procedure with a boy in his Contemporary World Issues class. Daniel was in serious danger of failing the course; although he was not disruptive, Daniel was consistently inattentive and rarely completed assignments. Fred and Daniel discussed self-evaluation, and Daniel was enthusiastic about trying it. Together, they designed a simple sheet, which they agreed Fred would keep and give to Daniel to fill out at the end of each class period. As you can see from Figure 6-4, the form requires Daniel to describe and evaluate his behavior.

During one meeting with all the teachers, Fred describes how the self-evaluation procedure worked out:

> We did it faithfully for three weeks, and it really worked. Sometimes I forgot to give Daniel the self-evaluation sheet at the end of the period, and he actually reminded me. I took that as a sign of his commitment. His behavior really improved; he started paying attention and completing assignments for the first time all year. At the end of three weeks, Daniel was out for several days. When he got back, we didn't pick it up again, and I didn't push it. He was doing what he was supposed to be doing, without any monitoring.

FIGURE 6-4
Darren's Self-Evaluation Form

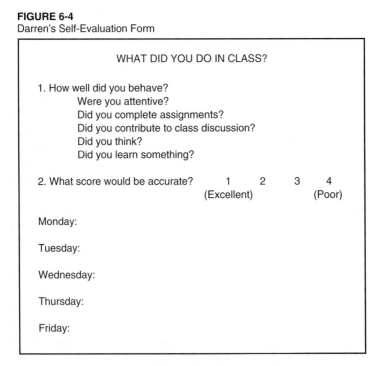

```
                    WHAT DID YOU DO IN CLASS?


    1. How well did you behave?
            Were you attentive?
            Did you complete assignments?
            Did you contribute to class discussion?
            Did you think?
            Did you learn something?

    2. What score would be accurate?        1      2     3     4
                                          (Excellent)     (Poor)


    Monday:


    Tuesday:


    Wednesday:


    Thursday:


    Friday:
```

Self-instruction   The third self-management approach is self-instruction, in which youngsters learn to give themselves silent directions about how to behave. Most self-instruction strategies are based on Meichenbaum's (1977) five-step process of cognitive behavior modification: (1) an adult performs a task, while talking aloud about it, carefully describing each part; (2) the youngster performs the task while the adult talks aloud (overt, external guidance); (3) the youngster performs the task while talking aloud to self (overt self-guidance); (4) the youngster performs the task while whispering (faded, overt self-guidance); (5) the youngster performs the task while thinking the directions (covert self-instruction). This approach has been used to teach impulsive students to approach tasks more deliberately, to help social isolates initiate peer activity, to teach aggressive students to control their anger, and to teach defeated students to try problem-solving instead of giving up (Brophy, 1983).

There is evidence that even seriously emotionally disturbed adolescents can learn to engage in self-instruction. In a study (Ninness, Fuerst, Rutherford, and Glenn, 1991) conducted in a self-contained special education class, three teenage males who displayed high rates of off-task and inappropriate behaviors (running, fighting, fondling, spitting, throwing objects, jumping, or inappropriate language) were given formal instruction in social skills and self-management for one hour a day. Students were taught to raise their hands to ask questions, to avoid distractions of other students, and to talk politely to teachers and students. While others played the role of distractors, students rehearsed overt statements such as "I'm not going to let him or her bother me. I'm going to keep doing my work," and they practiced avoiding eye contact with those who annoyed them. In addition, students were taught to evaluate their own on-task and socially appropriate behavior, using a scale ranging from one to four. A bonus point was awarded on any occasion in which a student's self-assessment was within one point of the teacher's assessment.

After five weeks, the training in social skills and self-management was discontinued, and a series of experimental conditions was begun. In one condition ("instructed"), students were left alone for 20 minutes in the classroom with instructions to assess and record their behavior. In a similar condition ("instructed under provocation"), students were told to self-manage, while others deliberately tried to provoke and distract them. Two other conditions investigated students' behavior when the teacher left ("uninstructed" and "uninstructed under provocation").

The results of the study demonstrated that training in self-management can dramatically improve students' behavior. Prior to the training, off-task and socially inappropriate behavior in the classroom averaged 92 percent, 95 percent, and 76 percent for Subjects 1, 2, and 3, respectively. All three subjects improved substantially during the course of the five-week self-management training—and all three demonstrated *near-zero off-task or socially inappropriate behavior* during the experimental situations.

Before we leave the discussion of self-monitoring, self-evaluation, and self-instruction, it is important to note that only a small number of studies has been conducted in secondary schools, and few of these involve students in regular, mainstream classes. For this reason, we cannot yet be certain that these strategies are either feasible or effective in regular secondary settings (Hughes, Ruhl, and Misra, 1989). Nonetheless, the studies described here suggest that these three strategies can be useful ways of dealing with chronic inappropriate behavior. If you decide to try one of these self-management strategies, it would be a good idea to consult with your school's psychologist, a counselor, or a special education teacher.

Contingency contracting   A contingency or behavior contract is an agreement between a teacher and an individual student that specifies what the student must do to earn a particular reward. Contingency contracts are negotiated with students; both parties must agree on the behaviors students must exhibit, the period of time involved, and the rewards that will result. To be most effective, contracts should be written and signed. And, of course, there should be an opportunity for review and renegotiation if the contract is not working (Evans, Evans, and Schmid, 1989).

In South Brunswick High School, the guidance counselors, the Vice-Principal for Student Affairs (the school's disciplinarian), and the attendance officers regularly use contracts to deal with students who exhibit serious problems (e.g., extremely disruptive behavior, poor attendance, failing grades). An example of a typical contract appears in Figure 6-5.

CONCLUDING COMMENTS

One day, during Carmen's free period, she and I talked about the problems her students bring to school. She displayed both sadness and compassion when she spoke about their home situations, but she also expressed a considerable amount of pride in their ability to behave appropriately:

> The problems many of these kids face are unbelievable. Tommy was abused as an infant; he was beaten and kept in a closet. Jorge's grandparents take care of him. His parents are both drug addicts. Raymond's been in one foster home after another; his mother's a drug addict and his father's in and out of jail. As a teacher, you've got to understand what some of these kids are coping with at home. But you can't just let them act however they want and say "They can't help it." I'm the teacher in this room and I have to see that they follow our rules. Actually, I think they behave very well. . . . They're really beautiful, aren't they?

Carmen's comments recall findings from a study on the ways teachers cope with problem students (Brophy and Rohrkemper, 1981). One basic factor that distinguished more-effective teachers from less-effective teachers was their *willingness to take responsibility.* They used a variety of strategies: some used behavioral approaches—negotiating contracts, providing rewards, praising desirable behavior—while others tried to build positive relationships, provide encouragement, and foster self-esteem. Regardless, effective teachers were willing to assume the responsibility for managing youngsters' behavior. In sharp contrast, *less-effective teachers tended to disclaim responsibility and to refer problems to other school personnel* (e.g., the principal, guidance counselor, etc.).

SOUTH BRUNSWICK HIGH SCHOOL
STUDENT PERSONNEL SERVICES

CONTRACT

TO: WHOM IT MAY CONCERN

DATE:

RE: AGREEMENTS FOR XXX XXXXXX TO REMAIN IN/SUCCEED IN
        QQ QQQQQ'S CLASS

AFTER A FRUITFUL DISCUSSION BETWEEN XXXX, YYYYY, AND ZZZZZ,
THE FOLLOWING DECISIONS WERE REACHED:

1.   XXX WILL BE IN CLASS ON TIME WITH BOOK, NOTEBOOK, AND
     WRITING UTENSIL.

2.   ALL HOMEWORK ASSIGNMENTS WILL BE TURNED IN ON TIME
     AND COMPLETE.

3.   QQ QQQQQ WILL MEET WITH XXX AFTER SCHOOL ON
     THURSDAYS TO ASSIST XXX WITH THE QUARTERLY PROJECT.

4.   XXX WILL CHANGE HIS SEAT AWAY FROM RRRRR, AND PAY
     ATTENTION DURING CLASS.

5.   OTHER:

UPON SUCCESSFUL COMPLETION OF THIS CONTRACT, XXX WILL PASS
THIS CLASS WITH A "C" OR BETTER FOR THIS QUARTER.

STUDENT_____   TEACHER_____
PARENT_____   COUNSELOR_____

FIGURE 6-5
An example of a contract

Clearly, our four teachers are willing to take responsibility for the behavior of their students. Like Carmen, they recognize they are accountable for what happens in their classrooms. Furthermore, they are willing to admit when they themselves have contributed to problems that occur. Listen to Sandy:

A while back I asked my students a question that took some critical thinking. They just stared at me. There was absolutely no response. I was getting really upset. I gave them a hard look and said, "Didn't you people look over your notes last night?" There was still no response. My lesson was falling apart. Finally, a student raises his hand, motions for me to come over, and whispers to me, "Mrs. K., you never taught us this stuff." I looked down at his notes and realized he was right. I had jumped ahead to the next lesson. No wonder they didn't know what I was talking about! I told them, "My objective for today's lesson has just changed." We laughed, and I apologized. It's important for teachers to admit when they make mistakes. Kids have to know you're human too.

I agree with Carmen, Sandy, Donnie, and Fred that teachers need to assume responsibility for students' behavior problems, and I hope this chapter will help you to feel more competent in this area. Nonetheless, there are times when you have to acknowledge that an individual's problem is so deeply rooted that interventions like the ones discussed in this chapter just don't work. As Donnie observes: "Teachers have to recognize that there are kids you can't help by yourself. Then it's important to go to guidance and try to get assistance." We return to this topic in Chapter Twelve, when we discuss "helping students with serious problems."

SUMMARY

Inappropriate behavior threatens order by interrupting the flow of classroom activity. In this chapter we discussed ways of responding to a variety of problems—from minor, nondisruptive infractions to chronic, more serious misbehavior.

Guidelines for Dealing with Misbehavior

- Match your disciplinary strategy to the misbehavior.
- Try to keep the instructional program going with a minimum of disruption.
- Consider the *context* of students' actions. Behavior that is acceptable in one context may be unacceptable in another.
- Use disciplinary strategies that preserve the dignity of the student.
- Separate the student's *character* from the specific *misbehavior.*
- Encourage students to take responsibility for regulating their own behavior.

Strategies for Dealing with Minor Misbehavior

- Nonverbal interventions
- Verbal interventions
    Direct student to the task at hand.
    State student's name.
    Remind student of rule.
    Call on student.
    Use gentle humor.
    Use an I-message.
- Ignore misbehavior that is fleeting

Strategies for Dealing with More Serious Misbehavior

- Plan penalties ahead of time.
- Choose penalties that are logically related to misbehavior.

- Impose penalties calmly and quietly.
- Re-establish a positive relationship with the student as quickly as possible.
- Develop a range of alternative consequences.

Strategies for Dealing with Chronic Misbehavior

- Thomas Gordon's no-lose problem-solving method:
  - Step 1: Define the problem.
  - Step 2: Brainstorm possible solutions.
  - Step 3: Evaluate solutions.
  - Step 4: Decide on a solution to try.
  - Step 5: Determine how to implement the decision.
  - Step 6: Evaluate the solution.
- Behavior-modification approaches:
  - Self-monitoring
  - Self-evaluation
  - Self-instruction
  - Contingency contracting

Effective teachers are willing to take responsibility for managing students' behavior. Work on developing a system for dealing with misbehavior that suits your personality and your teaching style. You may have a student whose problems are too severe for you to deal with. If so, it is your responsibility to get this individual outside help.

ACTIVITIES

1. Beginning teachers sometimes overreact to misbehavior or take no action at all because they simply don't know what to do or say. Read each of the following situations and devise a nonverbal intervention, a verbal cue, and an I-message.

Example	Nonverbal	Verbal	I-Message
A student writes on the desk.	Hand the student an eraser.	"We use paper to write on."	"When you write on the desk, the custodian complains to me, and I get embarrassed."
A student makes a big show of looking through her book bag for her homework, distracting other students and delaying the start of the lesson.	Give the "look."	"We're ready to begin."	"When you take so long to get your things out, I can't begin the lesson, and I get very frustrated by the lost time."

    a. A student is copying from another student's paper.

    b. A student takes another student's notebook.

    c. A student purposely steps on another student's homework assignment, which had fallen on the floor.

    d. A student spreads rumors about a friend.

2. When a misbehavior occurs, there usually isn't much time for careful consideration of logical consequences. I've listed a few typical misbehaviors for your practice. What are two logical consequences for each example?

    a. As part of a small group, Lou monopolizes the discussion and tells everyone what to do in an authoritarian manner.

    b. At the end of the year, Arianna returns her book with ripped pages and the cover missing.

    c. Shemeika yells out answers throughout your class discussion, even though you have instructed students to raise their hands.

    d. Whenever you're not looking, Tom practices juggling with three small bean-bags he has brought to school.

    e. Instead of working on the class activity, Tanya examines the contents of her cosmetics kit.

3. Develop a behavior modification plan (such as self-monitoring or a contingency contract) to deal with the following problems:

    a. Arthur is a seventh grader who exhibits aggressive behavior. Hardly a day goes by that another student hasn't come to you complaining of Arthur's pushing, teasing, or name-calling. You've talked to his parents, but they are at a loss about what to do.

    b. Cynthia, an eleventh grader, rarely completes her work. She daydreams, socializes with others, misunderstands directions, and gets upset when you speak to her about her incomplete work. The problem seems to be getting worse.

REFERENCES

Allen, J. D. (1986). Classroom management: Students' perspectives, goals, and strategies. *American Educational Research Journal, 23*(3), 437–459.

Alpert, B. (1991). Students' resistance in the classroom. *Anthropology & Education Quarterly, 22,* 350–366.

Anderson, L. M., and Prawat, R. S. (1983). Responsibility in the classroom: A synthesis of research on teaching self-control. *Educational Leadership, 40,* 62–66.

Broden, M., Hall, R. V., and Mitts, B. (1971). The effect of self-recording on the classroom behavior of two eighth-grade students. *Journal of Applied Behavior Analysis, 4,* 191–199.

Brophy, J. E. (1983). Classroom organization and management. *The Elementary School Journal, 83*(4), 265–285.

Brophy, J., and Rohrkemper, M. (1981). The influence of problem ownership on teachers' perceptions of and strategies for coping with problem students. *Journal of Educational Psychology, 73,* 295–311.

Cairns, L. G. (1987). Behaviour problems. In M. J. Dunkin (Ed.), *The International Encyclopedia of Teaching and Teacher Education.* New York: Pergamon Press, 446–452.

Canter, L., and Canter, M. (1992). *Assertive discipline: Positive behavior management for today's classroom.* Santa Monica, CA: Lee Canter & Associates.

Center for Education Statistics (1987). *Public school teacher perspectives on school discipline. OERI Bulletin.* Washington, D.C.: U.S. Department of Education.

Creton, H. A., Wubbels, T., and Hooymayers, H. P. (1989). Escalated disorderly situations in the classroom and the improvement of these situations. *Teaching & Teacher Education,* 5(3), 205–215.

Curwin, R. L., and Mendler, A. N. (1988). *Discipline with dignity.* Alexandria, VA: Association for Supervision and Curriculum Development.

Doyle, W. (1986). Classroom organization and management. In M. C. Wittrock (Ed.), *Handbook of research on teaching.* New York: Macmillan, 392–431.

Doyle, W. (1990). Classroom management techniques. In O. C. Moles (Ed.), *Student discipline strategies: Research and practice.* Albany, NY: SUNY Press.

Dreikurs, R., Grunwald, B. B., and Pepper, F. C. (1982). *Maintaining sanity in the classroom: Classroom management techniques* (2nd edition). New York: Harper & Row.

Emmer, E. T., and Aussiker, A. (1990). School and classroom discipline programs: How well do they work? In O. C. Moles (Ed.), *Student discipline strategies.* New York: SUNY Press, 129–165.

Emmer, E. T., Evertson, C. M., Clements, B. S., and Worsham, M. E. (1994). *Classroom management for secondary teachers.* Boston: Allyn and Bacon.

Epanchin, B. C., Townsend, B., and Stoddard, K. (1994). *Constructive classroom management: Strategies for creating positive learning environments.* Pacific Grove, CA: Brooks/Cole.

Evans, W. H., Evans, S. S., and Schmid, R. E. (1989). *Behavior and instructional management: An ecological approach.* Boston: Allyn and Bacon.

Evertson, C. M. (1989). Classroom organization and management. In M. C. Reynolds (Ed.), *Knowledge base for the beginning teacher.* New York: Pergamon Press, 59–70.

Evertson, C. M., and Emmer, E. T. (1982). Effective management at the beginning of the school year in junior high classes. *Journal of Educational Psychology,* 74(4), 485–498.

Good, J. E., and Brophy, T. L. (1994). *Looking in classrooms* (6th edition). New York: HarperCollins

Gordon, T. (1974). *T.E.T.—Teacher Effectiveness Training.* New York: Peter H. Wyden.

Graziano, A. M., and Mooney, K. C. (1984). *Children and behavior therapy.* New York: Aldine.

Hughes, C. A., Ruhl, K. L., and Misra, A. (1989). Disordered students in school settings: A promise unfulfilled? *Behavioral Disorders, 14,* 250–262.

Kneedler, R. D., and Hallahan, D. P. (1981). Self-monitoring of on-task behavior with learning disabled children: Current studies and directions. *Exceptional Education Quarterly, 2,* 73–81.

Kounin, J. S. (1970). *Discipline and group management in classrooms.* New York: Holt, Rinehart & Winston.

Lasley, T. J., Lasley, J. O., and Ward, S. H (1989). Activities and desists used by more and less effective classroom managers. Paper presented at the annual meeting of the American Educational Research Association, San Francisco.

Meichenbaum, D. (1977). *Cognitive behavior modification.* New York: Plenum.

Ninness, H. A. C., Fuerst, J., Rutherford, R. D., and Glenn, S. S. (1991). Effects of self-management training and reinforcement on the transfer of improved conduct in the absence of supervision. *Journal of Applied Behavior Analysis, 24*(3), 499–508.

Pittman, S. I. (1985). Cognitive ethnography and quantification of a first-grade teacher's selection routines for classroom management. *The Elementary School Journal, 85*(4), 541–558.

Smith, D. J., Young, K. R., West, R. P., Morgan, D. P., and Rhode, G. (1988). Reducing the disruptive behavior of junior high school students: A classroom self-management procedure. *Behavioral Disorders, 18,* 231–239.

Sparzo, F. J., and Poteet, J. A. (1989). *Classroom behavior: Detecting and correcting special problems.* Boston: Allyn and Bacon.

Turco, T. L., and Elliott, S. N. (1986). Assessment of students' acceptability ratings of teacher-initiated interventions for classroom misbehavior. *Journal of School Psychology, 24,* 277–283.

FOR FURTHER READING

Canter, L., and Canter, M. (1992). *Assertive discipline: Positive behavior management for today's classroom.* Santa Monica, CA: Lee Canter & Associates.

Charles, C. M. (1989). *Building classroom discipline: From models to practice* (3rd edition). New York: Longman.

Curwin, R. L., and Mendler, A. N. (1988). *Discipline with dignity.* Alexandria, VA: Association for Supervision and Curriculum Development.

Dreikurs, R., Grunwald, B. B., and Pepper, F. C. (1982). *Maintaining sanity in the classroom: Classroom management techniques* (2nd edition). New York: Harper & Row.

Epanchin, B. C., Townsend, B., and Stoddard, K. (1994). *Constructive classroom management: Strategies for creating positive learning environments.* Pacific Grove, CA: Brooks/Cole.

Gordon, T. (1974). *T.E.T.—Teacher Effectiveness Training.* New York: Peter H. Wyden.

Sparzo, F. J., and Poteet, J. A. (1989). *Classroom behavior: Detecting and correcting special problems.* Boston: Allyn and Bacon.

Chapter Seven

Making the Most of Classroom Time

On the first day of school, the academic year seems to stretch out endlessly. If you're a beginning teacher, you may wonder how you'll ever fill all the hours of school that lie ahead—especially if you're not even certain what you're going to do *tomorrow.* And yet, as the days go by, you may begin to feel that there's never enough time to accomplish all you need to do. With assemblies, fire drills, announcements over the intercom, standardized testing, snow days, holidays, and clerical tasks, the hours available for instruction seem far fewer than they did at first. Indeed, by the end of the year, you may view time as a precious resource—not something that has to be filled (or killed), but something that must be conserved and used wisely. (Of course, your students may not share this view—as Figure 7-1 illustrates!)

This chapter discusses issues of time and time management. First, we look at the amount of school time actually available for teaching and learning. Then we consider strategies for using classroom time efficiently, focusing on three complementary approaches—maintaining activity flow, minimizing transition time, and holding students accountable. As Linda Shalaway (1989) has commented, "Students only have so much time to learn in your classroom and you only have so much time to teach them" (p. 51). The wise use of time will maximize opportunities for learning and minimize opportunities for disruption.

HOW MUCH TIME IS THERE, ANYWAY?

Although this seems like a straightforward question, the answer is not so simple. In fact, the answer depends on the kind of time you're talking about (Karweit, 1989). Most states mandate a school year of approximately 180 days. Let's suppose you're teaching in a high school that has divided each of these days into 42-minute periods. (Actually, our four teachers' classes range from a low of 40 minutes, in Carmen's case, to a high of 45 minutes, in Fred's case.) This amounts to 126 hours of *mandated time* for each of your classes. But students are absent, and special assembly programs are scheduled; snowstorms cause delayed openings, and parent conferences require early closings. Factors like these immediately reduce the time you

Calvin and Hobbes   by Bill Watterson

FIGURE 7-1
Calvin doesn't agree that time passes quickly in classrooms. *(Calvin and Hobbes © Watterson. Dist. by Universal Press Syndicate. Reprinted with permission. All rights reserved.)*

have for teaching, so the *time available for instruction* can be substantially less than mandated time. Listen to the reflections of a student teacher who has learned to deal with the constant interruptions and cancellations:

"Well, at least you're learning to be flexible!" If I heard that once, I heard it a million times. I believe every teacher I've had contact with this semester has made this statement to me. A record snowfall, proficiency testing, marine biology field trips, half-day inservice days, pep rallies, assemblies . . . The actual amount of time I have had a full class of students . . . for more than two consecutive days is minimal. Nowhere is the realization that I must be flexible more evident than in my lesson plan book. When I began student teaching, my lesson plans were typed and clipped into a binder (and labeled "Monday," "Tuesday," etc.). A short time later I began calling each day "Day One," "Day Two," "Day Three," and so on. A short time after that I began writing the lessons in a plan book in pencil. About halfway through my student teaching experience I began doing my lessons on Post-it™ paper which I could arrange as needed. I only transferred the lesson to the blocks in the book as I became absolutely sure that they would not be disrupted. I have continued to use this practice with great success and have actually started one of my cooperating teachers on the same method.

Even when school is in session, students are present, and you have your class for the full 42 minutes, some portion of the available class time must be spent in non-instructional activities. This means that only part of the 42-minute period actually constitutes *instructional time.* In *A Place Called School* (1984), John Goodlad reports that the senior high school teachers he studied generally spent about 76 percent of available class time on instruction, 20 percent on routines, and 1.3 percent on behavior control; the remaining 2.2 percent was spent on socializing. Interestingly, the figures varied by subject area: foreign language classes ranked first in terms of time spent on instruction (83 percent at the senior high level), while English ranked last (73 percent). School-to-school differences were also apparent, with instructional time varying from 68 percent to 84 percent at the senior-high level. There was similar variation at the junior-high level. At "Crestview Junior High," for example, teachers spent 69 percent of class time on instruction and 25 percent on routines, while "Fairfield Junior High" teachers spent 87 percent on instruction and only 9 percent on routines.

Even within a school and a subject area, there can be considerable variation from teacher to teacher. In some classes, settling in at the beginning of the period, taking attendance, distributing materials, collecting homework, and reprimanding misbehaving students consume an inordinate amount of time. Karweit (1989) describes a "one-hour" math class, for example, in which the first ten minutes were typically used to collect lunch money, and the last ten were used to line up the students for lunch—leaving only 40 minutes for actual instruction.

Situations like this are not unusual in the classrooms of teachers who lack efficient strategies for carrying out routine, noninstructional tasks. Leinhardt and Greeno (1986) provide us with a glimpse into the difficulties encountered by one beginning teacher, Ms. Twain, as she attempted to check homework at the beginning of math. Ms. Twain had two goals—to identify who had done the homework and to correct it orally. She began by asking, "Who doesn't have their homework?" In response, students did one of three things: they held up their completed work, called out that they didn't have it, or walked over the teacher and told her whether they had done it or not. Ms. Twain then talked about the importance of homework and marked the results of this check on a posted sheet of paper.

Next, Ms. Twain chose students to give the correct answers to the homework problems:

> She called out a set of problem numbers (1-10) and assigned a child to call out the answers as she called the problem number. The student slowly called out the answers in order. (The first child chosen was the lowest in the class, did not have her work done, and was doing the problems in her head.) Thus, for the first ten problem answers, the teacher lost control of pace *and* correctness of answer; however, it was only when the child failed on the sixth problem that Twain realized the student had not done her homework. . . . (p. 87)

Ms. Twain continued to call on students to give the answers, while the rest of the class checked their work. The last student chosen went through the sequence of problems quickly, but gave both the problem number and the answer, a situation that caused some confusion (e.g., "24, 27; 25, 64"). Ms. Twain's entire homework check took six minutes—and it was clear to the observers that she was never certain which students had done their homework.

In contrast, Leinhardt and Greeno describe a homework check conducted by Ms. Longbranch, a successful, experienced teacher. Ms. Longbranch first gave a cue, "Okay, set 43," and then began to call the students' names. Those who had done the homework simply responded, "yes." Those who hadn't done the work got up and wrote their names on the chalkboard. In 30 seconds—with a minimum of fuss— Ms. Longbranch was able to determine who had completed the assignment.

The next goal was to correct the work:

> The students took colored pencils out and responded chorally with the correct answer, a fraction in lowest terms. As the teacher called the problem, "1/12 + 1/12," they responded "2/12 or 1/6." Time to complete was 106 seconds. (p. 85)

Ms. Longbranch's homework check is not presented as a model to be copied in your classroom; indeed, her procedure may not be appropriate for your particular class. The important point is that Ms. Longbranch has established a routine that enables her to check homework efficiently, almost automatically, while Ms. Twain does not yet have a workable strategy. Although the difference in the time used by the two teachers is only about four minutes, it is probably symptomatic of the ways they managed class time in general.

As you can see, the answer to the question "How much time is there, anyway?" depends on whether we are talking about the number of hours mandated by the state and district (mandated time), the number of hours your class is actually in session and students are in attendance (available time), or the time actually used for instruction (Karweit, 1989). But even when teachers are actually teaching, students are not necessarily paying attention. We must consider still another kind of time— *engaged time* or *time-on-task.*

Let's suppose that while you are teaching, some of your students choose to pass notes about last Saturday night's party, do their homework for the next period, comb their hair, or stare out the window. In this case, the amount of time you are devoting to instruction is greater than the amount of time students are directly engaged in learning. This is not an atypical situation. Research documents the fact that students tend to be "on task" about 70 percent of the time (Rosenshine, 1980). Again, there are sizable variations from class to class. A study of 30 middle and high school science teachers (McGarity and Butts, 1984) found that some classes had an engagement rate of 54 percent (i.e., the average student was attentive about half the time), while in other classes the engagement rate was 75 percent.

To a large extent, variations like these reflect teachers' ability to manage classroom events and to get students involved in learning activities (McGarity and Butts, 1984). (Recall our discussion of fostering students' motivation to learn in Chapter Five.) But other factors also come into play—the achievement level of the students (Evertson, 1980), time of day, and day of week. And some teachers insist that attention falls off (and misbehavior increases) when there is a full moon!

There are also substantial differences in engagement from activity to activity. During seatwork, for example, engagement is usually about 70 percent, while discussions led by the teacher yield engagement rates of 84 percent (Rosenshine, 1980). Why should this be so? Paul Gump (1982) suggests that some classroom activities prod students to be involved and "push" them along, while others do not. In a class discussion, external events (i.e., the teachers' questions, the other students' answers, and the teacher's responses) press students to pay attention. In seatwork and silent reading, materials (e.g., worksheets, textbooks) are simply made available; students must depend on their own internal pacing to accomplish the task. In other words, students must provide their *own* push—and sometimes the push just isn't there. (This topic is pursued further in Chapter Eight.)

The last type of time we need to consider is the *amount of time students spend on work that is meaningful and appropriate.* We sometimes get so caught up in trying to increase students' time-on-task that we overlook the tasks themselves. I once saw students in a ninth-grade general science class spend 15 minutes coloring a worksheet that showed diagrams of flower parts. The students seemed absorbed; indeed, an observer coding time-on-task would have recorded a high engagement rate. But what was the purpose of the activity? In first grade, coloring may be useful for developing children's fine motor skills, but it is hard to imagine why it would be worthwhile in high school. Coloring flower parts is not science, and in this case, one-third of the science period was allocated to a nonscientific activity.

It also makes no sense to have students spend time working on tasks they don't understand and are unable to complete successfully. This was vividly demonstrated in the Beginning Teacher Evaluation Study (BTES; Fisher, Berliner, Filby, Marliave, Cahen, and Dishaw, 1980), an influential project that examined the use of time in schools. BTES researchers created the term *academic learning time* (ALT) to refer to the proportion of engaged time in which students are performing academic tasks with a high degree of success. When students can accomplish a task with relatively few errors, it suggests the task is appropriately matched to their level of achievement and the teacher has provided sufficient preparation.

This chapter began by asking, "How much time is there, anyway?" Figure 7-2 depicts the answer to this question. The bar at the far left shows the number of hours that a typical 42-minute class would meet in the typical mandated school year—126 (180 days × 42 minutes). For the sake of argument, let's assume that student absences and assembly programs reduce this figure by ten days or 7 hours (10 days × 42 minutes). Thus, the second bar indicates that available time is 119 hours (bar 2). To be consistent with Goodlad's (1984) findings on the use of available class time, let's also assume that clerical and administrative tasks consume 20 percent of each class, leaving only 34 minutes each day for actual instruction. This yields 96 hours (bar 3). If students pay attention 80 percent of that time, engaged time is 77 hours (bar 4). And assuming that students work on meaningful, appropri-

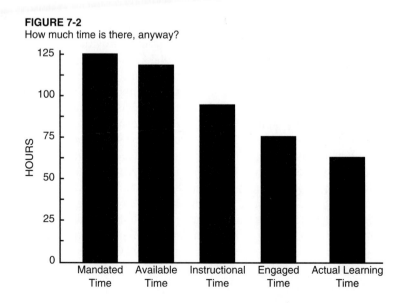

FIGURE 7-2
How much time is there, anyway?

ate tasks for 80 percent of the time they are engaged, we see that actual learning time is only 62 hours—*about half the "mandated" school time for this typical secondary class* (bar 5).

Obviously, these figures are estimates. As I have stressed, there are substantial variations from subject to subject, school to school, and classroom to classroom (Karweit, 1989). Nonetheless, the graph illustrates the fundamental point: *the hours available for learning are far more limited than they initially appear.*

INCREASING OPPORTUNITY TO LEARN

In addition to contributing the concept of ALT, the Beginning Teacher Evaluation Study (BTES) also demonstrated the relationship between time and achievement. The findings are not surprising. *As allocated time, engaged time, and academic learning time increase, so does student learning;* of the three, academic learning time is the best predictor of achievement.

The BTES data made time a popular topic for reform-minded educators. In 1983, for example, the National Commission on Excellence in Education declared that we were "a nation at risk" because of "a rising tide of mediocrity" in our educational system. The report advocated a variety of reforms, including recommendations to extend the school day to seven hours and to lengthen the school year to 200 or 220 days.

Other educators argued that there was sufficient time for learning, but that it was used inappropriately (Karweit, 1989). These educators urged teachers to increase time-on-task and to eliminate "wasted" time. In some districts (including New Brunswick), supervisors armed with clipboards and stopwatches visited classrooms to monitor students' engagement rates—and the results were used in evaluations of teaching effectiveness. I know teachers who became wary of doing anything that was not directly related to the standardized achievement tests given at the end of the year. They eliminated "frivolous," time-consuming activities like discussions, debates, role plays, mock trials, and experiments in order to provide more time for the practice of basic skills and the acquisition of factual knowledge.

It's easy to go overboard in this search for more hours. First, expecting students to be on task 100 percent of the time is foolish, even inhumane. Total engagement is not easy for *anyone;* it is especially difficult for students who must work on tasks they have not selected and sometimes find tedious. Second, eliminating activities like discussions and debates results in a curriculum devoid of interest, vitality, and variety; this might actually cause a loss of engaged time, since students are likely to become bored or disruptive. Third, some loss of instructional time to activities like taking attendance, collecting homework, and distributing materials is unavoidable.

With these qualifications in mind, it is still essential to consider reasonable ways of increasing students' academic learning time. We will discuss three strategies for achieving this goal: *maintaining activity flow, minimizing transition time,* and *holding students accountable.* (See Table 7-1 for a summary.) Of course, these strategies not only maximize time for learning, they also help to create and maintain classroom order.

TABLE 7-1
STRATEGIES FOR INCREASING STUDENTS' LEARNING TIME

1. Maintain activity flow	Avoid flip-flopping
	Avoid "stimulus-bounded events":
	being pulled away from the ongoing activity by an event or object that doesn't really need attention
	Avoid overdwelling and fragmentation
2. Minimize transition time	Prepare students for upcoming transition
	Establish clear routines
	Have clear beginnings and endings
	(bring first activity to a halt, announce the transition, monitor the transition, make sure everyone is attentive, begin second activity)
3. Hold students accountable	Communicate assignments clearly
	Monitor students' progress
	Provide feedback

Maintaining Activity Flow

Good and Brophy (1994) observe that "four things can happen" when students must wait with nothing to do, and "three of them are bad: (1) students may remain interested and attentive; (2) they may become bored or fatigued, losing interest and ability to concentrate; (3) they may become distracted or start daydreaming; or (4) they may actively misbehave" (p. 138). Given the three-to-one odds that waiting will result in undesirable behavior and a loss of valuable learning opportunities, it's essential for teachers to learn how to maintain the flow of classroom activities.

Once again, we turn for guidance to the work of Jacob Kounin (1970). Kounin investigated differences in teachers' ability to initiate and maintain activity flow in classrooms. He then looked for relationships between activity flow and students' engagement and misbehavior.

Kounin's research identified many differences in the ways teachers orchestrated classroom activities. In some classrooms, activities flowed smoothly and briskly, while in others activities were "jerky" and slow. Kounin even developed a special vocabulary to describe the problems he observed. For instance, he found that some ineffective managers would terminate an activity, start another, and then return to the first activity. Kounin called this *flip-flopping.* It is illustrated by the following situation: A foreign language teacher finishes reviewing homework with the class and tells students to turn to the next chapter in their textbook. She then stops and says, "Wait a minute. How many got all the homework problems right? . . . Very good. . . . Okay, now let's talk about the imperfect tense."

Kounin also observed *stimulus-bounded events,* situations in which teachers are "pulled away" from the ongoing activity by a stimulus (an event or an object) that really doesn't need attention. Kounin describes the case of a teacher who is explaining a math problem at the board when she notices a student is leaning on his left elbow as he works the problem. She leaves the board, instructs him to sit up straight, comments on his improved posture, and then returns to the board.

Sometimes, teachers slow down the pace of activity by *over-dwelling*—continuing to explain when students already understand or preaching at length about appropriate behavior. Another type of slow down is produced when a teacher breaks an activity into components even though the activity could be performed as a single unit—what Kounin called *fragmentation:*

> The teacher was making a transition from spelling to arithmetic as follows: "All right, everybody, I want you to close your spelling books. Put away your red pencils. Now close your spelling books. Put your spelling books in your desks. Keep them out of the way." [There's a pause.] "All right now. Take out your arithmetic books and put them on your desks in front of you. That's right, let's keep everything off your desks except your arithmetic books. And let's sit up straight. We don't want any lazy-bones, do we? That's fine. Now get your black pencils and open your books to page sixteen."

Flip-flops, stimulus-boundedness, over-dwelling, fragmentation—these are all threats to the flow of classroom activities. Not only do they result in lost learning time, they can also have a significant impact on students' behavior. When activities proceed smoothly and briskly, students are more involved in work and less apt to misbehave. Indeed, as Kounin concluded two decades ago, activity flow plays a greater role in classroom order than the specific techniques that teachers use to handle misbehavior.

During one visit to Sandy's classroom, I watched the skillful way she maintained the flow of activity in her class. It was the end of October, and students were in the middle of a very intriguing lab that involved the production of silver. As you read the vignette, note how Sandy ensures there will be no "down time" by preparing the board for the homework review before class begins, by starting class promptly, by having students put homework problems on the board during the lab activity, and by ensuring that students will have something to do if they finish the lab before others.

11:21   Sandy writes the numerals 4 through 11 on the chalkboard, evenly spacing them across the entire width.

11:22   She positions herself by the classroom door to greet students as they enter the room.

11:23   The bell rings. Sandy moves from the door to the front of the room. "Hats off, please. We have a lot to do today. First,we have to finish the lab. You need not wear your goggles. Second, I want to review the chemical equation sheet you did. You'll put the final balanced equations on the board. And third, you'll learn to solve problems associated with the balanced equations. So let's get going."

11:24   The students move to lab tables, get their equipment, and begin working. While students are doing the lab, Sandy moves around the room, assisting, questioning, and monitoring. The atmosphere is very relaxed. Sandy smiles, laughs, and jokes with students about the silver they're producing. While she circulates, she also notes which students are just about done with the lab and selects them to put the homework problems on the board: "Joe, are you finished? You have all your data? Okay, put number four up. Kim, you're done? Please put number five on the board." They leave their lab tables, get their homework, and put their assigned problems on the board. By the time the lab is over, numbers four through eleven are up on the chalkboard.

11:33 Sandy notices that students are nearing the end of the lab. She tells them: "When you're finished, take your seats so I know you're finished." One by one, students begin to move back to their seats; they take out their homework and begin to compare their answers to the work on the chalkboard.

11:37 The equipment is all put away, the lab tables have been cleaned, and the class is all seated.

11:38 Sandy introduces the problems on the chalkboard: "Okay, let's turn to the equations on the board. Let me preface this by saying that you should not panic if you're having trouble writing formulas. You don't have to be able to write formulas until December. But what you do need to know now is how to balance the equations. All right, let's look at the first one." She turns to the first problem written on the board and begins the review.

12:00 All the problems have been discussed, and Sandy moves to the third activity of the morning. "Now I want you to listen very carefully. Do not take notes. I know this sounds strange, but I want you to be able to watch and listen and think. I'm going to show you a new type of problem." She writes a chemical equation on the board and challenges them to think about it. The students are stuck. Sandy lets them ponder the problem; she asks some easier questions to help them get started, and suggests they use paper if they want to. She walks around the room to see how they're doing, commenting on their efforts, encouraging them to consult with one another.

12:07 The bell rings. Students are still involved in trying to solve the problems. Sandy tells the class, "Think about this tonight, and come back with your ideas tomorrow."

Later, Sandy reflected on the day's lesson and talked about her very deliberate attempts to maintain the flow of activities:

Some people would regard this as obsessive. Many teachers have kids finish the lab, sit down, and *then* put all the problems on the board. But what do you do when students are sitting there and others are putting things on the board? Even during labs, if they have to boil something for 10 minutes, I'll give them a problem to do. Kids can't just sit and watch something boil for 10 minutes. That's when they'll start squirting water bottles. Maybe I'm strange, but I just can't stand any down time. There's so much to accomplish and so little time.

Minimizing Transition Time

From the perspective of time management, transitions between classes and activities can be very problematic. An analysis by Paul Gump (1982, 1987) helps us to understand the reasons. First, Gump observes, there may be difficulty "closing out" the first activity—especially if students are deeply engaged. (Ironically, the very involvement that teachers strive to achieve makes it more difficult to get students to switch activities!) Second, transitions are more loosely structured than activities themselves (Ross, 1985). Since there's usually more leeway in terms of socializing and moving around the room, there is also more opportunity for disruption. In fact, in a study of 50 classes taught by student teachers, Marshall Arlin (1979) found that there was almost twice as much disruption during transitions (e.g., hitting, yelling, obscene gestures) as during nontransition time.

Third, students sometimes "save up" problems or tensions and deal with them during the transition time (Gump, 1982). They may seek out the teacher to complain about a grade, ask for permission to retrieve a book from a locker, or dump out the contents of their book bags in search of a lost homework assignment. Although these behaviors are legitimate—and help to protect the adjacent activities from disturbance—they also make transitions more difficult to manage. Finally, there may be delays in getting students started on the second activity (Gump, 1982). Students may have difficulty settling down, or teachers may be held up because they are dealing with individual students' concerns or are busy assembling needed materials.

Gump's analysis suggests that teachers can reduce the potential for chaos by *preparing students for upcoming transitions, by establishing efficient transition routines, and by clearly defining the boundaries of lessons* (Ross, 1985). Let's consider each of these guidelines, drawing on the practices of our four teachers.

Advance preparation   Marshall Arlin's (1979) research revealed that transitions were far more chaotic when student teachers failed to warn students about the imminent change of activity. This often occurred at the end of the period because student teachers didn't even realize that time was up:

> The lesson was still continuing when the bell would ring. Not having reached any closure, the teacher, with some degree of desperation, would say something like "Okay, you can go," and pupils would charge out of the room, often knocking each other over. (Sometimes, pupils did not even wait for the signal from the teacher.) The teacher might then remember an announcement and interject to the dispersing mob, "Don't forget to bring back money for the trip!" (p. 50)

In contrast, other student teachers in Arlin's study were able to prepare students for the upcoming transition. If they were about to dismiss the class, they made sure that desks were in order and that students were quiet and ready to leave. They made announcements while students were still seated and then made sure students left the room in an orderly fashion.

Our four teachers are very diligent "clock watchers." They take care to monitor time and to inform students when the class period is drawing to a close. This is not as easy as it sounds—even for these experienced teachers. During one visit to Donnie's class, I watched both teacher and students get caught up in the lesson and lose track of time. When the bell rang, one girl actually blurted out, "Dang! That went fast!" Donnie laughingly agreed, broke off the lesson, and gave the homework assignment. Fortunately, she had taught her students early in the year that *she,* not the bell, dismissed them, so students stayed seated and attentive until she was finished.

In addition to warning students about the end of the period, it's also helpful to prepare them for changes in class activities during the period. In the following scene, we see Fred explain to students what they will be doing that day and remind them periodically about how much time is left before they will be changing activities.

> The bell rings. Fred tells his students to take out paper and pencil while he distributes an article from *Newsweek* magazine regarding human rights and China. "While I meet with people one by one to go over grades, you will read and take notes on this article. You'll have about 12 minutes. At the end of that time, we will discuss these questions: What is the problem we're trying to solve between China and the United States? And is this just a case of western arrogance? Take good notes—I'm going to collect them—and I will ask you to give an oral presentation of your views."

> As students settle down to read, Fred gets out his grade book and sits at his desk. He quietly signals for individuals to come up to discuss their marking quarter grades. A few minutes later, he checks his watch. "Ladies and gentlemen, you have about seven more minutes to finish reading and taking notes."

> Later, he issues another warning about the time: "About two more minutes, so you should be finishing up." At the end of 12 minutes, he gets up from his desk. "Okay, you've had enough time now to read the article and take some notes. At the bottom of the paper, please summarize in 25 words or less what the basic problem is between China and the United States. What is the problem we're trying to solve between China and the United States?"

The use of routines   In Chapter Four we talked about the importance of having clear, specific routines in order to keep the classroom running smoothly. At no time is the use of routines more important than during transitions (Ross, 1985). Well-established routines provide a structure to transitions that helps to prevent confusion and lost time.

In Carmen's class, the routine for entering the room is very clear. Her seventh and eighth graders come in, get their chairs, and assemble in the small instructional area. Here they wait quietly for Carmen to provide directions for the day's activities. Having an efficient routine like this is especially important when time is so precious (remember that Carmen sees her students only 40 minutes a week!) and when distributing materials and cleaning up can consume so much of the period.

Donnie also has a routine for beginning the period that helps to get students settled quickly. It's the "Do Now," and she uses it once or twice a week.

It's period 6 geometry. As students enter the room, they see the "do now" assignment on the board—Pages 57–58, #10–13. Instead of heading for their desks, most of the students go over to the side of the room and get calculators and workbooks. Donnie stands at the side of the room, watching silently. The stragglers notice her standing there; they glance at the board, and then get their materials. When everyone has settled down, Donnie announces, "Okay, you have four or five minutes to finish those problems. Then we'll talk about them." While students are working, she takes attendance silently. Then she begins to circulate.

Clear beginnings and endings   Arlin's (1979) study demonstrated that transitions proceed more smoothly if teachers bring the first activity to a halt, announce the transition, allow time to make sure that everyone is attentive, and then begin the second activity. In other words, smooth transitions are characterized by well-defined boundaries.

In the following vignette, we see Carmen implement a transition with well-defined boundaries. Watch the way she prepares her students for the transition from whole-class instruction to individual art-making. She also helps ease the transition from one phase of the activity to another by displaying the steps on a large piece of cardboard mounted on an easel. Finally, note how she reminds her students about the passage of time and prepares them for the end of class.

Carmen's eighth-grade students are gathered around her in the back of the room. She has been demonstrating the steps they will use to make their own masks, referring to a cardboard display mounted on an easel. She then prepares students to begin working on their individual masks: "Okay, are you ready? [She scans the group, making sure students are paying attention.] Any questions? What are you going to do first? [A student responds.] Yes, the first thing is to get your paper and move back to your tables. You know where the scissors are. I've put out the tape on the front table. If you finish cutting your mask, you can start your drawing. Just refer to the easel if you forget what to do. Okay, get to work."

Students get their paper and scissors and sit down at their tables. They begin to fold their cardboard and outline their masks. As they work, Carmen circulates, helping and encouraging: "That's great. Are you going to make a three-dimensional mouth out of the cardboard or are you going to paint one on?" "These scissors aren't working well. Why don't you get another pair?" She looks at the clock. "You have 17 minutes. There's a lot to do in 17 minutes." She continues to circulate. Later, "Okay, you've got eight minutes. Use your time wisely."

Five minutes before the end of class, Carmen holds up her hand with two fingers extended. "Listen. Look at me. There are only five more minutes. Put your name on the cardboard or on the mask and begin to clean up. If you didn't finish all the steps today, it's okay. Don't worry. You'll finish next time."

Two minutes before the end of class, Carmen turns the lights out. "Okay, it's time. Everyone should be ready to go. [Students quiet down.] Push your chairs in and bring your masks to me. I'm going to put them in this cabinet. Then I want you to line up for Mr. Green" [their homeroom teacher, who comes to pick them up].

The class exits promptly at 11:40, and the next class comes in—immediately!

Holding Students Accountable

Walter Doyle (1983) has commented that students tend to take assignments seriously only if they are held accountable for them. Your own school experiences probably testify to the truth of this statement. Even as adults, it takes a good deal of self-discipline, maturity, and intrinsic motivation to put your best effort into work that will never be seen by anyone else. And secondary students are *adolescents*. Unless they know they will have to account for their performance, it is unlikely they'll make the best use of class time.

Furthermore, students are *unable* to make good use of their time if they are confused about what they're supposed to be doing. Teachers sometimes tell students to "get to work" and are immediately bombarded by questions: "Can I use pen?" "Do I have to write down the questions or can I just put the answers?" "Do we have to show all our work?" "Can I work at the lab table?" When this happens, precious class time has to be spent clarifying the original instructions.

In order to help students use their time wisely, teachers must *communicate assignments and requirements clearly, monitor students' progress,* and *provide feedback about performance* (Emmer, Evertson, Clements, Sanford, and Worsham, 1994). These practices minimize students' confusion and convey the message that school work is important. Let's see what our teachers and the research have to say about these three practices.

Communicating assignments and requirements   One finding of the BTES study (Fisher et al., 1980) was that students were more likely to have success on assignments when teachers provided clear, thorough directions. Interestingly, the number of explanations given *in response to students' questions was negatively associated with high student success.* What could account for this curious finding? One possibility is that when many students have to ask about an assignment, their teachers failed to provide sufficient preparation. In other words, the original instructions were not clear or thorough enough.

Before students begin to work, it's a good idea to explain what they'll be doing and why, how to get help, what to do with completed work, what to do when they're finished, and how long they'll be spending on the task (Jones and Jones, 1986). You also need to make sure students are familiar with your work standards—for example, what kind of paper to use, whether they should use pencil or pen, how to number the page, whether or not erasures are allowed, and what it means to "show all their work." Once you've given your instructions, it's also a good idea to have students explain what they will be doing in their own words and to give students a chance to ask questions. Asking "Does everyone understand?" rarely yields useful information.

Sometimes, in an effort to maintain activity flow, teachers rush into instructions and activities without checking that students are "with them." Arlin (1979) writes: "Several times I noticed over 15 children continuing the previous activity while the teacher was giving directions for the new activity" (p. 50). Needless to say, those teachers then became exasperated when students asked questions about what to do.

On the other hand, Paul Gump (1982) warns that waiting *too long* can cause a

Carmen carefully explains the art activity before students begin to work.

loss of momentum. He writes: "Waiting for absolute and universal attention can sometimes lead to unnecessarily extended transition times" (p. 112). Gump reminds us that by keeping the instructional program going, teachers can often "pull in" students whose attention has momentarily wandered.

This lesson was brought home to me on a lovely day in April, as I watched Fred's Contemporary World Issues class. As soon as the bell rang, Fred scanned the room and then announced he was going to divide the class into six groups of four or five each (by having students count off). Once students had moved into their groups, Fred distributed paper and atlases, appointed a chairperson for each group, and gave students the following instructions: "Put your name at the top of the page. Turn to page 81 in your atlas—the map of Africa. Your first task is to find the country of Burkina Faso and to write down the names of the countries that surround it." Students immediately started working, and I sat at the side of the room wondering why Fred had not explained why they were doing this and what they would be doing for the rest of the period. Only when students had finished this first task, did Fred provide more elaborate instructions:

> Ladies and gentlemen, give me your attention so you'll know what we're doing today. You'll remember that after we saw the film on Africa, we talked about how the problems seem so big, so paralyzing. What can an ordinary person do? The situation is just too overwhelming. Well, I found some readings about two ordinary people, Minata in Burkina Faso and Keko in Tanzania. Today, you'll read about these two people and the prob-

lems they face. Then I want you to think about the best thing for them to do. What would *you* do if you were in their shoes? [He distributes the readings.]

Here's how you're going to do it. First read the articles and jot down your own notes to the questions. Then share your reactions in your small group. Then each of you will write out final answers that represent the thinking of the whole group. The chairperson will turn in the notes and the final answers at the end of the period. You already did the first question when you found the countries surrounding Burkina Faso. You'll do the same thing for Tanzania when you read about Keko. Any questions about what you're going to do? [There are a few questions, and he answers them.] This is worth eight points.

Later, I asked Fred why he had started students on the activity *before* explaining what they would be doing for the period and giving general instructions (clearly a departure from "standard operating procedure"). He answered without hesitation:

Look, it's spring, and they're juniors and seniors suffering from spring fever. If I had tried to give instructions when they first came in, half of them wouldn't have been listening, and I would have had to say everything all over again. This way, I got them into groups and got them going on an easy task—finding the countries surrounding Burkina Faso. They got focused, and *then* I could give instructions and they'd all be listening.

In addition to providing explicit directions for in-class activities, teachers need to communicate homework assignments in a clear, organized manner. This is particularly important if you are working with students who have difficulty remembering what they are supposed to do. Sandy has devised a routine for assigning homework that she first developed to help her learning disabled students. She soon realized, however, that the routine was helpful for everyone:

When I first write a homework assignment on the board, I write it really big in the middle of the board and tell students to copy it down *now*. Then I move it to the left-hand corner of the board where it remains until the due date. Periodically, I remind students about it. I'm also really clear about the numbers of the problems that students have to do. For example, if the assignment is to do numbers 1 through 5, and then 7, 9, 11, and 13 through 16, I'll write out 1, 2, 3, 4, and 5, because some kids (especially my learning disabled students) don't see the difference between the comma and the dash.

Monitoring student progress   Once you've given directions for an assignment and your class gets to work, it's important to monitor how students are doing. The BTES study found that teachers with high-achieving classes circulated around the room while students were working at their seats (Fisher et al., 1980). This practice enables you to keep track of students' progress, to identify and help with problems, and to verify that assignments are matched to students' ability. Circulating also helps to ensure that students are using their time well.

Observations of our four teachers revealed they rarely sit down, unless they're working with a small group.

Donnie's class is working with rulers and protractors to "discover" the properties of parallelograms. As students work, Donnie continually circulates. She keeps up a steady stream of comments, questions, and praise: "Very good, Veronica." "Everybody finished with that first question?" "Answer the questions as you go, so you'll have all the answers when you finish." "Anyone need help?" "What does consecutive mean, José?" "Is there anyone who's having problems with the protractor?"

After class, Donnie talked about the fact that she is constantly on the move:

> I don't see how a person can teach math and sit down. I just wouldn't feel comfortable sitting down. You have to write on the board, you have to guide students through the problems, you have to see they're on the right track. By walking around the room, I can catch mistakes. I can ask, "What were you doing here? Explain your reasoning." I can talk them through the problem. I have to be up and moving when I'm teaching.

In addition to circulating while students are working, it's essential to monitor whether students are regularly completing assignments. This requires you to *establish routines for collecting and checking classwork and homework.* For example, at the beginning of class, Donnie has students take out their homework and put it on their tables. While they review the assignment, she circulates around the room and notes in her grade book who has done the homework. The whole procedure takes just a few minute and there's no loss of instructional time, since the class is simultaneously going over the homework problems.

Sandy uses a different system. She has a folder for each class that she keeps on the front table. Homework assignments are to be placed in the folder at the very beginning of class. She gives a "last call for homework," and then closes the folder. Sometime during the period, Sandy checks the papers to see if any assignments are missing. This allows her to verify immediately that she does not have an assignment from a particular student and to find out what happened. As she puts it, "This way I can avoid the situation where a student says, 'But I *did* do the homework. You must have lost it.' "

It's especially important to *keep track of students' progress on long-term homework assignments.* By establishing intermediate check points, you can help students develop a "plan of attack." For example, if they are writing a research paper, you can set due dates on which they have to submit each stage of the assignment (e.g., the topic; preliminary notes; a list of references; the first draft; the final draft). Not only does this allow you to monitor students' progress, it also helps to lessen the anxiety that adolescents sometimes feel when faced with a large assignment.

Fred tells an ironic story that points out the value of this approach:

> Last year, my students did a long research paper. I had them turn in each piece to show me how they were coming along—a working outline, a bibliography, their notes, a rough draft, and then the final copy. I used a point system. The first four parts of the assignment were worth 10 points each; the final copy was worth 60 points.

> This year, I decided it was babyish to do this, so I didn't do it. I told my classes, "I'm going to treat you like adults," and they said, "Great. We can do it." Well, they didn't get their papers in. They told me, "We messed up. We let it go, we procrastinated." They asked me to do what I had done last year! I trusted them to be mature, and they said, "We're not."

Finally, you need to *maintain records of what students are accomplishing.* In some districts, teachers can develop their own system for recording students' progress; others require teachers to follow a prescribed format. For example, Donnie's grade book has to reflect her weekly lesson plans and the "quarterly topic plans" she has to submit four times a year; following the district's objectives for her courses, these plans describe what she will be teaching day-by-day. For each marking period, Donnie must have two grades per week for homework and at least one test grade per objective. If five objectives are to be covered during a particular marking period, then Donnie would have to have at least five test grades.

In contrast, Fred is allowed to develop his own record-keeping system. Fred doesn't even have a regular grade book; instead he records his students' grades on the computer. Nonetheless, like Donnie, he is careful to keep up-to-date records of students' progress. He explained his record-keeping system to students at the very beginning of the year:

> I want to take a minute or two to discuss grades with you. I don't have a grade book. I keep your grades on the computer. We can go any time after school and check out your grades. What I use is homework, class work, projects, tests, and quizzes. Each in-class assignment is about four points. A big exam would be worth about five in-class assignments—about 20 points. The total point value for the marking period is 120–130 points. You can always find out what your point total is, what your grade is at any time. . . . It's important to me that everyone in here passes this class and does well. If you need me to get on your case, so you'll do okay in here, let me know. Remember, the grades are yours. You can see them at any time.

Checking or grading all the work students do each day is an arduous, time-consuming task. One student teacher in English recently wrote about "the looming mountain of paperwork that a teacher must perpetually climb":

> Sometimes I'm not sure if I'm a teacher or a certified [public] accountant! However, my experience . . . has enabled me to find ways to reckon with the ponderous load. Simple things like color-coordinated folders for each class, or writing the names of absent students on quiz sheets to keep track of make-up work, are "tricks" I am extremely grateful to have been shown along the way.

Like this student teacher, you need to find ways to "make a molehill out of a mountain" (Shalaway, 1989). I asked Sandy, Donnie, and Fred how they handle the paperwork. Their ideas are listed in Figure 7-3.

Providing feedback   Sometimes, turning in work to a teacher is like dropping it down a black hole. Assignments pile up in huge mounds on the teacher's desk, and students know their papers will never be returned—graded or ungraded. From a student's perspective, it's infuriating to work hard on an assignment, turn it in, and then receive no feedback from the teacher. But a lack of academic feedback is not simply infuriating. It is also detrimental to students' involvement and achievement. The BTES (Fisher et al., 1980) study documented the importance of providing feedback to students:

Fred: Check that students do in-class assignments and routine homework, but don't spend a lot of time reading and grading these. Develop a simple system for keeping track of students' routine assignments (e.g., four points for full credit; 3.5 points for an almost completed assignment, etc.).

Spend your time on the assignments that require higher-level thinking. These are harder to grade!

On tests, create "structured essay" questions. Construct your own answer to the essay. (Know what the essay is "supposed to say.") Look for key words when grading.

Refuse to grade papers that contain more than three technical errors (spelling, punctuation, etc.). I tell students, "I have 100 of these to grade; it's not fair for me to sit here and correct your spelling mistakes. I'm not here to proofread. . . . Have a smart person proofread your papers before you turn them in."

Sandy: With homework, grade on attempt/effort, not whether it's right or wrong.

For the first few assignments, read *everything* really carefully. Go over lab reports with a fine-tooth comb. That way, students come to see that you have really high expectations and that they have to be clear and thorough. Then, later, you can skim the first few pages (objectives, procedures, materials), and spend the bulk of your time on the data section.

Sometimes, in long labs, have students present their data in table form.

Donnie: Review homework everyday, but have students check their own work. In your grade book, enter a check (as opposed to a grade) to show who has done the assignment.

Have students grade one homework assignment each week that you record in your grade book.

Collect one homework assignment each week to grade yourself.

FIGURE 7-3
Ideas for Handling Paperwork

One particularly important teaching activity is providing academic feedback to students (letting them know whether their answers are right or wrong, or giving them the right answer). Academic feedback should be provided as often as possible to students. When more frequent feedback is offered, *students pay attention more and learn more. Academic feedback was more strongly and consistently related to achievement than any of the other teaching behaviors.* (p. 27; emphasis added)

If you circulate while students are working on assignments, you can provide them with immediate feedback about their performance. You can catch errors, assist with problems, and affirm correct, thoughtful work. In the following vignette, we see Sandy help two girls having problems pouring a solution into a funnel. Only a clear, colorless solution was supposed to come out into the beaker, but the solution was yellow and had particles of the solid in it.

SANDY: Why did this happen?

TANYA: Because I poured too fast and too much.

SANDY: Right. [She calls all the students over to see the problem that the two girls had.] So what happened?

LISA: The yellow stuff got over the filter paper, behind the fold.

SANDY: Okay, so what can you do?

TANYA: Pour it back in, but we're going to lose some.

SANDY: (To the other students) Can they pour it back in?

STUDENT: Yeah.

SANDY: Sure. It was good you washed the beaker.

Sometimes you're unable to monitor and correct work while it's being done. In this case, you need to check assignments once they've been submitted and return them to students as soon as possible. You might also decide to allow your students to check their own work. Donnie believes this has numerous educational benefits:

> I like to go over the homework in class and have students check their own work. This gives them the chance to see how they're doing, where they're confused. If I just had them turn in the work and I graded it, they'd know which problems were right and

Sandy provides feedback to a small lab group.

which were wrong, but they wouldn't know why. Once a week, though, I do collect the homework and go over it myself. That way I can see for myself how students are doing.

Whether you correct work while it's being done, at home over a cup of coffee, or together with your students, the important point is that students *need to know how they are progressing.* If you don't provide them with frequent, specific, informative feedback, they may spend valuable time doing assignments incorrectly. Furthermore, a lack of feedback can be interpreted as a sign that you don't take their work seriously—and that provides a good excuse for fooling around.

CONCLUDING COMMENTS

Tracy Kidder's book, *Among Schoolchildren* (1989), describes one year in the life of Chris Zajac, an elementary teacher who's feisty, demanding, blunt, fair, funny, and hard working. At the very end of the book, Kidder describes Chris's thoughts on the last day of school. Although she is convinced she belongs "among schoolchildren," Chris laments the fact she hadn't been able to help all her students—at least not enough:

> Again this year, some had needed more help than she could provide. There were many problems that she hadn't solved. But it wasn't for lack of trying. She hadn't given up. She had run out of time.

Like Chris, we all run out of time. The end of the year comes much too quickly, and some children's needs are much too great. Hopefully, the concepts and guidelines presented in this chapter will help you make good use of the limited time you have.

SUMMARY

This chapter described time as a "precious resource." First, we looked at the amount of school time actually available for teaching and learning. Then the chapter discussed three strategies for increasing students' academic learning time. I reviewed research by Kounin demonstrating that activity flow plays a greater role in classroom order than the specific techniques teachers use to handle misbehavior. I stressed the importance of minimizing transition times. Finally, I outlined ways of holding students accountable and helping them to use their time wisely.

Types of Time

- *Mandated time:* the time the state requires school to be in session
- *Available time:* mandated time minus the time lost to absences, special events, half-days
- *Instructional time:* the time actually used for instruction
- *Engaged time:* the time a student spends working attentively on academic tasks

- *Academic Learning Time (ALT):* the proportion of engaged time in which students are performing academic tasks with a high degree of success

The Relationship between Time and Learning

- As allocated, engaged, and academic learning time increase, so does student learning.
- Of the three, ALT is the best predictor of achievement.

How to Increase Hours for Learning

- Maintain activity flow by avoiding:
    flip-flopping
    stimulus-bounded events
    over-dwelling
    fragmentation
- Minimize transition time by:
    defining boundaries to lessons
    preparing students for transitions
    establishing routines
- Hold students accountable by:
    communicating assignments and requirements clearly
    monitoring students' progress
    establishing routines for collecting and checking classwork and homework
    maintaining good records
    providing feedback about performance

By using time wisely, you can maximize opportunities for learning and minimize occasions for disruption in your classroom. Think about how much time is being spent on meaningful and appropriate work in your room, and how much is being eaten up by business and clerical tasks. Be aware that the hours available for instruction are much fewer than they first appear!

ACTIVITIES

1. While you are visiting a class, carefully observe the way the teacher uses the time. Keep an accurate record for a complete period, noting how much of the available time is actually used for *instructional* purposes. For example, let's suppose you elect to observe a 50-minute mathematics class. The *available time is 50 minutes.* But while you are observing, you note that the first five minutes of the period are spent checking to see who does or does not have the homework (a clerical job). In the middle of the period, the teacher asks students to get into groups of four, and moving into groups takes up another five minutes that is not actually spent in instruction. Then an announcement comes on over the loudspeaker, and the class discusses the announcement for another three minutes. Finally, the teacher wraps up class five minutes before the end of the period and

gives everyone free time. *Conclusion: Out of 50 minutes of available time, 18 minutes was spent on nonacademic or noninstructional activities, leaving 32 minutes of actual instructional time.*

2. Read the following vignette and identify the factors that threaten the activity flow of the lesson. Once you have identified the problems, rewrite the vignette so that activity flow is maintained OR explain how you would avoid the problems if you were the teacher.

Mrs. P. waits while her sophomore "A" level students take out the ten mixed number addition problems she had them do for homework last night. Jack raises his hand. "I brought the wrong book by mistake, Mrs. P. My locker is right across the hall. Can I get my math book?"

"Be quick, Jack. We have ten problems to go over, and the period is only 50 minutes long." Jack leaves, and Mrs. P. turns back to the class. "Okay, this is what I want you to do. Switch papers with your neighbor." She waits while students figure out who will be partners with whom. She scans the room, trying to make sure everyone has a partner. "Okay, now write your name at the bottom of the page, on the right-hand side, to show that you're the checker. When I collect these papers, I want to know who the checkers were, so I can see who did a really accurate, responsible job of checking." She circulates while students write their names at the bottom of the page. "Ariadis, I said the right-hand side." Ariadis erases her name and rewrites it on the right side. "Okay, now let's go over the answers. If your neighbor didn't get the right answer, put a circle around the problem and try to figure out what they did wrong so you can explain it to them. Okay, number one, what's the right answer?" A student in the rear of the class raises his hand. "Billy?"

"I don't have a partner, Mrs.P. Can I go to the bathroom?"

"Jack will be right back, and then you'll have a partner. Just wait until we finish going over the homework." Jack returns. "Take a seat near Billy, Jack, and exchange homework papers with him."

Jack looks sheepishly at Mrs. P. "It's not in my book, Mrs. P. I must have left it on my desk last night. I was working on it pretty late."

"Class, go over the answers to problems one and two with your neighbors. See if you agree, and if you did the problems the same way. Jack, step outside."

Billy waves his hand again. "Mrs. P., can I *please* go to the bathroom now?"

"Yes, Billy. Fill out a pass, and I'll sign it. Just get back quickly." Leaving the door open so she can keep an eye on the other students, Mrs. P. follows Jack out of class. "You haven't had your homework done three times in the last two weeks, Jack. What's the problem?"

"Well, Mrs. P., my mother's been . . . " The office intercom phone buzzes.

"Want me to get that, Mrs. P.?" a student calls from the class.

"Yes, tell them I'll be right there."

"They said to just tell you that Billy has to go to the office if he's not doing anything right now."

"Go take your seat, Jack. I'll talk to you after class." Mrs. P. moves to the front of the room again. "I'm sorry, class, let's begin again. Did you all do numbers one and two?" The class murmurs assent. "Okay, number three. Let's start with problem three. Joan?"

Joan gives the correct answer. Mrs. P. gets responses and explanations for three more homework problems. As the class reviews the homework, Mrs. P. wanders up and down the rows. As she passes Tanya's desk, she notices a pink slip of paper. "Class, I almost forgot to collect the slips for the Academic Fair. This fair is a chance for us to show how much progress we've made this year in math. How many of you remembered to fill out the slip, describing the project you're going to do?" Students proceed to hunt through their backpacks and flip through their math books. Those who find their pink slips give them to Mrs. P. She reminds the others to return them tomorrow. "Okay, let's get back to problems . . . six, no seven. We were on seven, right? Shakia." Shakia begins to respond. Then Billy returns. A student in a seat by the door reminds Mrs. P. that Billy has to go to the office. "Billy, go to Mr. Wilkins' office."

"Why, Mrs. P.? All I did was to go to the john."

"I don't know, Billy. Just go and make it quick. We're trying to have a class." Billy leaves, and Mrs. P. turns to the class. "Pass your papers to the front. I'll check the rest for you and give you credit for your homework. We need to move on to subtraction with fractions. Who can think of a real-life problem where you would need to subtract fractions? Missy?"

"Can I go to the nurse, Mrs. P? I don't feel good."

3. Develop a routine or transition activity for each of the following situations. Remember, your goal is to use time wisely.
   a. Beginning class each day
   b. Taking attendance
   c. Checking homework
   d. Collecting papers
   e. Returning papers
   f. Moving from the whole group into small groups
   g. Ending class each day
   h. Students leaving class
4. You want to have your students do a research report that will be due in four weeks. As you explain this long-term project, you will need to consider how to hold your students accountable. How will you:
   a. Convey requirements clearly and thoroughly?
   b. Monitor student progress?
   c. Maintain interest?
   d. Provide feedback to students?

REFERENCES

Arlin, M. (1979). Teacher transitions can disrupt time flow in classrooms. *American Educational Research Journal, 16,* 42–56.

Doyle, W. (1983). Academic work. *Review of Educational Research, 53*(2), 159–200.

Evertson, C. (1980, April). Differences in instructional activities in high and low achieving junior high classes. Paper presented at the annual meeting of the American Educational Research Association, Boston.

Emmer, E. T., Evertson, C. M., Clements, B. S., Sanford, J. P., and Worsham, M. E. (1994). *Classroom management for secondary teachers.* Boston: Allyn and Bacon.

Fisher, C. W., Berliner, D. C., Filby, N. N., Marliave, R., Cahen, L. S., and Dishaw, M. M. (1980). Teaching behaviors, academic learning time, and student achievement: An overview. In C. Denham and A. Lieberman (Eds.), *Time to learn.* Washington, D.C.: U.S. Department of Education, 7–32.

Good, T. L., and Brophy, J. E. (1994). *Looking in classrooms* (6th edition). New York: HarperCollins.

Goodlad, J. I. (1984). *A place called school.* New York: McGraw-Hill.

Gump, P. (1982). School settings and their keeping. In D. L. Duke (Ed.), *Helping teachers manage classrooms.* Alexandria, VA: Association for Supervision and Curriculum Development, 98–114.

Gump, P. V. (1987). School and classroom environments. In D. Stokols and I. Altman (Eds.), *Handbook of environmental psychology.* New York: John Wiley & Sons, 691–732.

Jones, V. F., and Jones, L. S. (1986). *Comprehensive classroom management: Creating positive learning environments.* Boston: Allyn and Bacon.

Karweit, N. (1989). Time and learning: A review. In R. E. Slavin (Ed.), *School and classroom organization.* Hillsdale, NJ: Lawrence Erlbaum Associates.

Kidder, T. (1989). *Among schoolchildren.* Boston: Houghton-Mifflin.

Kounin, J. (1970). *Discipline and group management in classrooms.* New York: Holt, Rinehart & Winston.

Leinhardt, G., and Greeno, J. G. (1986). The cognitive skill of teaching. *Journal of Educational Psychology, 78*(2), 75–95.

McGarity, Jr., J. R., and Butts, D. P. (1984). The relationship among teacher classroom management behavior, student engagement, and student achievement of middle and high school science students of varying aptitude. *Journal of Research in Science Teaching, 21*(1), 55–61.

National Commission on Excellence in Education (1983). *A nation at risk: The imperative for educational reform.* Washington, D.C.: Government Printing Office.

Rosenshine, B. (1980). How time is spent in elementary classrooms. In C. Denham and A. Lieberman (Eds.), *Time to learn.* Washington, D.C.: U.S. Department of Education.

Ross, R. P. (1985). Elementary school activity segments and the transitions between them: Responsibilities of teachers and student teachers. Unpublished doctoral dissertation, University of Kansas.

Shalaway, L. (1989). *Learning to teach . . . not just for beginners.* Cleveland, OH: Instructor Books, Edgell Communications.

FOR FURTHER READING

Shalaway, L. (1989). *Learning to teach . . . not just for beginners.* Cleveland, OH: Instructor Books, Edgell Communications.

PART III

MANAGING SUBSETTINGS OF THE ENVIRONMENT

Chapter Eight

Managing Seatwork

Chapter One discussed the assumption that the tasks of classroom management vary across different classroom situations. I pointed out that the classroom is not a "homogenized glob" (Kounin and Sherman, 1979), but is composed of numerous "subsettings" such as opening routines, homework routines, teacher presentations, transitions, and whole-class discussions. How order is defined in each of these subsettings is likely to vary. For example, during transitions students may be allowed to sharpen pencils and talk with friends, but these same behaviors may be prohibited during a whole-group discussion or a teacher presentation.

Variations in behavioral expectations are understandable, given the fact that subsettings have different goals and pose different challenges in terms of establishing and maintaining order. To be an effective manager, you must consider the unique characteristics of your classroom's subsettings and decide how your students need to behave in each one in order to maximize opportunities for learning.

This chapter focuses on the subsetting known as *seatwork,* the situation in which students are assigned to work independently at their desks with their own materials, while the teacher is free to monitor the total class (Doyle, 1986)—to observe students' performance, provide support and feedback, engage in mini-conferences, and prepare students for homework assignments. Seatwork is often used to provide students with the chance to practice or review previously presented material (Emmer, Evertson, Clements, and Worsham, 1994). For example, in "direct instruction" or "explicit teaching" (Rosenshine, 1986), the teacher reviews previous material, presents new material in small steps, and then gives students the opportunity to practice, first under supervision ("guided practice") and then independently ("independent practice").

To be honest, this chapter almost didn't get written. When I sat down with Donnie, Sandy, Fred, and Carmen to discuss their views on seatwork, I found heated differences of opinion. On one hand, Fred argued that seatwork could be a valuable activity:

I use seatwork to give kids the opportunity to practice skills like making predictions, valid inferences, generalizations. . . . Intellectual skills like these benefit from practice just like a backhand stroke in tennis. If I have 27 kids doing an assignment in class, I can walk around, see immediately what they're dong, give individual critiques, catch them if they're having a problem. I can't give that individual immediate feedback if the work is done as homework.

On the other hand, Sandy was vehemently negative: "I hate seatwork," she told us. "As far as I'm concerned, it's just a way of killing time." Similarly, Donnie claimed she never used seatwork. I pointed out that I had frequently observed her using a pattern of direct instruction, beginning class with a review of the homework, then introducing a small segment of the new lesson, and having students do one or two problems at their seats while she circulated throughout the room. Donnie readily acknowledged her use of "guided practice," but argued that this was not seatwork:

It's not like elementary school, where you have different reading groups, and you have to find a way for kids to be busy for long periods of time while you're working with a small group. Most of my instruction is done with the whole group, so there's no need for all the kids to be sitting there quietly working on worksheets.

Finally, Carmen didn't see how she could contribute anything to such a chapter: "Since this is an art class, I never have students sitting there doing dittoes. If you write a chapter like this, it won't be about me."

We debated, we moralized, and we shared anecdotes about the awfulness or the usefulness of seatwork. Eventually, we came to realize that there was no fundamental difference of opinion among us, that our dissension arose from the negative connotations of the term "seatwork." We all agreed that teachers sometimes need to assign work that provides students with the opportunity to practice. But we also agreed that seatwork is too often busywork, that it frequently goes on for too long, and that too many teachers use seatwork as a substitute for active teaching. As Donnie put it:

Some teachers think of seatwork as "give them something to do all period so I can do something else." They'll teach for ten minutes, then give their students 30 minutes of seatwork, and sit down. That's not seatwork—that's a free period.

We also agreed that seatwork didn't have to mean silence; in fact, all the teachers felt strongly that students should generally be allowed to help one another. And we came to see that many of the managerial problems that crop up when Carmen's class is engaged in their art projects are parallel to those that exist during seatwork assignments.

This chapter begins by discussing the problems that occur when seatwork is misused—when teachers do not reflect on ways to organize seatwork so that it is appropriate and meaningful for students. We then go on to consider the ways Donnie, Sandy, Fred, and Carmen try to avoid, or at least minimize, these problems. The intent is *not* to encourage you to spend large amounts of time in seatwork activities, but rather, to provide you with a way of thinking about seatwork so that you can make better decisions about when and how to use it.

WHAT'S WRONG WITH SEATWORK?

Seatwork—the term itself conjures up images of bored, passive students doing repetitive, tedious worksheets, while teachers sit at their desks calculating grades or reading the newspaper. Consider the following description of a typical seatwork situation. It was observed by Robert Everhart (1983), who spent two years conducting fieldwork in a junior high school. His book, *Reading, Writing and Resistance: Adolescence and Labor in a Junior High School,* is a chronicle of the daily routine experienced by students, and to some extent, by teachers. This scene takes place in Marcy's English class, where students are supposed to be learning about the proper form of business letters.

> First, Marcy asked the class to turn to the chapter on business letters in their grammar books and read that section. After five minutes Marcy asked the class, "How many have not yet finished?" Initially about one-third of the class raised their hands. Roy, sitting in the rear near where I was sitting, nudged John. John then spoke up, "I'm not finished."
>
> "I ain't finished either," Roy added, smiling. Needless to say, they both had finished; I had seen them close their books a few minutes earlier and then proceed to trade a *Mad* magazine back and forth.
>
> "Well, I'll give you a few more minutes, but hurry up," said Marcy. Those not finished continued reading while the rest of the class began engaging in different activities: looking out the window, doodling, and pulling pictures from their wallets and looking at them. Roy then pulled a copy of *Cycle* magazine from beneath his desk and began leafing through it. After a few minutes Marcy went to the blackboard and began outlining the structure of the business letter.
>
> "Ok, first thing we do is to place the return address—where, class?"
>
> "On the paper," said one boy slouched in his chair and tapping his pencil.
>
> "All right, comedian, that's obvious. Where else?"
>
> "On the front side of the paper."
>
> "Come on, class, get serious! Where do you place the return address? Larry?"

Marcy eventually gets through a description and explanation of the form of the business letter. She then informs students that they will be writing their own business letters, which will be due at the end of the following week. Today, they are to write the initial paragraph:

> After about ten minutes of writing, Marcy asked, "How many are not finished with their paragraph?" About six students raised their hands. "OK, I'll give you a few minutes to finish up. The rest of you, I want you to read your paragraphs to each other because I want you to read them to the class tomorrow and they'd better be clear; if they aren't clear to you now they won't be clear to the class tomorrow."
>
> One of the students at the back of the room seemed somewhat surprised at this. "Hey, you didn't say anything about having to read these in front of the class."
>
> "Yeah, I don't want to read mine in front of the class," added Phil.
>
> Marcy put her hands on her hips and stated emphatically, "Now come on, class, you'll all want to do a good job and this will give you a chance to practice and improve your paragraphs before they're submitted for grades. And you all want to get 'A's,' I'm sure." There was a chorus of laughs from most of the class and Marcy smiled.
>
> "I don't care," I heard one girl say under her breath.

"Yeah, I don't care either, just so I get this stupid thing done."

After saying that, Don turned to Art and said, "Hey, Art, what you writing your letter on?"

"I am writing the Elephant Rubber Company, telling them that their rubbers were too small."

"Wow," Ron replied.

"Don't think I'll write that letter though. Marcy will have a bird."

"For sure," Art replied.

The students continued talking to each other, which finally prompted Marcy to get up from her desk and say, "Class, get busy or some of you will be in after school."

Analysis of this scenario allows us to identify five problems that are frequently associated with seatwork. (These are summarized in Table 8-1.) First, it is clear that *the assignment is not meaningful to students.* Don calls the business letter a "stupid thing," Art jokes about writing to the Elephant Rubber Company, and an unnamed girl mumbles that she doesn't care about getting an A. In Fred's terms, Marcy has given her students a "garbage assignment":

> Seatwork has a well-deserved bad reputation. The typical assignment is not well-thought through. It's mindlessly assigned and mindlessly done. "Read and answer the questions on page 287." "Fill in the blank." "Read and outline the chapter." What's *really* scary is when the kids don't even think assignments like that are so bad! That tells me that they're so used to that kind of thing, they don't realize it's a waste of time. *But seatwork doesn't have to be that way.* Look, I'm human. I can't be creative and wonderful five periods a day, five days a week, week after week. There are times when I'll give kids seatwork assignments that are less than wonderful, assignments that I'm not especially proud of. But I really try to make that the exception, not the rule, and to come up with seatwork that's meaningful to kids and educationally useful.

"Garbage assignments" are not only a waste of precious learning time, they also foster boredom, alienation, and misbehavior. Clearly, if students do not perceive the value of a seatwork assignment, they are unlikely to become invested in it. That's when teachers have to resort to threats about detention or extrinsic incentives like grades. Recall Marcy's words. First she tells her class, "And you all want to get 'A's,' I'm sure." Later she warns, "Class, get busy or some of you will be in after school."

Second, it appears that Marcy's assignment *does not match students' varying*

TABLE 8-1
THE PROBLEMS WITH SEATWORK

All too often:

1. Assignments are not meaningful, educationally useful, or motivating.
2. Assignments are not matched to students' achievement levels.
3. Directions are not clear and thorough.
4. Teachers do not circulate and monitor students' comprehension and behavior.
5. Some students finish early, while others do not finish.

Calvin and Hobbes

by Bill Watterson

FIGURE 8-1
Calvin's response to seatwork that is too difficult for him. *(Calvin and Hobbes © Watterson. Dist. by Universal Press Syndicate. Reprinted with permission. All rights reserved.)*

achievement levels. (Figure 8-1 depicts Calvin's rather special strategy for dealing with seatwork that is too difficult for him.) For some students, the reading assignment seems too easy; they finish reading quickly and fill their time by doodling, looking out the window, and reading magazines. Others seem to find the reading more difficult and need "a few more minutes." Similarly, writing one paragraph in ten minutes doesn't seem like a particularly challenging assignment for most of Marcy's secondary school students, yet six students indicate they are not finished when Marcy checks their progress. (Of course, it's possible they have just been wasting time.)

Assigning work that does not match students' achievement levels is typical of the behaviors exhibited by the less-effective managers studied by Carolyn Evertson and Ed Emmer (1982; see Chapter Four for a fuller description of this study). You may recall that Evertson and Emmer observed mathematics and English teachers at the junior high level and identified those who were more effective managers and those who were less effective. The observations led Evertson and Emmer to conclude that the more-effective teachers had greater awareness of students' entering skills:

> An example of an activity showing low understanding was an assignment in one of the lower achieving English classes to "Write an essay from the perspective of an inanimate object." The problem was compounded by an unclear explanation of the term, perspective. Narratives noted more instances of vocabulary beyond some of the students' comprehension. As a consequence of being more aware of student skills . . . , the more effective teachers' classes had more success in participating in class activities and completing assignments.

A third problem is that Marcy *does not provide her students with clear, complete directions.* At the beginning of the period, Marcy tells the students to read the chapter on business letters, but she says nothing about why they are to read the chapter, how long they have, or whether they should take notes. In other words, she merely tells them to "do it"—without explaining the purpose for reading or suggesting strategies that might be used. Nor does Marcy explain they will be writing their own letters later in the period. It is only after reviewing the form of the business letter that Marcy instructs her students to write the initial paragraph, and once again, she neglects to tell them what will be coming next—namely, they will be reading the paragraphs aloud the following day. (Marcy might have made this decision at the last minute, in order to provide an activity for students who finished early.) Not surprisingly, some of the students react with displeasure. One complains, "Hey, you didn't say anything about having to read these in front of the class," while another protests, "Yeah, I don't want to read mine in front of the class."

Marcy's lack of clarity and thoroughness is reminiscent of the less-effective managers studied by Evertson and Emmer (1982). In addition to differing in their awareness of students' entering abilities, teachers also differed in terms of skill in communicating information. More-effective English teachers were clearer in giving directions and stating objectives than less-effective teachers. (Interestingly, this difference did not appear in comparisons of more- and less-effective math teachers.) According to Evertson and Emmer, more-effective managers

> were better able to segment complex tasks into step-by-step procedures and to help students understand their tasks, and how to accomplish them. When students knew what to do and had the skills to do it, they were more likely to stay on task. . . . (p. 496)

A fourth problem evident in Marcy's class is her *lack of monitoring*. Although the vignette doesn't explicitly describe what Marcy is doing while her students are reading and writing, the last paragraph does state that Marcy gets up from her desk to admonish students who are talking. Furthermore, Marcy not only has to ask how many students have not yet finished, she also seems unaware that students in the rear of the room are reading *Mad* magazine. These are sure signs that Marcy is not circulating through the room, checking on students' progress, helping them with problems, and providing feedback. If Marcy is not going to provide this supervision and support, she might as well have her students do the assignment at home.

Finally, Marcy does not really plan for the fact that *students work at different paces*. They may *begin* seatwork at the same time, but they never *finish* at the same time. "Ragged" endings can upset a schedule that looked beautiful on paper. Students who cannot complete assignments in the allotted time may have to do the assignment for homework. Students who complete their work earlier than you expected need something to keep them occupied; if they must sit and wait with nothing to do, they may distract students who are still working. In Marcy's class, students who finish earlier than their peers are actually quite well behaved: they read *Mad* and *Cycle* magazines, look out the window, doodle, and look at pictures from their wallets. Nonetheless, they are wasting time that could be spent on more profitable activities.

IMPLICATIONS FOR CLASSROOM PRACTICE

Analysis of Marcy's seatwork sheds light on the special problems associated with this particular subsetting of the classroom. How can you avoid or at least minimize these problems? In this section of the chapter, we consider four guidelines derived from both the research on seatwork and the collected wisdom of our four teachers. (See Table 8-2.)

Assign Work That Is Clear, Meaningful, and Appropriate

Secondary textbooks generally have questions, activities, and exercises at the end of each chapter, and some come with supplemental study guides, workbooks, or activity sheets. Since these materials may not always be clear, let alone meaningful and motivating, it is essential that you evaluate the activities you assign. If you don't, you may encounter situations like this one, related by a student teacher in a foreign language class:

> I decided to use this worksheet that listed in random order ten statements from a short story we had read (e.g., "The gardener reported that the dandelions were growing furiously"). Underneath the list were ten lines, numbered from one through ten, and students were instructed to put the statements or events in sequential order. A lot of the students thought that the numbers (1–10) referred to the order of events, so next to each number, they wrote the number of the statement. (So "1–7" was meant to indicate that the first thing that happened in the story was the seventh item in the list). Other kids figured that the one through ten referred to the number of the statement. When they put "1–7," they meant that the first statement in the list occurred seventh. Needless to say, lots of kids "failed" the assignment! I couldn't understand how it could be, until we went over the papers. Then I realized how confusing it was. I learned a good lesson. Don't assume that everything printed on an "official" worksheet is clear!

Many teachers prefer to create their own assignments, rather than rely on commercially prepared materials. In this way, they can target particular problems that students are having and can provide greater individualization. For example, when Fred wants students to become familiar with the resources in the library, he asks them to do tasks like these:

Use an almanac to find a country that begins with the first letter of your last name and tell the population of that nation.

List three facts on one topic that interests you using *Information Plus*. Cite your source.

List the headline from the *Central Post* that appeared on your birthday. (Use another paper if the *Central Post* is unavailable.)

TABLE 8-2
GUIDELINES FOR MINIMIZING THE PROBLEMS WITH SEATWORK

1. Provide assignments that are clear, meaningful and appropriate.
2. Present assignments clearly and thoroughly, explaining norms for peer assistance.
3. Monitor behavior and comprehension.
4. Plan for ragged endings.

Use *The New York Times* microfilm index to identify an important event in the year 1962.

Locate a biography about a person whose last name begins with the same letter as your first name.

According to Fred, this simple way of individualizing the assignment has a very positive effect on students' motivation. And there's an added bonus: students have to do their own work.

Fred also likes to use open-ended assignments that allow students working on a variety of levels to complete the work successfully. For example, when his students read a chapter in their texts, Fred often foregoes the end-of-chapter questions (which often have one correct answer); instead, he may ask students to create their own questions. At other times, he asks a question that is broad enough to allow a variety of responses. When students discussed the plight of United States troops in Somalia (March 1993), for example, Fred asked them to read an article from *Newsweek* and "tell how and why you would vote on sending troops to Somalia today." Almost everyone in his extremely diverse class was able to respond—in some fashion—to this question, although answers obviously varied in terms of length, substance, and coherence. Fred calls this the "slanty rope theory of seatwork":

> If we set a rope across a room at four feet, some kids can get over it and some can't. But if we slant the rope, then everyone can find their way over at some point. I firmly believe that people don't all want to go over at the lowest level. We can encourage kids to stretch—and once you teach kids to stretch, you've taught something more important than the subject matter.

Present Seatwork Assignments Clearly

In Chapter Seven, I talked about the need to provide clear, thorough directions for assignments so that classroom time is not wasted. This general guideline certainly applies to seatwork situations. Recall that one of the problems with Marcy's letter-writing activity was that she didn't tell students why they were to read the chapter on business letters or how long they would have; nor did she explain they would be writing their own letters later in the period. Contrast this with the way Donnie introduces a brief seatwork assignment on rearranging equations to solve for different variables. Even though the assignment will take just a few minutes, she explains what students are to do, how much time they will have, and what they will be expected to do when they're finished:

> What I need you to do now is turn to page 178. Get out some paper and a pencil or pen. We're going to look at the chapter review, up through #15. I'm going to begin by making an assignment to each person. Problem #1, Ernest; Problem #2, Damika; Problem #3, Latoya; Problem #4, Jerome. [She continues until everyone has been assigned a problem to do.] Now I want you to solve the problem you were assigned. These are just

like the homework problems we just reviewed. You're going to be rearranging equations to solve for the different variables. . . . I'll give you approximately two minutes to
do this. When we come back, make sure you can give us the answer and explain the
problem to the rest of the class.

Sometimes, written instructions about the assignment are included in the textbook or on the worksheet, so teachers think they don't have to explain orally what
students are to do. It's certainly important for students to read written instructions,
but don't assume they'll do this automatically; this may be a skill you'll have to
teach. Consider the lesson learned by this student teacher:

> These kids don't instinctively read something when it is given to them: they wait to have
> it explained. . . . I know that I'm supposed to state all the objectives and explain things
> carefully, but there are times when I want them . . . to be curious enough to take a look
> at what's in front of them. I try to pepper my handouts with cartoons and some of my
> own spectacular drawings just to make them more attractive and engaging. I'm so used
> to the college mentality—something is passed out and you read it rather than listen to it
> being explained. I have to remember it's usually the opposite in high school. . . .

When you're presenting directions for seatwork assignments, you also need to
make it clear whether or not students can ask peers for assistance. In some classes,
teachers encourage students to work collaboratively, while in other classes giving
or receiving help is tantamount to cheating (Rizzo, 1989). This latter situation can
present a real dilemma for students. On one hand is their need to follow the
teacher's directions and to stay out of trouble. On the other hand is their need to
complete the assignment successfully and to assist friends who are having difficulty
(Bloome and Theodorou, 1988).

In general, all of our four teachers not only allow, they encourage students to
help one another. As Donnie puts it, "I can't possibly get around to everybody. The
kids would constantly be calling me to come over and help them. For my own sanity, I have to have students help one another. But I think they learn better that way
anyway."

It's important to note that all of the teachers work hard to explain what "helping"
really means. They take pains to explain to students that simply providing the answer or doing the task for someone else is not helping, and they stress the futility of
copying. Donnie says she has "parasites" in her geometry class who don't want to
do anything on their own; they just want someone else to give them the answer.
(This often irritates more diligent students, as Figure 8-2 illustrates.) In order to
avoid this from happening, she'll sometimes assign different problems to students
sitting next to each other; this allows them to help each other, but not to copy.

Although all the teachers firmly believe in the value of peer assistance, there are
also times when they do *not* allow students to help one another. In these situations,
they are careful to explain that the ground rules are different. Listen to Sandy:

> Most of the time, I stress that scientists do not work in isolation, that it's necessary to
> look at everyone's data and ask, "Did anyone else get these results?" But four or five

Calvin and Hobbes   by Bill Watterson

FIGURE 8-2
Sometimes students don't like to help classmates who haven't tried to do the assignment on their own. *(Calvin and Hobbes © Watterson. Dist. by Universal Press Syndicate. Reprinted with permission. All rights reserved.)*

times a year, I run "quiz labs" where students are *individually* responsible for listening to instructions, carrying out the procedures, and drawing conclusions. This is my way of making certain that every single person knows how to light the bunsen burner, handle the equipment, etc. These are not discovery or inquiry lessons, but opportunities for students to apply what has been learned in class. During these lab activities, students cannot speak to one another. This is a real departure from regular lab activities, so I have to make it really clear that they are not to consult with one another—that the norms are different.

Monitor Behavior and Comprehension

As mentioned in Chapter Seven, students' engagement rate during seatwork is often lower than the engagement rate during teacher-directed activities. Why should this be so? Apparently, even when they do find the activity meaningful and comprehensible, seatwork requires students to pace themselves through assignments. Since there are no external signals such as teachers' questions to push students along (Gump, 1982), they may begin to doodle, pass notes, comb their hair, and sharpen pencils—until the teacher reminds students to get back to work. In fact, research has shown that engagement in seatwork often follows a predictable cycle (deVoss, 1979): Students begin their assignments; attention wanes; the noise level increases; the teacher intervenes; the students return to the assignment. This cycle can repeat several times, until a final spurt when students rush to complete their tasks before the time is over.

In order to avoid having students lose momentum, it's important that you monitor their behavior. As we've already learned (in Chapter Seven), our four teachers rarely sit down while students are working. In the following example, also taken from Donnie's lesson on rearranging equations, we see the way she circulates throughout the room while students are working. Notice how she is also able to

Donnie circulates while students are working so that she can provide immediate assistance.

"overlap" (Kounin, 1970)—to monitor the behavior of students doing seatwork while she also works with an individual.

> Students are working on the problems Donnie has just assigned. She walks around the room, peering over students' shoulders, commenting, helping, prodding them along. Then she heads over to three students who were absent and are making up the assignment that everyone else did the day before. She checks what they are doing, and helps one girl who is having particular difficulty. While she is working with this student, she periodically looks up and scans the room to monitor the rest of the class. One boys appears to be doing nothing. "Jerome, are you finished with your problem?"

The purpose of circulating is not simply to monitor behavior. Roving around the room allows you to monitor students' *understanding of the assignment.* Clearly, it's not enough for students to remain busy and on task. They must also understand what they are supposed to do and carry out their tasks successfully. This requires monitoring. Sandy comments:

> When I give a seatwork assignment, I never sit at my desk doing paperwork. I give an assignment for an instructional reason, not just to keep kids busy while I grade papers. This means that I need to be moving around, seeing what they're doing. For example, at the end of the period, I might say, "Let's try problems 1, 2, and 3." I walk around and help. If I see that students are doing all right, then I know I can have them complete four through six for homework.

Plan for Ragged Endings

During one visit to Carmen's eighth-grade special education class, the lesson about "ragged endings" was made especially vivid to me. Fortunately for Carmen, several students were absent, so there were only five students that day, but they were working on four different activities! After checking attendance, Carmen got students started on their individual projects. It was almost dizzying:

> Billy, you have to finish making your clay sculpture, right? Yasim, you're about ready to start the stained glass, but first you have to coat your sculpture. You two girls are going to put the puff paint on your stained glass [a paper project that uses puff paint for the leading and colored cellophane for the glass], and Teresa, you're going to paint your sculpture and then start on your stained glass. Okay, everyone know what they're going to do?

Students settled down with their materials, and Carmen flitted around, giving instructions, assisting, and encouraging. Whenever students finished their current activity, she quickly got them started on the next:

> Yasim, let's glue this leg first, before you apply the coating. Billy, wet your hands; it'll make it easier to work with the clay. Here are your tools. Ebony, you're done with the puff paint? Okay, how about working on these decorations for the hallway? Teresa, how're you doing with that paint? Were you able to make the color you want? Remember to put newspaper down. Okay, Yasim, you're done with the coating? Then let's get you started with the drawing for your stained glass. Nice job with the puff paint, Nicole.

Although it's essential to think about the possibility of ragged endings and to plan assignments for students who finish early, you need to think carefully about the approach you will take. In Marcy's class, Roy and John both reported they hadn't finished reading the chapter, when they had. Obviously, they wanted time to read *Mad,* rather than move on to a new activity about business letters. And behavior like this isn't limited to school-smart teenagers; even very young students learn to dawdle if they know they'll only be given more (uninteresting) work to do when they finish. Jones and Jones (1986) report the following anecdote:

> During a visit to a second-grade classroom, a student in one of our courses reported observing a child who was spending most of his time staring out the window or doodling on his paper. The observer finally approached the child and asked if she could be of any assistance. Much to her surprise, the child indicated that he understood the work. When asked why he was staring out the window rather than working on his assignment, the boy pointed to a girl several rows away and said, "See her? She does all her work real fast and when she's done she just gets more work." (p. 234)

In the classrooms of our four teachers, ragged endings are rarely a problem, since class activities are structured so that students rarely finish early. Listen to Sandy:

> Not only do students have to understand what to do and why they're dong it, they need to know what's expected upon completion. If you don't do this, some kids may rush

through, thinking I'll finish real fast and then I'll have time to do my homework. If they know they'll have a follow-up related assignment, they keep going. I never make it a closed assignment. I'll say, "Today you're going to do an analysis of knowns. Once you've completed the analysis, formulate the flow chart for your unknowns." I know it usually takes a complete double period to do this. When time is about to run out, I'll say, "If you're not done, do it tonight." If they know at the beginning that it's a homework assignment, they may relax, figure they'll just do it for homework. So I never let them know that they won't be able to finish. If they see that they have a lot to do, they'll say, "Wow, I really need to work." If it's a ten-minute task, they may drag it out. I suggest that teachers predict how long something will take and then tack on a related assignment.

Fred takes a similar approach. He tells us:

I make sure that my seatwork assignments will more than fill the period so kids can't get done early. At the end of the period, I'll say, "You can either hand this in now for partial credit, or you can take it home and finish it in order to get full credit. It's up to you."

CONCLUDING COMMENTS

In this chapter, I have tried to provide you with an understanding of the pitfalls and problems associated with seatwork, as well as suggestions for avoiding, or at least minimizing, these problems. I hope you will keep these in mind as you decide on the kinds of activities students will do during seatwork time, the way you will introduce seatwork assignments, and the rules and procedures you will establish to guide behavior.

It is important to note that this chapter has focused exclusively on the situation in which seatwork is assigned to the entire class, while the teacher circulates and assists students in accomplishing the tasks. But this is only one way that seatwork can be used. Another option is to assign seatwork to the majority of the class, while you work with individuals who need additional help or a more challenging assignment.

This use of seatwork is common at the elementary level. Most of us recall our primary teachers meeting with the "Cardinals," the "Butterflies," or the "Tigers," while the rest of the class worked independently. But independent seatwork combined with small-group instruction is far more unusual at the high school level, where instruction often tends to be conducted in a large group.

Research (Anderson, 1985; Fisher, Filby, Marliave, Cahen, Dishaw, Moore, and Berliner, 1978) suggests that elementary students spend far too much time doing seatwork assignments that have questionable value, so I am certainly not suggesting that you replicate this situation at the secondary level. Nonetheless, there are times when it may be appropriate to have the majority of students work on an independent assignment, while you meet with individuals. This format may be particularly useful if you have an extremely heterogeneous class. But take heed: If you are going to be unavailable for circulating and assisting, your assignments need to be even clearer and more meaningful than usual. You also need to hone the skill of overlapping. This is a situation that truly requires you to have "eyes in the back of your head."

SUMMARY

This chapter examined the subsetting known as seatwork, the situation in which students work on assignments that provide practice or review of previously presented material. Seatwork provides teachers with the opportunity to observe students' performance, to provide support and feedback, to engage in mini-conferences with individuals, and to prepare students for homework assignments. But it can also be misused. Too often, seatwork is synonymous with images of bored, passive students doing repetitive, tedious worksheets, while teachers sit at their desks calculating grades or reading the newspaper.

The first part of this chapter examined the problems that are frequently associated with seatwork:

- the assignment is not meaningful to students
- the assignment does not match students' varying achievement levels
- the teacher does not provide students with clear, complete directions
- the teacher does not monitor what students are doing
- students work at different paces, so that some finish early, while others do not finish

The chapter then considered some guidelines for minimizing the problems of seatwork:

- Provide assignments that are meaningful and appropriate
- Present assignments clearly and thoroughly
- Explain the norms for peer assistance
- Monitor behavior and comprehension
- Plan for ragged endings

This chapter focused exclusively on the situation in which seatwork is assigned to the entire class, but it may sometimes be appropriate to give a seatwork assignment to the majority of the class, while you work with individuals who need additional help or a more challenging assignment. This use of seatwork is rare at the secondary level; however, it may be a useful strategy if you need to work with small groups (e.g., if you have an extremely heterogeneous class). But be careful: If you are going to use seatwork this way, you truly need to have "eyes in the back of your head."

ACTIVITIES

1. Obtain a workbook (preferably in your content area), and select three pages to examine closely. For each page, note the topic, describe the format of the worksheet, identify the skill being practiced or extended, and generate an alternative activity that would accomplish the same goal. An example is provided.

Topic	Description of Worksheet	Skill	Alternative
Who fired the first shot at Lexington and Concord?	3 accounts by individuals who observed or participated in events at Lexington and Concord; students are to determine point of view for each account	identifying point of view and bias	Choose two of the following characters (a British officer, an American militiaman, a French reporter, the minister's wife at Lexington, a maid at the inn in Concord) and tell the story of the events at Lexington and Concord from their respective points of view

2. Select a workbook page or a ditto sheet (preferably in your content area). Examine it, using the following questions as a guide. Suggest ways to improve the page.

Question	Response	Suggested Improvement
Are the directions clear?		
How does the page organization facilitate or hinder students' understanding of the task?		
To what extent does the activity reinforce the intended skill?		
How meaningful is the task?		
If there are illustrations, to what extent do they help or distract?		

3. Interview two to four high school students to learn their perceptions about seatwork. If possible, select students who vary in terms of achievement level. Include the following questions in your interview:

In what classes is seatwork used most? least?
To what extent is seatwork used in your academic classes?
Under what circumstances is seatwork useful/useless? interesting/boring?
What do your teachers generally do when the class is doing seatwork?
Are there consistent differences among teachers in this regard?
Are you generally allowed to ask for help from peers or do you have to work alone?

REFERENCES

Anderson, L. (1985). What are students doing when they do all that seatwork? In C. W. Fisher and D. C. Berliner (Eds.), *Perspectives on instructional time.* New York: Longman, 189–202.

Bloome, D., and Theodorou, E. (1988). Analyzing teacher-student and student-student discourse. In J. E. Green and J. O. Harker (Eds.), *Multiple perspective analyses of classroom discourse.* Norwood, NJ: Ablex, 217–248.

deVoss, G. G. (1979). The structure of major lessons and collective student activity. *Elementary School Journal, 80,* 8–18.

Doyle, W. (1986). *Classroom organization and management.* In M. C. Wittrock (Ed.), *Handbook of research on teaching.* New York: Macmillan, 392–431.

Emmer, E. T., Evertson, C. M., Clements, B. S., and Worsham, M. E. (1994). *Classroom management for secondary teachers.* Boston: Allyn and Bacon.

Everhart, R. B. (1983). *Reading, writing, and resistance: Adolescence and labor in a junior high school.* Boston: Routledge and Kegan Paul.

Evertson, C. M., and Emmer, E. T. (1982). Effective management at the beginning of the school year in junior high classes. *Journal of Educational Psychology, 74*(4), 485–498.

Fisher, C. W., Filby, N. N., Marliave, R. S., Cahen, L. S., Dishaw, M. M., Moore, J. E., and Berliner, D. C. (1978). *Teaching behaviors, academic learning time and student achievement. Final report of Phase III-B, Beginning Teacher Evaluation Study.* San Francisco, CA: Far West Laboratory for Educational Research and Development.

Gump, P. V. (1982). School settings and their keeping. In D. L. Duke (Ed.), *Helping teachers manage classrooms.* Alexandria, VA: Association for Supervision and Curriculum Development.

Jones, V. F., and Jones, L. S. (1986). *Comprehensive classroom management. Creating positive learning environments.* Boston: Allyn and Bacon.

Kounin, J. S. (1970). *Discipline and group management in classrooms.* New York: Holt, Rinehart & Winston.

Rizzo, T. A. (1989). Friendship development among children in school. Norwood, NJ: Ablex.

Rosenshine, B. V. (1986). Synthesis of research on explicit teaching. *Educational Leadership, 43*(7), 60–69.

FOR FURTHER READING

Rosenshine, B. V. (1986). Synthesis of research on explicit teaching. *Educational Leadership, 43*(7), 60–69.

Chapter Nine

Managing Groupwork

Keep your eyes on your own paper.
Don't talk to the person sitting next to you.
Pay attention to the teacher.
If you need help, raise your hand.
Do your *own* work.

For most of us, these are familiar instructions. We have heard them time and time again, spoken by teachers trying to instill the norms of the traditional classroom. (See Figure 9-1.) Phrases like this are so much a part of the way we view classrooms that four-year-olds who have never even attended kindergarten use them when playing school.

As these instructions suggest, students in most classrooms work either alone or in competition. There are few opportunities for students to interact, to assist one another, or to collaborate on tasks (Gerleman, 1987; Goodlad, 1984; Graybeal and Stodolsky, 1985); in some classrooms, helping may even be construed as cheating. This lack of interaction is unfortunate. Letting students work together in pairs or small groups has many advantages. Donnie alluded to one advantage in Chapter Eight: If students can help one another during classwork, they are less likely to "get stuck," to have to sit and wait for the teacher's assistance, and to become uninvolved and disruptive.

There are other benefits to groupwork. Working with peers on tasks can enhance students' motivation (Good and Brophy, 1994; Sharan, 1990). Groupwork also allows students to take an active role in their own learning—to ask questions, to allocate turns for speaking, to evaluate the work of others, to provide encouragement and support, to debate, and to explain—and some of these behaviors have clear academic payoffs. For example, research has consistently demonstrated that providing explanations to peers is beneficial to achievement (Swing and Peterson, 1982; Webb, 1985); in other words, the more students explain, the more they learn.

Opportunities for interaction also have social payoffs. When students work in heterogeneous groups, they can develop relationships across gender, racial, and ethnic boundaries (Slavin, 1988). Groupwork can also help to integrate individuals

"This class will stimulate your ideas and thoughts. And remember — no talking."

FIGURE 9-1
Students are rarely allowed to work together. (Reprinted with permission.)

with disabilities into the regular, mainstream classroom (Johnson and Johnson, 1980; Madden and Slavin, 1983). As our school-age population becomes increasingly diverse, fostering positive intergroup relationships grows more and more important.

Given all these benefits, why is there so little groupwork in secondary classrooms? The answer has to do with the teacher's responsibility for keeping order and covering curriculum. In the crowded, complex world of the classroom, it's easier to keep order and cover curriculum when teachers do the talking, and students do the listening. Furthermore, like classwork, groupwork has its own set of "built-in hazards" (Carter, 1985) that can make it difficult for teachers to manage.

This chapter examines the special pitfalls associated with groupwork. It then considers ways they can be minimized, drawing on the experiences of our four teachers, as well as the research and scholarly literature on groupwork. In the last part of the chapter, four specific approaches to groupwork are described—STAD, Jigsaw and Jigsaw II, Group Investigation, and the structural approach to cooperative learning.

THE PITFALLS OF GROUPWORK

Let's begin by considering the recent experience of Ralph, a student teacher in social studies. During a recent meeting, Ralph recounted his first attempt to use groupwork with his third-period U.S. History I class:

We were working on sectional differences—the period from 1800 to 1850, when the Northeast, the West, and the South were like three different countries. I wanted my kids to research the views that each section of the country had on three topics—tariffs, slavery, and the role of the federal government. I didn't want to just lecture, or have them read out of the textbook and then discuss the material, and it seemed like this could be a great cooperative learning activity. My kids haven't had much experience working in groups, but my cooperating teacher is really good about letting me try new things, and he said, "Sure, go ahead and see what happens."

I decided to do this over two days. On the first day, I planned to divide the class into the three sections of the country and have each group learning about its section's position on the three topics. I only have 20 kids in this class, so I figured that would be about six or seven kids in each group, which seemed about right. At the end of the first day, they were supposed to pick someone to be their section's spokesman—Daniel Webster from the Northeast, John C. Calhoun from the South, and Henry Clay from the West. The second day, these three spokesmen would debate the issues.

So I come into class all fired up about this great thing we're going to do. It didn't seem important to have the groups be absolutely equal in size, and I figured if the kids could choose their own section they'd be more motivated. So I told them they could decide what section of the country they wanted to study. I told them, "If you want to do the Northeast move to this corner, and if you want to do the South move to that corner, etc. Ready, move." Well, it didn't work out. First of all, most of the kids wanted to be the West or the South—there were like nine people in the West and six people in the South and only four people in the Northeast. Plus—I couldn't believe it—the West was all girls (white and Asian-American), the South was this really juvenile group of white boys (I just knew they would never get anything done), and the Northeast was my three African-American kids and Rick Moore, this white basketball player! And this really quiet, insecure kid just kind of stood there in the middle of the room, not knowing where to go. I had to start asking people to switch and they weren't very happy about that and started making comments about how I didn't know what I was doing and when was Mr. M going to come back and do some "real teaching."

Well, I finally got some of the girls from the West to move into the Northeast group so the sections were about the same size, and I explained what they were going to do. I told them to use their text, and I showed them all the resource materials I had gotten from the library, and told them to use them too. I explained that they were all supposed to help one another research their section's views on tariffs, slavery, and the role of the federal government. Then they were to work together to write a position paper outlining these views and choose someone to be Webster, Calhoun, or Clay for tomorrow's debate. By this time there's only about 25 minutes left, so I tell them to get to work right away. Well, most of them just sat there and stared and kept saying things like, "I don't understand what we're supposed to do." A few kids got up and went back to their desks to get their textbooks and pencils (of course, I had forgotten to tell them to take their books and stuff with them when they moved), and I went around giving out paper, but a lot of the kids just sat there.

I kept going around and trying to get them to work. When I'd come over, they'd begin to jot down notes, but I think they were really just *acting* like they were working, to get me off their back. Finally, some of the kids in the West and the Northeast began looking up stuff in their texts and taking notes, but they weren't helping each other much. I just could not get them to work together! And some of the kids never did anything—they just sat and let the other kids do it. I even heard comments like, "Let Allison be Clay— she's the smartest one in history." Meanwhile, the guys in the South spent most of the time fooling around and laughing. And they kept putting each other down, saying things like, "He's too dumb to be Calhoun. . . . We don't have any smart kids in this group," and yelling, "Hey Mr. G, we need some smart kids in this group." I kept asking them to be quiet and get to work but they just ignored me.

At the end of the period I told them they'd have to finish looking up their section's views for homework. Then I told them to decide on their spokesman, and of course nobody wanted to do it. In the West, they decided that this one kid who's really conscientious should do it. In the South, they fooled around a lot and then finally this real wiseguy says okay, he'll do it. Well, he was absent the next day, so there was no Calhoun, which they seemed to think was really funny.

All in all, these were two of the worst days of my student-teaching experience. After reading all these education theorists who say that cooperative learning is such great stuff, I had been real excited, but now I'm not so sure. Maybe if your class is really motivated to begin with, it would work, but my class is not all that great (the really smart kids are in Honors History), and maybe they just can't work together like this.

Unfortunately, Ralph's story is not unusual. It illustrates all too vividly what can happen when teachers don't understand the problems associated with groupwork and don't work to prevent them from occurring. Let's take a closer look at four of these problems.

First, as Ralph discovered, allowing students to form their own groups often leads to *segregation* among students in terms of gender, race, and ethnicity. Have you ever had lunch in the cafeteria of a desegregated school? One glance is enough to see that members of each ethnic and racial group tend to sit together (Slavin, 1985). It is important to recognize that strong forces operate against the formation of cross-ethnic friendships; left to their own devices, most students will choose to be with those they perceive as similar. An even greater barrier to friendship exists between students with disabilities and their nondisabled peers (Slavin, 1988). Public Law 94-142, passed in 1975, encourages the inclusion of students with disabilities in regular mainstream classrooms, but mere physical presence is not enough to ensure that these individuals will be liked, or even accepted.

A second problem of groupwork is the *unequal participation of group members.* Sometimes, this is due to the "freeloader" phenomenon, where one or two students in the group end up doing all the work, while the others sit back and relax. We saw this happen in Ralph's class, when only a few of the students took the research assignment seriously, and one group decided to let Allison, the "smartest" history student, be her group's spokesperson. Although this might be an efficient approach to the task, it's not exactly a fair distribution of responsibility. And those who were freeloading were unlikely to learn anything about sectional differences.

Unequal participation can occur for other reasons as well. Catherine Mulryan (1992) studied students' involvement in cooperative small groups in mathematics and identified six types of passive students (outlined in Table 9-1). It is worth keep-

TABLE 9-1
SIX CATEGORIES OF PASSIVE STUDENTS (FROM C. MULRYAN, 1992)

Category	Description	Typical Achievement Level
Discouraged student	The student perceives the group task to be too difficult and thinks it better to leave it to others who understand.	Mostly low achievers
Unrecognized student	The student's initial efforts to participate are ignored or unrecognized by others, and he/she feels that it's best to retire.	Mostly low achievers
Despondent student	The student dislikes or feels uncomfortable with one or more students in the group and does not want to work with them.	High or low achievers
Unmotivated student	The student perceives the task as unimportant or "only a game," with no grade being assigned to reward effort expended.	High or low achievers
Bored student	The student thinks the task is uninteresting or boring, often because it is seen as too easy or unchallenging.	Mostly high achievers
Intellectual snob	The student feels that peers are less competent and doesn't want to have to do a lot of explaining. Often ends up working on the task individually.	High achievers

ing these in mind; although a desire to freeload may be at the root of some students' passivity, it is also possible that uninvolved students are feeling discouraged, despondent, unrecognized, bored, or superior.

Just as some individuals may be passive and uninvolved in the group activity, others may take over and dominate the interaction (Cohen, 1986). Frequently, the dominant students are those with high "academic status" in the classroom—those who are recognized by their peers as successful, competent students. At other times the dominant students are those who are popular because they are good athletes or are especially attractive. And sometimes dominance simply reflects the higher status our society accords to those who are white and male. Indeed, research has shown that in heterogeneous groups, males often dominate over females (Webb, 1984), while whites dominate over African-Americans and Hispanics (Cohen, 1972; Rosenholtz and Cohen, 1985).

A third pitfall of groupwork is *lack of accomplishment.* In Ralph's class, a significant amount of instructional time was wasted while students formed groups, and most people didn't get much done even once the groups had formed. A number of students, particularly those in the group doing the South, seemed to view the opportunity to interact as an opportunity to fool around and socialize. (Mulryan, 1992, calls these the "social opportunists.") Their behavior undoubtedly distracted students who were trying to work. Furthermore, the disruption was upsetting to Ralph, who repeatedly asked students to quiet down—without success.

Finally, a fourth problem associated with groupwork is students' *lack of cooperation* with one another. Ralph tells us that the students tended to work alone, and the boys in the "juvenile" group spent a lot of time "putting each other down." Although these kinds of behavior are certainly disappointing, they are not surprising. As we have pointed out, most students have little experience working in cooperative groups, and the norms of the traditional classroom are dramatically different from the norms for successful groupwork (Cohen, 1986):

Ask peers for assistance.
Help one another.
Explain material to other students.
Check that they understand.
Provide support.
Listen to your peers.
Give everyone a chance to talk.

Students who are used to keeping their eyes on their own papers may find it difficult to follow these new norms. Those who are used to asking the teacher for help may be reluctant to turn to their peers, perhaps because they don't want to appear "dumb" (Newman and Schwager, 1993). Some may have difficulty giving clear, thorough explanations to their peers (O'Donnell and O'Kelly, 1994; Webb and Kenderski, 1984). Those who are not "effective speakers" may lack the skills needed to obtain assistance (Wilkinson and Calculator, 1982). Students whose cultural backgrounds have fostered a competitive orientation may have difficulties functioning in cooperative situations (Kagan, Zahn, Widaman, Schwarzwald, and Tyrrell, 1985). And students who are used to being passive may be unwilling to assume a more active role (Lazarowitz, Baird, Hertz-Lazarowitz, and Jenkins, 1985). As Elizabeth Cohen (1986) reminds us, "It is a great mistake to assume that children (or adults) know how to work with each other in a constructive collegial fashion" (p. 34).

The next section of this chapter considers some general strategies for managing groupwork. Remember, *successful groupwork will not just happen.* If you want your students to work together productively, you must plan the groups and the tasks carefully, teach students the new norms, and provide opportunities for them to practice the behaviors that are required. As Sandy comments:

Sometimes, when beginning teachers do groupwork, they think, "I'll divide my students into groups and that's it. That's all I have to do." They don't plan the groups and they don't plan the group *work.* That's where they get into trouble. You not only have to think about how you're going to get your kids *into* groups, but what you're going to do after they're *in* the groups. You have to plan it so carefully, and it's not an easy thing to do.

DESIGNING SUCCESSFUL GROUPWORK

Decide on the Type of Group to Use

Students can work together in a variety of ways. Susan Stodolsky (1984) has identified five different types of groupwork: helping permitted, helping obligatory, peer tutoring, cooperative, and completely cooperative. The first three groups all involve students assisting one another on individual assignments. In a *helping-permitted group,* individuals work on their own tasks, and they are evaluated as individuals; however, they are allowed—but not required—to help one another. *Helping-obligatory* situations differ only in that students are now *expected* to offer mutual assistance. In *peer tutoring,* the relationship between the students is not equal: an "expert" is paired with a student who needs help, so assistance flows in only one direction.

Cooperative groups differ from these helping situations in that youngsters now share a common goal or end, instead of working on completely individual tasks. In a simple *cooperative group,* some division of responsibilities may occur. For example, a group researching the Civil War might decide that one student will learn about the causes of the War, while another learns about famous battles, and a third learns about important leaders. Tasks are carried out independently, but everyone's assignment has to be coordinated at the end in order to produce the final joint product.

More complex is a *completely cooperative group.* Here, students not only share a common goal, there is little or no division of labor. All members of the group work together to create the group product. This was the type of groupwork that Ralph used when he directed his history students to research their section's views on tariffs, slavery, and the role of the federal government and then develop a position paper. (Of course, his students could have decided to divide up the research assignment, and then coordinate their findings, but Ralph did not direct them to do so.)

It is important to keep these distinctions in mind as you plan groupwork. *Different types of groups are suitable for different types of activities, and they require different kinds of skills.* (See Table 9-2.) In helping situations, for example, students are ultimately responsible for completing individual tasks. Although these students need to know how to ask for help, how to explain and demonstrate (rather than simply providing the right answer), and how to provide support and encouragement, they do not need the more complex skills required in truly cooperative situations where they share a common goal.

As an example of a helping situation, let's consider the following activity I observed in Carmen's class:

> Carmen's seventh graders are working on clay sculptures—mythical beasts associated with their study of medieval monsters and gargoyles. Some of the beasts have several heads (emanating from various parts of their bodies); some have dragon tails and dinosaur arms; others have wings and feathers. There is lots of discussion about the sculptures. Much of the talk is commentary on progress, not directed to anyone in particular: "I'm gonna paint the head dark brown and the body light brown." "I want this to be really, really nice so I can put it somewhere." "My tail is coming off." But there are also

TABLE 9-2
DIFFERENT TYPES OF GROUPS

Type of Group	Skills Required	Example of an Activity

Helping permitted
Helping obligatory
	How to ask for help
	How to explain
	How to provide support and
	   encouragement
		Creating clay sculptures: students
		   ask each other for assistance
		   and opinions, but everyone com-
		   pletes an individual sculpture

Peer tutoring	How to ask for help
	How to explain
	How to provide support
	   and encouragement
		Tutor helps tutee to complete a
		   set of chemistry problems

Cooperative group	Divide group task into
	   individual tasks
	Coordinate individual
	   efforts to produce
	   final group product
		Survey on what students do after
		   school: each group member
		   interviews students at one grade
		   level; then pool figures to make
		   a group graph

Complete cooperative	Take turns
	Listen to one another
	Coordinate efforts
	Share materials
	Collaborate on a single
	   task
	Solve conflicts
	Achieve consensus
		Determining political party
		   affiliation: as a group, decide if
		   hypothetical person is Democrat
		   or Republican

requests for assistance and opinions: "Do you think I should make the wings bigger?" "Do you think that head looks straight? I can't make it straight. Could you hold it on for a minute?" "How did you attach your arms? Would you help me attach my arms?"

In contrast to helping situations, cooperative groups require skills beyond requesting and giving appropriate assistance. Students must be able to develop a plan of action; they must be able to coordinate efforts toward a common goal; they must be able to evaluate the contributions of their peers and give feedback in a constructive way; they must monitor individuals' progress toward the group goal; they must be able to summarize and synthesize individual efforts. Consider the following example, provided by Donnie:

> In my basic skills class, I work on collecting, analyzing, and depicting data. I have the students work in groups of four. Each group has to create a survey designed to learn what high school kids do after school—for example, how much they watch TV, just hang around, play basketball, have an after-school job, do homework. Then, each group has to interview 80 students in the high school, and each person in the group is responsible for interviewing 20 students at one grade level (in other words, one person interviews all freshmen, one interviews all sophomores, and so on). Each person has to collect his or her own information, but then they have to come together to make a group graph showing how people at all four grade levels manage their time. Kids know that they can't complete the project unless everybody does their part, so they really get on each other's case if somebody isn't working.

Completely cooperative groups with no division of labor present even greater challenges. Not only must students be able to take turns, listen to one another carefully, and coordinate efforts, but they must also be able to collaborate on a single task, reconcile differences, compromise, and reach a consensus. During one visit to Fred's class, I observed a good example of a completely cooperative group activity. The class was divided into groups of four or five to consider profiles of eight hypothetical Americans (e.g., "A union member working in an automobile plant in one of the large factories located in the Industrial Belt that includes Buffalo, Cleveland, Toledo, Detroit, Chicago, and Milwaukee. He is a college graduate"; "A bank executive in a small county seat in Colorado. She is concerned about her career, is unmarried, and is about to buy her own home"). For each profile, students had to determine the probable party affiliation (or lack of one), the kinds of issues that would be important to the individual in a campaign, and whether the individual was likely to be a voter or a nonvoter. Although students were required to carry out individual tasks, they had to coordinate their individual efforts if the groups were to be successful:

> Fred hands out the worksheet describing the eight hypothetical American voters (or nonvoters). He explains that students will first do the task individually, taking notes for each profile. When everyone is finished, he divides the class into groups of four or five. Fred explains that students are to share their opinions, being sure to provide their reasoning. He encourages the groups to work toward consensus on each hypothetical voter and suggests that a different person serve as recorder for each voter. Each group will be expected to report on its results to the rest of the class.

> Students begin to go through the eight profiles, sharing their responses. Fred circulates, asking students to explain their reasoning ("Why do you think he's a Democrat?"), commenting on their responses ("I can't believe how confident you people are!"), and checking on group process ("What number are you on? Has everyone had a chance to be a recorder for at least one profile?").

> When the groups have finished, Fred announces that Group B will be the first group to report out. The four members of Group B stand in the front of the room. Sandra reports on the group's opinions about the first two profiles: "We think he's a Democrat. He definitely votes. We think he cares about auto safety. . . ." The reports continue, with Fred interjecting questions and comments.

Although this activity first required students to think through their responses as individuals, they then had to work together to construct a group report. They had to decide who would be the recorder and reporter for each profile, take turns explaining the reasons for their ideas, listen respectfully to one another, reject ideas without being destructive, and reach consensus on what to report. These are not easy skills to learn—even for adults.

As these three examples illustrate, the more interdependent students are, the more skills they need to cooperate successfully. It's a good idea to use simpler types of groups when you are just starting out. In Ralph's case, we can see that he began with the most complex kind of groupwork. He set up a situation in which students who were not even used to helping one another were expected to cooperate completely.

Decide on the Size of the Group

To some extent, the size of the group you use depends on the task you assign. Pairs are appropriate when foreign language students are drilling one another on vocabulary words, or when home economics students are reviewing weights and measures in preparation for a test. Groups of two maximize students' opportunity to participate (Webb, 1989). They are also easier for beginning teachers to manage (Johnson, Johnson, Holubec, and Roy, 1984), and teachers of younger or less mature students often prefer pairs over larger groups that require more elaborate social skills (Edwards and Stout, 1989-1990). Even with senior high school students, Sandy makes sure to provide students with experiences in pairs before using cooperative groups.

In the following vignette, we see Donnie use pairs of students in a helping situation:

> Donnie is reviewing problems that involve different kinds of angles (supplementary, complementary, and vertical). After going through a number of problems on the board, Donnie announces that students will be doing the next set by themselves. She explains: "Please listen to what you're going to do next. On this assignment, you may confer with one other person. You're going to count off: one, two, three. [The students do so.] If you are a number one, you will start with problem number 19, and then go up by 3's (22, 25, 28, 31, 34, and 37). If you are a number two, your problems will start with 20, and go up by 3's. If you are a number three, your problems will start with 21, and go up by 3's. Pair yourself up with someone who has the same number you have. Your job is to help one another understand the problems. You have 20 minutes to do these. Please have them ready to be passed in at the end of the period."

In situations where the task is an ambitious one that requires a division of labor (e.g., the survey on what high school students do after school), it makes sense to form groups larger than two. Groups of three are still relatively easy to manage, but you need to make sure that two students don't form a coalition, leaving the third isolated and excluded (Cohen, 1986).

In general, educators recommend cooperative groups of four or five (Cohen, 1986), and six is usually the upper limit (Johnson, Johnson, Holubec, and Roy, 1984). Keep in mind that as group size increases, the "resource pool" also increases; in other words, there are more heads to think about the task and more hands to share the work. It is also true, however, that the larger the group, the more difficult it is to develop a plan of action, allocate turns for speaking, share materials, and reach consensus.

Assign Students to Groups

In addition to deciding on the type and size of your groups, you must think carefully about group composition. As I mentioned earlier in this chapter, groupwork allows students to develop relationships with those who differ in terms of gender and ethnicity. Groupwork also helps to integrate students with disabilities into the mainstream classroom. For these reasons, groups should be heterogeneous with respect to gender and ethnicity, and disabled students should be included in groups with their nondisabled peers.

You also need to consider whether groups will be homogeneous or heterogeneous with respect to ability level. At times, homogeneous groups can be useful, for example, you may want to form a helping group of several students who are all working on a particular mathematics skill. In general, however, educators recommend the use of heterogeneous groups (Cohen, 1986; Johnson, Johnson, Holubec, and Roy, 1984; Slavin, 1988). One reason is that they provide more opportunities for asking questions and receiving explanations (Johnson, Johnson, Holubec, and Roy, 1984; Webb, 1985).

Just how heterogeneous your groups should be is still not clear. Research by Noreen Webb and her colleagues (1985) has shown that in junior-high math groups composed of high-, medium-, and low-achieving students, those of medium-ability tend to get left out of the interaction. In fact, Webb (1985) argues that two-level groups (high-medium or medium-low) are most beneficial for all students. In contrast, other proponents of cooperative learning (e.g., Slavin, 1988) recommend that four-person teams consist of a high-achiever, a low-achiever, and two average-achievers.

Another variable you need to consider when deciding on group composition is social skill. After observing a completely cooperative learning activity in Sandy's class, she and I talked about how she had decided on the groups. Her comments emphasized the importance of considering more than ability:

> When I form groups, I consider kids' personalities more than their ability, although I do try not to put just one bright kid in a group. (If I do, the others expect that person to tell them what to do.) I think about how they interact with other people and try to think about where they'll feel comfortable and where they'll work best. For example, I would never pair Kahlil and Michael. Michael is impulsive—he blurts out the first thing that comes into his mind—while Kahlil is very deliberate and careful. He would retreat into himself and not say a word if I put him in a group with Michael. So I put Kahlil with Laura. Laura is kind of insecure and quiet. But Kahlil draws her out. During today's lesson, he said to her, "What's the matter? Why are you so quiet?" She said, "I'm thinking," and he said, "Well say something, we need to work together." He was really showing good leadership, but he would never have done that with Michael. On the other hand, I was able to put Michael with Nathan. When Michael blurts out, Nathan says, "Wait a minute. Slow down."

As Sandy's comments indicate, groups work better when students' personalities and social skills are taken into consideration. Some students have difficulty working with others—they may be unusually volatile, or angry, or bossy—and it makes sense to distribute them across the groups. On the other hand, some students have unusual leadership abilities; others are particularly adept at resolving conflicts; still others are especially alert to injustice and can help to ensure that everyone in the group has a chance to participate. When forming groups, it generally makes sense to disperse students like these too, so that each group has the benefit of their talents. All four teachers follow this practice; however, Sandy and Donnie occasionally find it useful to put all of the leaders in one group. Donnie explains:

At first, the kids in the other groups say, "Oh, we don't have anybody good in our group. This isn't fair." They sort of sit there aimlessly, wondering what to do. But with encouragement, they begin to get their act together. It doesn't always work, of course, but sometimes this creates a chance for new leaders to emerge.

Teachers develop different systems for assigning students to groups. Some teachers of academic subjects write each student's name on a note card, along with information about achievement and interpersonal relationships (e.g., with whom the student doesn't get along). Then they rank students in terms of achievement level and assign a top-ranked student and a bottom-ranked student to each of the groups. Next, the average students are distributed, keeping in mind the need to balance the groups in terms of gender, ethnicity, and social skill. Having each student's name on a note card allows you to shuffle students around as you try to form equivalent groups that will work well together.

Fred has developed a different system. Like Sandy, he focuses more on social skills and personalities than on academic ability:

First I think about who *can't* be in the same group, and I say, "Okay, he goes in Group 1, and she goes in Group 2, etc." Then I think about who the *nicest* people in the class are—the people who can get along with everybody, and I spread them out too. Then I separate the *loudmouths*—the kids who are not good listeners and who tend to talk a lot. Finally, I think about the kids who need "*special handling.*" Maybe somebody who doesn't speak English, or maybe someone who's very sensitive or shy. I think, "Which group will not destroy this person?" and I try to put that kid in a group that will be most supportive.

When Carmen determines group assignment, she considers not only personality and social skills but also artistic ability. If an activity involves drawing, painting, and cutting, for example, she may try to ensure that each group has a student who is skillful in each of these areas. According to Carmen, working in groups like this can actually be a relief to some students who are not especially talented:

Art class can be hard for students if they always have to work individually. Kids who are just not that talented are under a lot of pressure. When they work in groups, they don't have to do everything themselves. They can pool their individual strengths.

Since group composition is so important, it is risky to allow students to select their own groups. On the other hand, a brief group activity might not warrant lengthy reflection on group composition. One approach is to use a random assignment strategy, like having students count off by four's (although Fred is reluctant to use a random assignment strategy early in the year, when he doesn't know his students well). As I mentioned in Chapter Five, I once observed Donnie take a deck of playing cards from her desk, walk toward a student, and ask him to help her shuffle:

"I've never been very good at this. I never learned how." [A few students tease her about her inability to shuffle.] After the cards are shuffled, Donnie moves from student to student, directing each one to "pick a card." As she makes her way around the room, the students and I wonder what she is up to. When everyone has a card, Donnie tells the students to pay close attention. "Now, I need you to find the people with the same number or face card that you have. When you find your partners, chose a table and sit down in a group. Then I'll tell you what you're going to do and pass out the materials." The students get up and walk around the room to find their partners. Once the groups have all formed, Donnie proceeds to give directions for the problem-solving activity they are to do as a group.

After class, Donnie and I talked about this strategy for forming groups:

> This was the first time I ever tried this. My main reason was to get them talking and working with people other than their normal neighbors. They're in seats they chose on the first day, and some of them are very quiet and shy. They don't like to move around or interact with new people. This made them get up and form some new groups.

Finally, there are times when Donnie, Fred, Sandy, and Carmen allow their students to form their own groups, but only for certain kinds of tasks, and not until the students have had substantial experience working in various kinds of groups with almost everyone in the class. As Fred observes:

> It really depends on the task. If we're doing something new and I have very specific goals for the activity, then I make sure that I put the kids together. This way I can put a kid in a particular group that I know will be a good place for him.

Structure the Task for Interdependence

If you want to ensure that students cooperate on a task, you have to create a situation in which they need one another in order to succeed. In other words, you need to structure the task so that students are *interdependent*. A simple way to do this is to require group members to *share materials* (Johnson, Johnson, Holubec, and Roy, 1984). If one member of a pair has a page of math problems, for example, and the other member has the answer sheet, they need to coordinate if they are both to complete the problems and check their answers.

Another way to create interdependence is to create a *group goal*. For example, you might have each group produce a single product, such as a report, a science demonstration, a poem, or a skit. When Carmen's students studied the middle ages, for example, she had students work in groups to construct medieval castles, complete with people wearing the dress of the period. Similarly, Donnie sometimes has groups turn in just one solution to a challenging problem, with the names of all group members on the page. A *group grade or group reward* is another way to stress the importance of collaborating. For example, suppose you want to encourage students to help one another with the symbols for chemical ions. You can do this by rewarding groups on the basis of the total number of ions correctly supplied by all members of the group. You can also give bonus points to every group in which all students reach a predetermined level of accomplishment.

Another way of promoting collaboration is to structure the task so that students are dependent on one another for *information* (Johnson, Johnson, Holubec, and Roy, 1984). In Donnie's lesson on collecting and displaying information, for example, group members had to pool their individual data on adolescents' after-school activities. Since each student was responsible for collecting data on one grade level, they needed each other in order to construct a graph depicting the activities of freshmen, sophomores, juniors, and seniors.

Finally, you can assign *different roles* to group members, requiring each role to be fulfilled if the group is to complete the task. For example, Fred sometimes designates a recorder, a timekeeper, an encourager (to facilitate participation), a taskmaster (to keep people on track), a summarizer (to report at the end of the group session), and an observer (to monitor group process). At times, the roles Fred assigns are integral to the activity itself. In a social studies simulation on reconstruction, students form "Presidential Advisory Committees" to advise President Andrew Johnson on a program for the South after the Civil War. Groups have to provide guidance on weighty issues:

Are the southerners who lately rebelled against us still citizens? Shall they have the same rights and privileges as other loyal Americans?

What shall we do with the leaders of the rebellion, especially General Lee and President Davis?

How can I make sure the South is governed by leaders loyal to the United States?

Are the soldiers who fought against us traitors?

What shall we do about the former slaves? Should they be given citizenship? Should they be allowed to vote? Should we pay former slave owners for the loss of their slave "property"?

Each Presidential Advisory Committee is composed of characters with very different backgrounds and points of view. Here are a few examples:

The Reverend Harry (Harriet) Stone, 43 years old, deeply religious, attended college in Virginia, not very active in the Abolition Movement. Believed slavery is immoral but felt John Brown took things "too far."

William (Mary) Hardwick, 52, a rich mill owner from Delaware, two sons fought in the war, the youngest was killed in the Wilderness while serving under Grant. Manufactures shirts and has profited from government war contracts, which have been cancelled since Lee's surrender at Appomattox. Southern distributors still owe you $40,000 for purchases made before the war began.

Having a variety of roles ensures that everyone has a role to play and that all students have to participate if the group is to succeed.

Ensure Individual Accountability

As discussed earlier in the chapter, one of the major problems associated with groupwork is unequal participation. Sometimes individuals refuse to contribute to the group effort, preferring to "freeload." Sometimes more assertive students dominate, making it difficult for others to participate. In either case, lack of participation is a genuine problem. Those who do not actively participate will not learn anything about the academic task; furthermore, the group is not learning the skills of collaboration.

One way to encourage the participation of all group members is to hold everyone responsible for a task or a level of performance. You can do this by giving individual quizzes, by grading each individual's part of the total group project, or by having each student complete an individual worksheet or project. One morning in May, I watched Sandy explain that students were gong to be working on understanding the idea of equilibrium. She divided the class into groups of three, explained the task, and reminded students that they needed to work together to discover the operative principle. Before she allowed them to begin work, however, she stressed that a group should not consider itself through until all group members understood. In other words, Sandy made it very clear that every student would be accountable for explaining the process of equilibrium.

In addition to planning tasks so that individuals are held accountable, you need to monitor students' effort and progress during groupwork time. Carmen, Donnie, Fred, and Sandy continually circulate throughout the room, observing each group's activity. In this way they can note problems, provide assistance, and keep students on task. During the cooperative learning activity on equilibrium, Sandy was especially vigilant because she knew that the task was difficult and that students might become frustrated:

> Students are working in groups of three, trying to predict the molecular behavior of three chemical systems. Sandy notices that one group is particularly quiet. She moves over and places her hand on one boy's shoulder. He looks up and tells her: "I don't know what I'm doing." Sandy responds: "Why don't you talk to your group members?" He moves closer to the other individuals. As Sandy approaches another group, a girl indicates that she's "got it." Excitedly, she tries to explain the process to her group and to Sandy, but then collapses in confusion. "I'm just babbling," she says. Sandy decides it's time to intervene: "Okay, let's go back to the question. You have to understand what the question is asking first. What's the question?" In another group, a boy doesn't like the idea offered by a teammate: "I don't want to argue; but I don't think that's right." Sandy reaffirms his behavior: "That's okay. You're *supposed* to question one another." At one point, Sandy divides one group and sends its members to temporarily join two adjacent groups. "Mrs. K. says I should ask you my question," one boy says to his new group. While Sandy is working with a group on one side of the room, two groups on the other side begin to fool around. One boy has a bottle of correction fluid that he is tossing into the air with one hand and trying to catch with the other (which is behind his back). Sandy notices the disruption: "Excuse me, I don't think you're done, are you?" One group finally discovers the principle that is involved and erupts in a cheer. A girl in another group expresses frustration: "We're clueless over here and they're cheering over there." A few minutes later, Sandy joins this group to provide some assistance.

After class, during her free period, Sandy reflected on the importance of monitoring cooperative learning activities:

> Since this was a difficult activity, I expected that there would be some frustration, so it was really important to keep close tabs on what the groups were doing. You can tell a lot just by watching students' physical positions. If kids' heads are down, or if they're facing away, those are good signs they're not participating or interacting with other group members. Today, I could tell that Richard was going to try the problem as an individual; he was off by himself—until he got frustrated and joined the other students.

But that group never really worked well. I thought that Sylvia would help the group along, but she never got completely involved.

I also try to listen closely to what they're saying to one another in terms of group process. Like Mark—he wasn't sure it was okay to disagree. I was glad I heard that so I could reassure him that he's supposed to do that. What's neat is to see how some kids begin to function as really good group leaders. For example, Sivan is really quiet, but she really listens, and she was able to bring in the other two boys she was working with.

You also have to monitor students' progress in solving the problem and try to prevent them from getting completely off track. Today I could see that one group got stuck; the kids were really in a rut, saying the same words over and over. So I split the group up and sent the kids to explain what they were thinking or to ask their questions to two

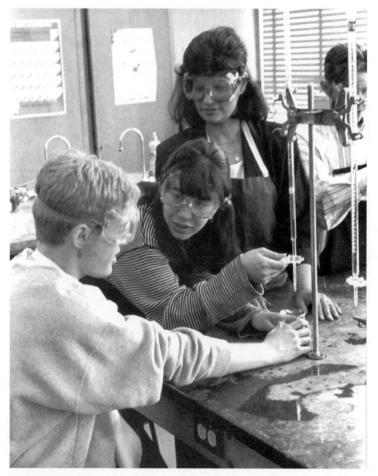

Sandy works with a small group.

other groups. Sometimes having them talk to other kids can help to move them forward. In this case, it seemed to work. By interacting with a different group, Roy got out of the rut and then he was able to go back and help the kids in his own group.

Occasionally, the four teachers also build in "progress checkpoints." For example, after two days of having his students try to rewrite South Brunswick's Human Dignity and Affirmative Action policies, Fred stopped the groups' activity and asked students to report on what they had accomplished and what problems they were having. Similarly, you can divide large assignments into components that are due every few days (see the section on "monitoring student progress" in Chapter Seven). This allows you to keep track of how well groups are functioning.

Teach Students to Cooperate

Recently, I read the following entry in a reflective paper written by a student teacher in English:

> I have tried to use cooperative learning activities as much as possible but I'm not at all sure it's been beneficial. It seems to me that instead of facilitating students' learning—as my education professors claim—these group activities have generally been a waste of time. Students spend more time socializing, goofing off, arguing, and procrastinating than getting anything done. I guess I'm not convinced that cooperative learning can work unless (1) students are mature enough to work without a teacher breathing down their necks and (2) they have the social skills to interact with peers. Given these criteria, I am skeptical about using cooperative learning with freshmen. . . .

This student teacher has come to understand the fact that students' social skills can make or break a groupwork activity. What he fails to understand, however, is the role of the teacher in teaching these skills. David and Roger Johnson (1989-1990), two experts on cooperative learning, warn teachers not to assume that students know how to work together. They write:

> People do not know instinctively how to interact effectively with others. Nor do interpersonal and group skills magically appear when they are needed. Students must be taught these skills and must be motivated to use them. If group members lack the interpersonal and small-group skills to cooperate effectively, cooperative groups will not be productive. (p. 30)

As the classroom teacher, *it is your responsibility to teach students to work together.* This is not a simple process; students do not learn to cooperate in one 45-minute lesson. Indeed, we can think about the process in terms of three stages: learning to value cooperation, developing group skills, and evaluation. Let's consider each of these briefly.

Valuing cooperation

Before students can work together productively, they must understand the value of cooperation. Sandy introduces cooperative groupwork early in the year by setting up a task that students are unable to do alone:

I tell the kids that they are to solve a particular chemical problem (it's different every year), and that they should go to the lab tables and get started. They look at me as if I'm crazy. They say, "But Ms. Krupinsky, you didn't tell us what procedure to use." I tell them I forgot to write out the procedure for them. I say, "Let's see if you can come up with the procedure. You'll get five extra points if you can figure out a procedure by yourself. If you do it in pairs, you'll split the five points, etc." They all start out working alone—they want that five points for themselves. But as the period goes on, they begin to work in groups. They realize they need each other, that they can really help one another and they don't care about the points.

At the end of the period, I say, "Let's talk about what happened here. Why did you start out by yourself?" They tell me, "I wanted the five points, but I had to ask for help because I didn't know enough." We talk about how helpful it is to work together when you're learning something new, and how the points don't matter.

When students are going to work in the same groups over a period of time, it's often helpful to have them engage in a nonacademic activity designed to build a team identity and to foster a sense of group cohesion. One idea is to have each team create a banner or poster displaying a group name and logo. In order to ensure that everyone participates in creating the banner, each group member can be given a marker of a different color; individuals can only use the marker they have been given, but the banner must contain all the colors.

Group skills training

Teaching a group skill is much like teaching students how to balance equations or use a pipette. It requires systematic explanation, modeling, practice, and feedback. *It's simply not enough to state the rules and expect students to understand and remember.* And don't take anything for granted: even basic guidelines like "don't distract others" and "speak quietly" may need to be taught.

It's helpful to begin by analyzing the groupwork task you have selected in order to determine the specific skills students need to know (Cohen, 1986). Will students have to explain material? Will they have to listen carefully to one another? Will they have to reach a consensus? Once you have analyzed the task, select one or two key behaviors to teach your students. Resist the temptation to introduce all the required group skills at once; going too far too fast is sure to lead to frustration.

Next, explain to your students that they will be learning a skill necessary for working in groups. Be sure to *define terms, discuss rationales,* and *provide examples.* Johnson and Johnson (1989-1990) suggest that you construct a "T-chart" on which you list the skill and then—with the class—record ideas about what the skill would look like and what it would sound like. Table 9-3 shows a T-chart for "encouraging participation."

Finally, you need to provide opportunities for students to practice the skill and to receive feedback. You might have students role play; you might pair the skill with a familiar academic task so that students can focus their attention on using the social skill (Carson and Hoyle, 1989-1990); or you might have students engage in exercises designed to teach particular skills. (Elizabeth Cohen's book, *Designing*

TABLE 9-3
A T-CHART FOR SHARING

Sharing	
Looks Like	Sounds Like
Leave the markers in the middle of the table where all can reach.	Anybody need the markers?
	Here's the marker.
Hand the markers to somebody else.	Thanks for handing me the marker.
Take turns with the markers.	I'm done with this marker; does anyone want it?
Return markers to middle of the table	

Groupwork, 1986, contains cooperative exercises, such as "Master Designer" and "Guess My Rule," which focus on helping and explaining, and Epstein's "Four-Stage Rocket," designed to improve group-discussion skills.)

Donnie sometimes teaches group skills in a more "devious" way. She secretly assigns individuals to act out different roles: the dictator, the nonparticipant, the person who tears down everybody else, and the facilitator who encourages participation and listens well. Students engage in some sort of nonacademic activity—perhaps the task of building a tower with pins and straws—and then debrief, sharing their reactions about the group process. An activity like this serves to heighten students' awareness of group skills—and they have fun at the same time.

Regardless of the type of practice you provide, you need to give students feedback about their performance. Fred has found that it's helpful to designate a "process person" or "observer" for each group. This individual is responsible for keeping track of how well the group is functioning; for example, he or she may monitor how many times each person speaks. At the end of the groupwork session, the process person is able to share specific data that the group can use to evaluate its ability to work together.

Evaluation

In order to learn from their experiences, students need the chance to discuss what happened and to evaluate how successful they were in working together. One approach is to ask students to name three things their group did well and one thing the group could do better next time (Johnson and Johnson, 1989-1990). You can also have students consider more specific questions, such as

Did everyone carry out his or her job?
Did everyone get a chance to talk?
Did you listen to one another?
What did you do if you didn't agree?

A simple checklist, like the ones in Figure 9-2, can be helpful.

After individual groups have talked about their experiences, it is often helpful to

Group-rating for younger or less mature students:
1. Did we get to work promptly?
2. Did we stick to the point?
3. Did we work quietly?
4. Did we all contribute?
5. Did we ask for help as soon as we needed it?
What did we accomplish?

Self-rating for younger or less mature students:
1. Was I prepared?
2. Did I follow directions?
3. Did I make good use of my time?
4. Did I work without disturbing other groups?
5. Did I listen to the other people in my group?
6. Did I contribute to my group's task?
My chief contribution to my group was:

Self-rating for older or more mature students:
1. Did I assume the responsibility the group wished?
2. Did I listen alertly?
3. Did I willingly express my own point of view?
4. Did I try to understand the viewpoint of others?
5. Did I attempt to assess the strengths and weaknesses of all opinions expressed?
6. Did I encourage those who seemed reluctant to speak?
7. Did I help maintain a friendly, businesslike atmosphere?
8. Did I keep the discussion moving purposefully?
My greatest contribution to the group was:

Adapted from Stover, L. T., Neubert, G. A., and Lawlor, J. C. (1993). *Creating interactive environments in the secondary school.* New York: National Education Association.
FIGURE 9-2
Checklists for Evaluating Group Skills

have groups report to the whole class (Lemlech, 1988). You can encourage groups to share and compare their experiences by asking, "Did your group have a similar problem?" "How many groups agree with the way they solved their problem?" "What do you recommend?"

Let's see what a groupwork evaluation session might look like in practice. During a visit to Fred's classroom early in the school year, I observed a lesson on U.S. policy toward Haiti. Students were working in groups of four or five, trying to reach consensus on a number of politically sensitive questions: Should the United States support the Dole Amendment (requiring the President to get permission from Congress before sending troops to Haiti)? Should the United States continue the oil and arms embargo of Haiti even if the people of Haiti suffer as a result? Should the President send in United States troops to protect President Aristide on his return to Port-Au-Prince? Before students began to work, Fred explained that students were to discuss each question and prepare a report for a special envoy advising the President on Haitian policy. The chairperson of each group was responsible for compiling the report and seeing that all members had an opportunity to participate. Fred made it clear that groups would not be evaluated solely on their reports, but also on how well they worked together—specifically, how quickly they got to work; how involved and engaged they looked; how well group members listened to each other; if members conducted themselves with maturity and decorum; and if all group members had a chance to express their views. During the activity, Fred roamed the room, watching and listening; in addition, the school's media specialist videotaped the entire class.

The following day, Fred spent about half the period evaluating the group activity his students had done. First, Fred talked about how difficult it is to work in groups and told a few "horror" stories about groups in which he had worked. Then he asked each student to complete a self-evaluation of his or her group's interaction. (See Figure 9-3 for one student's evaluation.) Finally, he played the videotape, commenting on the things he had noticed:

> [The tape shows students getting into groups, getting organized, and getting to work.] The first thing I did was watch you getting started. I actually timed you, from the moment you entered class to the time the last group was seated and working. It was less than three minutes. I think that was pretty good. [The camera zooms in on each group.] I also looked at how people were seated. [The tape shows a group where four people are clustered and one person is sitting away.] Your physical placement in the group is very important; if you have someone sitting outside the group, it's a good bet that person's not participating. I also tried to watch the way you took turns participating. Look at this. [William's group is shown on the tape.] William was a very organized chairperson. He went around to each person, asking "What do you think? What do you think?" It was very orderly, and everyone got a chance to speak. But what's a drawback? A drawback is you might be disengaged when you're not talking. [Camera shows Frank's group.] Now Frank here ran a more free-wheeling group. There was more arguing back and forth. What's a drawback here? [Student responds.] Yeah, someone can easily get left out. Now take a look at Jan's group. Jan really made an effort to draw people in. . . . I also tried to look at whether any people were dominating the discussion. It really ticks people off if you dominate the group. I'll say that again. *It ticks people off.* Now what did you people think about the composition of the groups? [Students comment.] I tried to put one person in each chair's group who I thought the chair could relate to. Instead of separating all the friends, I thought it might make it easier to chair. Did it? What do you think about having friends in the group? . . .

FOUR SPECIFIC APPROACHES TO GROUPWORK

Several structured approaches to cooperative learning have been developed to avoid the problems characteristic of groupwork and to encourage norms of effort

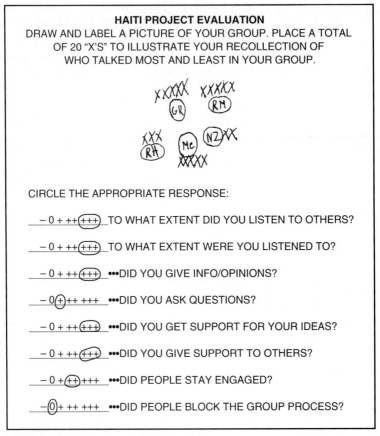

FIGURE 9-3
One student's evaluation of the groupwork activity

and mutual support. Designed for use at any grade level and in most school subjects, all of these cooperative learning strategies are characterized by heterogeneous groups working together to achieve a common goal (Slavin, 1985). This section of the chapter briefly examines four of these strategies: STAD, Jigsaw and Jigsaw II, Group Investigation, and the structural approach to cooperative learning. You can learn more about these by referring to the references listed in "For Further Reading."

STAD

Student Teams-Achievement Divisions (STAD) is a cooperative learning method developed and studied at Johns Hopkins University by Robert Slavin and his colleagues (Slavin, 1988). STAD is particularly appropriate for content areas where there are "right answers," such as mathematics, spelling, and grammar.

In STAD, the teacher presents a lesson, and students then work within their teams on an academic task. In other words, students help one another with the assignment instead of doing it individually. Suppose the task is to complete a set of math problems. Students may do the problems individually and then compare answers, or work together on each problem. Their objective is to ensure that all team members master the material. Team members are told they are not finished studying until everyone on the team feels confident about knowing the material.

Following team practice, students take individual quizzes on which they receive individual scores. In addition, a *team score* is calculated, based on team members' *individual improvement over their own past performance.* This is an extremely important feature: using improvement scores prevents low-achieving students from being rejected because they cannot contribute to the team. In STAD, the student whose quiz scores go from 57 to 67 contributes as much as the student whose scores go from 85 to 95.

Finally, teams that earn a designated number of points receive certificates recognizing their performance as either a "Superteam," a "Greatteam," or a "Goodteam."

Jigsaw and Jigsaw II

In Jigsaw, one of the earliest cooperative learning methods (Aronson, Blaney, Stephan, Sikes, and Snapp, 1978), heterogeneous teams work on academic material that has been divided into sections. Jigsaw is particularly appropriate for narrative material, such as a social studies chapter, a biography, or a short story. Each team member reads only one section of the material. The teams then disband, and students reassemble in "expert groups" with other people who have been assigned the same section. Working together, they learn the material in these expert groups and then return to their home teams to teach it to their teammates. Since everyone is responsible for learning all the material, successful task completion requires students to listen carefully to their peers. Jigsaw also includes team-building activities and training to improve communication and tutoring skills.

Jigsaw II (Slavin, 1985) is a modification developed by the researchers at Johns Hopkins. It differs from the original Jigsaw in that all students of a team read the entire assignment. Then they are assigned a particular topic on which to become an expert. Like STAD, Jigsaw II uses individual quizzes and team scores based on individual improvement.

Group Investigation

Group Investigation, developed by Shlomo Sharan and his colleagues at the University of Tel Aviv (Sharan and Sharan, 1976, 1989-1990) places students in small groups to investigate topics from a unit being studied by the entire class. Each group further divides their topic into individual subtopics and then carries out the research. Students work together to find resource materials, to collect and analyze information, and to plan and present a report, demonstration, play, learning center, or exhibition for the class. Evaluation focuses on both learning and affective experiences; assessment procedures may include comments from peers, students' self-evaluations, and questions submitted by groups for a common test, as well as evaluation by the teacher.

The Structural Approach to Cooperative Learning

The structural approach was developed by Spencer Kagan, a psychology professor at the University of California—Riverside and director of Resources for Teachers. According to Kagan (1989-1990), "structures" are content-free ways of organizing social interaction among students. Structures usually involve a series of steps, with prescribed behavior at each step. A traditional classroom structure, for example, is the "whole-class question-answer" situation. In this structure, the teacher asks a question, students raise their hands to respond, and the teacher calls on one person. If that person answers the question incorrectly, the other students get a chance to respond and to win the teacher's praise. Thus, students are often happy if a classmate makes a mistake, and they may even root for one another's failure.

Kagan has developed a number of simple cooperative structures that can be used at a variety of grade levels and in many content areas. He emphasizes the need for teachers to select the structures that are most appropriate for their specific objectives. Some structures are useful for team building or for developing communication skills, while others are most suitable for increasing mastery of factual material or for concept development.

"Numbered Heads Together" is a good example of a structure that is appropriate for checking on students' understanding of content. (It also provides a cooperative alternative to "whole-class question-answer.") In Numbered Heads, students "number off" within teams (e.g., one through four). When the teacher asks a question, team members "put their heads together" to make sure that everyone on the team knows the answer. The teacher then calls a number, and students with that number may raise their hands to answer. This structure promotes interdependence among team members: if one student knows the answer, everyone's chance of answering correctly increases. At the same time, the structure encourages individual accountability: once the teacher calls a number, students are on their own.

Some of Kagan's other structures are listed in Table 9-4.

CONCLUDING COMMENTS

Although this chapter is entitled "Managing Groupwork," we have seen that there are actually a number of different groupwork situations, each with its own set of uses, procedures, requirements, and pitfalls. As you plan and implement groupwork in your classroom, it's important to remember these distinctions. Too many teachers think that cooperative learning is putting students into groups and telling them to work together. They select tasks that are inappropriate for the size of the group; they use heterogeneous groups when homogeneous groups would be more suitable (or vice versa); they fail to build in positive interdependence and individual accountability; they fail to appreciate the differences between helping groups and co-

TABLE 9-4
SOME OF SPENCER KAGAN'S COOPERATIVE STRUCTURES

Name	Purpose	Description	Functions
Roundrobin	Teambuilding	Each student in turn shares something with teammates.	Expressing ideas and opinions. Getting acquainted.
Match Mine	Communication	Students try to match the arrangement of objects on a grid of another student using oral communication only.	Vocabulary building. Communication skills. Role-taking ability.
Three-Step Interview	Concept Development	Students interview each other in pairs, first one way, then the other. Students then share information they learned with the group.	Sharing personal information such as hypotheses, reactions to a poem, conclusions from a unit. Equal participation. Listening.
Inside-Outside Circle	Multifunctional	Students stand in pairs in two concentric circles. The inside circle faces out; the outside circle faces in. Students use flash cards or respond to teacher questions as they rotate to each new partner.	Checking for understanding. Review. Tutoring. Sharing. Meeting classmates.

Adapted from Kagan, S. (1989-1990). The structural approach to cooperative learning. *Educational Leadership, 47*(4), p. 14.

operative learning. The following example, taken from O'Donnell and O'Kelly (1994), would be funny—if it weren't true:

> One of our colleagues recently described an example of "cooperative learning" in his son's school. The classroom teacher informed the students that [they] would be using cooperative learning. His son was paired with another student. The two students were required to complete two separate parts of a project but were expected to complete the work outside of class. A grade was assigned to each part of the project and a group grade was given. In this instance, one child received an "F" as he failed to complete the required part of the project. The other child received an "A." The group grade was a "C," thus rewarding the student who had failed to complete the work, and punishing the child who had completed his work. In this use of "cooperative learning," there was no opportunity for the students to interact, and the attempt to use a group reward (the group grade) backfired. Although this scenario is not recognizable as cooperative learning to most proponents of cooperation, the classroom teacher described it as such to the students' parents. (p. 322)

This example illustrates the need for thorough training in cooperative learning. No three-hour class, no one-shot inservice workshop, and no chapter can adequately meet this need. Nonetheless, I hope this chapter has sensitized you to some of the problems that can arise with groupwork and has provided you with some strategies for minimizing these problems. Despite the pitfalls, groupwork should be an integral part of secondary classrooms. Like Donnie, Carmen, Fred, and Sandy, I believe students must learn to work together and that students learn from one another. As Sandy puts it:

> Having students do cooperative group activities takes a lot longer than just getting up there and telling them the material. But I really believe that this is the best way. When they've worked through the material in a group, they really understand.

Sandy's reflections focus on the academic benefits of groupwork. But as I mentioned at the beginning of the chapter, groupwork has social payoffs as well. It's important to remember that the classroom is not simply a place where students learn academic lessons. It's also a place where students learn *social lessons*—lessons about the value of helping one another, about relationships with students from other racial and ethnic groups, about accepting individuals with disabilities, and about friendship. As a teacher, you will determine the content of these lessons. If planned and implemented well, groupwork can provide students with opportunities to learn lessons of caring, fairness, and self-worth.

SUMMARY

I began this chapter by taking about the potential benefits of groupwork and about some of the special challenges it presents. Then I suggested strategies for designing successful groupwork. Finally, I described some structured programs of cooperative learning.

Benefits of Groupwork

- Less idle time while waiting for the teacher to help
- Enhanced motivation
- More involvement in learning
- Greater achievement
- Decreased competition among students
- Increased interaction across gender, ethnic and racial lines
- Improved relationships between mainstreamed students and their peers

Some Common Pitfalls

- Segregation in terms of gender, ethnicity, and race
- Unequal participation
- Lack of accomplishment
- Lack of cooperation among group members

Challenges of Groupwork

- Maintaining order
- Achieving accountability for all students

- Teaching new (cooperative) behavioral norms
- Creating effective groups

Designing Successful Groupwork

- Decide on the type of group to use (helping permitted, helping obligatory, peer tutoring, cooperative, completely cooperative)
- Decide on the size of the group
- Assign students to groups
- Structure the task for interdependence (e.g., create a group goal or reward)
- Ensure individual accountability
- Teach students to cooperate

Structured Programs of Cooperative Learning

- STAD
- Jigsaw I and II
- Group Investigation
- The Structural Approach to Cooperative Learning

Group work offers unique social and academic rewards, but it is important to understand the challenges it presents and not to assume that, just because a task is fun or interesting, the lesson will run smoothly. Remember to plan groupwork carefully, prepare your students thoroughly, and allow yourself time to develop experience as a facilitator of cooperative groups.

ACTIVITIES

1. For each of the following types of groupwork, give an example of an activity from your own content area:
   a. Helping permitted
   b. Helping obligatory
   c. Peer tutoring
   d. Cooperative group
   e. Completely cooperative group
2. Choose a topic from your own content area and create a completely cooperative activity. As you design the activity, keep in mind the following questions:
   How will you assign students to groups?
   How will you structure the activity to foster positive interdependence?
   What roles will you assign, if any?
   What forms of accountability will you build in?
   What are the social skills you need to teach, and how will you teach them?
   How will you monitor the groupwork?
   How will you provide an opportunity for students to evaluate the group process?
3. Choose two topics from your own content area. For each one, select an approach discussed in this chapter (STAD, Jigsaw, Group Investigation, or one of Kagan's cooperative structures). Briefly describe how you would use the cooperative learning strategy you selected. Use a different strategy for each topic.

REFERENCES

Aronson, E., Blaney, N., Stephan, C., Sikes, J., and Snapp, M. (1978). *The Jigsaw classroom.* Beverly Hills, CA: Sage.

Carson, L., and Hoyle, S. (1989-1990). Teaching social skills: A view from the classroom. *Educational Leadership, 47*(4), 31.

Carter, K. (March-April, 1985). Teacher comprehension of classroom processes: An emerging direction in classroom management research. Paper presented at the annual meeting of the American Educational Research Association, Chicago, Illinois.

Cohen, E. G. (1972). Interracial interaction disability. *Human Relations, 25,* 9–24.

Cohen, E. G. (1986). *Designing groupwork: Strategies for the heterogeneous classroom.* New York: Teachers College Press.

Edwards, C., and Stout, J. (1989-1990). Cooperative learning: The first year. *Educational Leadership, 47*(4), 38–41.

Gerleman, S. L. (1987). An observational study of small-group instruction in fourth-grade mathematics classrooms. *The Elementary School Journal, 88,* 3–28.

Good, T. L., and Brophy, J. E. (1994). *Looking in classrooms* (6th edition). New York: HarperCollins.

Goodlad, J. I. (1984). *A place called school.* New York: McGraw-Hill.

Graybeal, S. S., and Stodolsky, S. S. (1985). Peer work groups in elementary schools. *American Journal of Education, 93,* 409–428.

Johnson, D. W., and Johnson, R. T. (1980). Integrating handicapped students into the mainstream. *Exceptional Children, 47*(2), 90–98.

Johnson, D. W., and Johnson, R. T. (1989-1990). Social skills for successful groupwork. *Educational Leadership, 47*(4), 29–33.

Johnson, D. W., Johnson, R. T., Holubec, E. J., and Roy, P. (1984). *Circles of learning: Cooperation in the classroom.* Alexandria, VA: Association for Supervision and Curriculum Development

Kagan, S. (1989-1990). The structural approach to cooperative learning. *Educational Leadership, 47*(4), 12–15.

Kagan, S., Zahn, G. L., Widaman, K. F., Schwarzwald, J., and Tyrrell, G. (1985). Classroom structural bias: Impact of cooperative and competitive classroom structures on cooperative and competitive individuals and groups. In R. Slavin, S. Sharan, S. Kagan, R. Hertz-Lazarowitz, C. Webb, and R. Schmuck (Eds.), *Learning to cooperate, cooperating to learn.* New York: Plenum Press, 277–312.

Lazarowitz, R., Baird, J. H., Hertz-Lazarowitz, R., and Jenkins, J. (1985). The effects of modified Jigsaw on achievement, classroom social climate, and self-esteem in high-school science classes. In R. Slavin, S. Sharan, S. Kagan, R. Hertz-Lazarowitz, C. Webb, and R. Schmuck (Eds.), *Learning to cooperate, cooperating to learn.* New York: Plenum Press, 231–253.

Lemlech, J. K. (1988). *Classroom management: Methods and techniques for elementary and secondary teachers.* New York: Longman.

Madden, N. A., and Slavin, R. E. (1983). Cooperative learning and social acceptance of mainstreamed academically handicapped students. *Journal of Special Education, 17,* 171–182.

Mulryan, C. M. (1992). Student passivity during cooperative small groups in mathematics. *Journal of Educational Research, 85*(5), 261–273.

Newman, R. S., and Schwager, M. T. (1993). Students' perceptions of the teacher and classmates in relation to reported help seeking in math class. *The Elementary School Journal, 94*(1), 3–17.

O'Donnell, A., and O'Kelly, J. (1994). Learning from peers: Beyond the rhetoric of positive results. *Educational Psychology Review, 6*(4), 321–349.

Rosenholtz, S. J., and Cohen, E. G. (1985). Status in the eye of the beholder. In J. Berger and M. Zelditch, Jr. (Eds.), *Status, rewards, and influence.* San Francisco, CA: Jossey Bass.

Sharan, S. (1990). The group investigation approach to cooperative learning: Theoretical foundations. In M. Brubacher, R. Payne, and K. Rickett (Eds.), *Perspectives on small group learning.* Oakville, Ontario: Rubicon.

Sharan, S., and Sharan, Y. (1976). *Small-group teaching.* Englewood Cliffs, NJ: Educational Technology Publications.

Sharan, Y., and Sharan, S. (1989-1990). Group investigation expands cooperative learning. *Educational Leadership, 47*(4), 17–21.

Slavin, R. (1985). An introduction to cooperative learning research. In R. Slavin, S. Sharan, S. Kagan, R. Hertz-Lazarowitz, C. Webb, and R. Schmuck (Eds.), *Learning to cooperate, cooperating to learn.* New York: Plenum Press, 5–15.

Slavin, R. (1988). *Student team learning: An overview and practical guide* (2nd edition). Washington, D.C.: National Education Association.

Slavin, R. E. (1989-1990). Guest editorial: Here to stay or gone tomorrow? *Educational Leadership, 47*(4), 3.

Stodolsky, S. S. (1984). Frameworks for studying instructional processes in peer work groups. In P. L. Peterson, L. C. Wilkinson, and M. Hallinan (Eds.), *The social context of instruction.* New York: Academic Press, 107–124.

Swing, S. R., and Peterson, P. L. (1982). The relationship of student ability and small-group interaction to student achievement. *American Educational Research Journal, 19,* 259–274.

Webb, N. M. (1984). Sex differences in interaction and achievement in cooperative small groups. *Journal of Educational Psychology, 76,* 33–44.

Webb, N. M. (1985). Student interaction and learning in small groups: A research summary. In R. Slavin, S. Sharan, S. Kagan, R. Hertz-Lazarowitz, C. Webb, and R. Schmuck (Eds.), *Learning to cooperate, cooperating to learn.* New York: Plenum Press, 147–172.

Webb, N. M. (1989). Peer interaction and learning in small groups. *International Journal of Educational Research, 13,* 21–41.

Webb, N. M., and Kenderski, C. M. (1984). Student interaction and learning in small-group and whole-class settings. In P. L. Peterson, L. C. Wilkinson, and M. Hallinan (Eds.), *The social context of instruction.* New York: Academic Press, 153–170.

Wilkinson, L. C., and Calculator, S. (1982). Effective speakers: Students' use of language to request and obtain information and action in the classroom. In L. C. Wilkinson (Ed.), *Communicating in the classroom.* New York: Academic Press, 85–100.

FOR FURTHER READING

Cohen, E. G. (1986). *Designing groupwork: Strategies for the heterogeneous classroom.* New York: Teachers College Press.

Johnson, D. W., Johnson, R. T., Holubec, E. J., and Roy, P. (1984). *Circles of learning: Co-operation in the classroom.* Alexandria, VA: Association for Supervision and Curriculum Development.

Kagan, S. (1989). *Cooperative learning resources for teachers.* San Juan Capistrano, CA: Resources for Teachers.

Slavin, R. (1988). *Student team learning: An overview and practical guide* (2nd edition). Washington, D.C.: National Education Association.

Special issue of *Educational Leadership* (December 1989/January 1990). *Cooperative Learning, 47*(4), 1–67.

Chapter Ten _____

Managing Recitations and Discussions

_____

Much of the talk that occurs between teachers and students is unlike the talk you hear in the "real world." Let's consider just one example (Cazden, 1988). In the real world, if you ask someone for the time, we can assume you really need to know what time it is and will be grateful for a reply. The conversation would probably go like this:

> "What time is it?"
> "2:30."
> "Thank you."

In contrast, if a teacher asks for the time during a lesson, the dialogue generally sounds like this:

> "What time is it?"
> "2:30."
> "Very good."

Here, the question is not a request for needed information, but a way of finding out what students know. The interaction is more like a quiz show (Roby, 1988) than a true conversation: the teacher asks a question, a student replies, and the teacher evaluates the response (Mehan, 1979). This pattern of interaction (initiation-response-evaluation or I-R-E) is called *recitation,* and several studies (e.g., Stodolsky, 1988) have documented the substantial amount of time that students spend in this subsetting of the classroom.

The recitation has been frequently denounced as a method of instruction. Critics object to the active, dominant role of the teacher and the relatively passive role of the student. They decry the lack of interaction among students. They condemn the fact that recitations often emphasize the recall of factual information and demand little higher-level thinking. (See Figure 10-1 for an example of this kind of recitation.)

An additional criticism focuses on the public evaluation that occurs during recitation. When the teacher calls on a student, everyone can witness and pass judg-

> Mr. Lowe is conducting a "discussion" about Macbeth in his twelfth-grade English class. Students have just finished reading the first act.
>
> MR. LOWE: Okay, let's talk about the first act of this play. In the very first scene—which is very brief—three witches are on stage. What's the weather like, Sharon?
>
> SHARON: It's thundering and lightning.
>
> MR. LOWE: Right. What are the witches talking about, Larry?
>
> LARRY: How they're going to meet Macbeth.
>
> MR. LOWE: Good. When are they going to meet him? Jonathan?
>
> JONATHAN: When the battle's done.
>
> MR. LOWE: Right. Okay, let's jump to the third scene. The battle's done, and the three witches tell us that "Macbeth doth come." So we meet Macbeth and Banquo, two generals in the King's army. They've just returned from the battle. Who were they fighting? Missy?
>
> MISSY: Cawdor.
>
> MR. LOWE: Very good. Now we know that Cawdor was a traitorous rebel, right? Who was he rebelling against, Tanya?
>
> TANYA: King Duncan.
>
> MR. LOWE: Good. What country is Duncan king of? Melissa?
>
> MELISSA: Scotland.
>
> MR. LOWE: Yes. Now, when the witches first speak to Macbeth, what do they call him? Eric?
>
> ERIC: Thane of Glamis.
>
> MR. LOWE: Right. That's his title, so that makes sense. But then what do they call him?
>
> SUSAN: Thane of Cawdor.
>
> MR. LOWE: Right! So we know that Macbeth is going to be named the new thane of Cawdor. What happens to the old thane of Cawdor? Paul?
>
> PAUL: He's killed.
>
> MR. LOWE: Yes, he's put to death.

FIGURE 10-1
An example of a poor recitation: *Macbeth* as quiz show

ment on the response. In fact, as Phil Jackson (1968) comments, classmates are sometimes encouraged to "join in the act":

> Sometimes the class as a whole is invited to participate in the evaluation of a students' work, as when the teacher asks, "Who can correct Billy?" or "How many believe that Shirley read that poem with a lot of expression?" (p. 20)

Questions like these exacerbate the "negative interdependence" among students that recitations can generate (Kagan, 1989-1990). In other words, if a student is unable to respond to the teacher's question, the other students have a greater chance to be called on and to receive praise; thus, students may actually "root" for their classmates' failure.

Finally, critics observe that the format of the recitation is incompatible with the cultural background of some students. A vivid illustration comes from Susan Philips (1972), who wondered why children on the Warm Springs Indian Reservation in Oregon were so reluctant to participate in classroom recitations. Her analysis of life in this Native American community disclosed a set of behavioral norms that conflict with the way recitations are conducted. As I have noted, recitations permit little student-student interaction, but Warm Springs children are extremely peer-oriented. During recitations, the teacher decides who will participate, while Warm Springs traditions allow individuals to decide for themselves if and when to participate in public events. Recitations involve public performance and public evaluation—even if a student has not yet mastered the material—but Warm Springs children are used to testing their skills in private before they choose to demonstrate them in public. Understanding these disparities helps us to see why the children would find recitations unfamiliar and uncomfortable.

Despite the criticism, recitations remain an extremely common feature of secondary classrooms. What is there about this instructional strategy that makes it so enduring in the face of other, more highly touted methods (Hoetker and Ahlbrand, 1969)?

I thought hard about this question during one visit to Fred's classroom, and my observation of a recitation session that he conducted provided some clues. Students had just read an article from *Newsweek* magazine on whether the United States should renew China's most-favored-nation status. Fred then told them he wanted to hear what they thought about the basic issue described in the article:

FRED: Okay, I'm going to call on people, and I want to hear what you people think about the basic issue described in this article. Ms. Harnett, would you start, please?

HARNETT: I was really confused about this article. . . . I think it was talking about how in China there are a lot of political prisoners . . . and we don't like that . . . so we're trying to get them to change. . . . Oh, I don't know, it was confusing. . . .

FRED: You really understand more than you thought. Let's hear from someone else. Jenny.

JENNY: Well, like the United States doesn't like it that China has all these political prisoners . . . but China says leave us alone, our people are doing okay.

FRED: Okay, so China's saying that you have to look at the whole picture. You have to look at it from *their* perspective. [He calls on a student whose hand is raised.] Philip.

PHILIP: The Chinese are saying we keep talking about the dissidents, but they want to look at everyone. And like there's different ideas about human rights.

FRED: Hmmm. Let's talk about that. Let's talk about what we value as basic human rights in the United States. What are some of our basic human rights?

STUDENT: Equality.

FRED: What does that mean, equality? Come over here, Sally. [She comes up and stands next to him.] Are you my equal? Is she my equal?

Student: Well, she's not as big as you are [laughter], and she's probably not as strong, but she's equal in terms of rights.

FRED: Hmmm. So we're not equal in terms of size or strength. Are we equal economically? [Murmurs of "No . . ."] Probably not. Are we equal in terms of power? You bet we're not. [More laughter.] But we have *legal* equality; we've got equal rights under the law. What are some of those rights?

STUDENT: Freedom.

FRED: To do what?

STUDENT: To speak . . . freedom of speech.

FRED: Okay. What else?

STUDENT: Freedom of religion.

STUDENT: Freedom to vote.

FRED: Okay. In the United States, human rights means *individual* rights. We emphasize personal freedoms—the right of individuals to follow their own religion, to vote for who they want. But in China, the *group* is the focus of human rights. . . .

Fred's question-and-answer session helped me to identify five very useful functions of classroom recitations. First, the recitation allowed Fred to assess students' comprehension of the reading and to check their background knowledge on the issue of human rights and most-favored-nation status. Second, by asking intellectually demanding questions (e.g., "What do we mean by equality in the United States?"), Fred was able to prod his students to do some critical thinking and to guide them to some fundamental understandings (Good and Brophy, 1994). Third, the recitation permitted Fred to involve students in the presentation of material— what Roby (1988) calls "lecturing in the interrogatory mood." Instead of telling students directly about most-favored-nation status and the debate over human rights, Fred brought out the information by asking questions. Fourth, the recitation provided the chance to interact individually with students, even in the midst of a whole-group lesson. In fact, my notes indicate that Fred made contact with eight different students in just the brief interaction reported here. Finally, through his questions, changes in voice tone, and gestures, Fred was able to maintain a relatively high attention level; in other words, he was able to keep most of his students "with him."

Later, Fred reflected aloud on some other useful functions of recitation:

I'll use recitation a lot at the beginning of the year because it's a good way to get to know kids' names and to see how they handle themselves in class. It's also a tool for building self-confidence in a new class. They have a chance to speak in class, and I can provide them with opportunities for success early in the year. It's generally a pretty nonthreatening activity; since it doesn't ask for as much higher-level thinking as discussions, it's easier. I also try to emphasize that it's *okay not to know,* that we can figure out this stuff together. That's what education *is.*

As we can see, Fred's recitation session was hardly a "quiz show" in which passive students mindlessly recalled low-level, insignificant facts. On the other hand, both the pattern of interaction (I-R-E) and the primary intent (to assess students' understanding of the reading) set it apart from another type of questioning session: the *teacher-led discussion.* In order to make the distinction clear, let's consider another example from Fred's class. Here, students had been asked to read brief descriptions of hypothetical voters and determine if they were likely to be Democratic or Republican. (See Chapter Nine for a fuller description of this activity.) In this excerpt from the class, Fred was soliciting students' thoughts about the case of a retired school teacher living in New Jersey and dependent upon Social Security:

FRED: What are the indicators that the retired school teacher is left of center? Jeremy, what do you think?

JEREMY: She's from New Jersey.

FRED: Why would that affect her political views?

JEREMY: Well, New Jersey generally votes Democratic.

STUDENT: [Jumping in.] Wait a minute—we just elected a Republican governor.

JEREMY: Yeah, but there's a lot of diversity here, and like, I don't know, but I think people tend to be more liberal here.

FRED: What do other people think about this issue? Do you think living in New Jersey is an indicator that she's probably Democratic?

STUDENT: Well, I know this is going to sound dumb, but everybody I know around here is a Democrat, so I think if she's from New Jersey, she's probably Democratic.

FRED: Anything else here to indicate she might be liberal?

STUDENT: She's a teacher, so she's well educated.

FRED: Hmmmm. . . . Why would education be a factor that makes you more liberal?

STUDENT: Well, it just seems like the more you know, the more you understand about other people.

FRED: What other indicators might make you think that she's liberal?

STUDENT: Since she's a teacher, she probably cares about social issues. So that probably makes her more liberal.

STUDENT: Yeah, but she's older and she's retired. I think that would make her more conservative.

FRED: Let's consider that. Would age tend to make her more conservative?

STUDENT: Yeah. That happens.

FRED: Why? Why would age make her more conservative?

STUDENT: Older people are more set in their ways.

FRED: Okay, I tend to be more skeptical because I've been around more. I've been dumped on more. But of course, we've got to remember that these are generalizations. I'm going to bring in an older guy who's a far left liberal and a young guy who's real conservative, just to defy the generalizations. Okay, what other indicators are there that she's conservative?

STUDENT: She's living on Social Security, so she's probably real concerned about money.

FRED: So she's concerned about money. Why would that make her conservative?

STUDENT: She might vote against social programs that would cost her.

STUDENT: Yeah, like she'd probably vote against the school budget.

STUDENT: I don't agree with that. As a retired teacher, I can't see that she'd ever vote against a school budget.

Later in the interaction, after Fred and the students had decided that the retired teacher was probably a Democrat (but conservative on issues "close to the pocketbook"), Fred stressed the fact that there could be no right answers in this exercise:

Are we right? I don't know. All we can make are informed generalizations. If there's a right answer here, it's that there's *no right answer*. But this is not just an exercise in futility that we did. Lots of times in politics, people are given tasks where they are required to make judgments and they don't have enough data to know the right answer. But people can make better judgments—in the absence of complete data—by being more attuned to the indicators. The indicators are useful for making predictions, which is really important in politics. And if it turns out your predictions are right, you're considered a brilliant strategist; if you're wrong, you're fired.

Fred leads a whole class discussion.

As in the recitation presented earlier, Fred was still very much in charge of this interaction. He set the topic, posed the questions, and called on students to speak. Nonetheless, there are some obvious differences. In the discussion, Fred generally initiated the questions, and students replied, but he often dispensed with an evaluation of their responses. Thus, the predominant pattern was not I-R-E, but I-R, even I-R-R-R. Furthermore, students occasionally initiated questions of their own, both to Fred and to each other, and sometimes they commented on or evaluated the contributions of their peers. Finally, the purpose of this interaction was not designed to "go over material" or to "elaborate on a text" (Good and Brophy, 1994). Rather, the teacher-led discussion was intended to stimulate a variety of responses, to encourage students to consider different points of view, to foster problem-solving, to examine implications, and to relate material to students' own personal experiences (Good and Brophy, 1994).

Although educational critics frequently decry the use of recitation and promote the use of discussion, both types of interaction have a legitimate place in the secondary classroom—if done well. As Tom Good and Jere Brophy (1994) write: "The operative question about recitation for most teachers is not whether to use it but when and how to use it effectively" (p. 386).

This chapter begins by examining the managerial hazards associated with recitations and teacher-led discussions. Like seatwork and groupwork, these subsettings of the secondary classroom have their own set of "built-in hazards" (Carter, 1985)—unequal participation; loss of pace, focus, and involvement; and the difficulty of monitoring comprehension. Next, we consider what our teachers and the research have to say about minimizing these problems. The final section of the chapter takes a brief look at yet another type of questioning session—the student-centered discussion—and offers some guidelines for managing this third pattern of interaction.

THE PITFALLS OF RECITATIONS AND TEACHER-LED DISCUSSIONS

Unequal Participation

Imagine yourself in front of a class of 25 students. You've just asked a question. A few individuals have their hands up, conveying their desire (or at least their willingness) to be called on. Others are sitting quietly, staring into space, their expressions blank. Still others are slumped down as far as possible in their seats; their posture clearly says, "Don't call on me."

In a situation like this, it's tempting to call on an individual whose hand is raised. After all, you're likely to get the response you want—a very gratifying situation! You also avoid embarrassing students who feel uncomfortable speaking in front of the group or who don't know the answer, and you're able to keep up the pace of the lesson. But selecting only those who volunteer or those who call out may limit the interaction to a handful of students. This can be a problem. Students tend to learn more if they are actively participating (Morine-Dershimer and Beyerbach, 1987). Furthermore, since those who volunteer are often high achievers, calling only on volunteers is likely to give you a distorted picture of how well everyone understands. Finally, restricting your questions to a small number of students can communicate negative attitudes and expectations to the others (Good and Brophy, 1994): "I'm not calling on you because I'm sure you have nothing to contribute." Negative attitudes like this can be communicated even if you have the best of intentions. Listen to Sandy recall a situation in which she made a practice of not calling on a student who seemed painfully shy:

> It was my second year of teaching, but I still remember it clearly. My kids did course evaluations at the end of the year, and one kid said I didn't care about students. I was devastated. I tracked her down and asked her why she thought I didn't care. She said it was because I hadn't required her to participate in class discussions. Here I had been trying to avoid causing her embarrassment. She seemed so afraid to talk, so I left her alone. And she interpreted my behavior as saying I didn't care. That taught me a good lesson!

Losing It All: Pace, Focus, and Involvement

In the early 1960's, a popular television program capitalized on the fact that "Kids Say the Darndest Things." The title of the show aptly describes what can happen during a recitation or discussion. When you ask your question, you might receive the response you have in mind. You might also get answers that indicate confusion and misunderstanding, ill-timed remarks that have nothing to do with the lesson (e.g., "There's gum on my shoe" or "When are you going to give back the lab reports?"), or unexpected comments that momentarily throw you off balance. All of these threaten the smooth flow of a recitation or discussion and can cause it to become sluggish, jerky, or unfocused.

Threats like these require you to make instantaneous decisions about how to proceed. It's not easy. For example, if a student's answer reveals confusion, you need to determine how to provide feedback and assistance without losing the rest of the class. During recitations and discussions, you are frequently confronted with two incompatible needs: the need to stay with one person to enhance that individual's learning and the need to move on to avoid losing both the momentum and the group's attention. Donnie reflects on this common situation:

> There always seems to be one person who doesn't understand! While you're trying to help that student, the rest of the class begins to mumble things like, "Why are we still doing this? We know this stuff already." They become really restless. Of course, they want you to stay with them when *they* don't understand, but they get disgusted if you spend too long on someone else.

When "kids say the darndest things" during a recitation or discussion, you also need to determine if the comment is genuine or if it is a deliberate ploy to get you sidetracked. Fred has had first-hand experience with this particular hazard:

> I'll have kids try to get me off on a tangent by asking a question that's out of the blue. It's especially true with sharp kids. When that happens, I'll say, "What a great question. It's not what we're dealing with today, but I'd really like to discuss that with you. Is 2:30 okay or how about tomorrow?"

Sometimes, questioning sessions get sluggish because ambiguity in the teacher's question makes it difficult for students to respond. For example, Farrar (1988) analyzed a social studies lesson in which the teacher asked a yes-no question: "Did you read anywhere in the book that Washington's army was destroyed?" When students responded, "No," and "Uh-uh," he rejected their answers. The result was confusion and a momentary breakdown of the recitation. In retrospect, it appears that the teacher was not really expecting a yes or no answer, but wanted a restatement of information that had appeared in the reading. Students responded to his *explicit* question, while he was waiting for the answer to his *implicit* question: "What happened to Washington's army?"

Questioning sessions can also become bogged down if the teacher has not developed a set of verbal or nonverbal signals that communicate to students when they are to raise their hands and when they are to respond chorally. Without clear signals, students are likely to call out when the teacher wants them to raise their hands, or to remain silent and raise their hands when the teacher wants them to call out in a choral response.

Difficulties in Monitoring Students' Comprehension

Recitations and discussions provide an opportunity for teachers to check students' comprehension, but doing so is not always easy. Recently, a fifth-grade teacher talked about a lesson taught by her student teacher, Rebecca. The class had been studying the human body, and halfway through the unit, Rebecca planned to give her students a quiz. On the day of the quiz, she conducted a brief review of the material by firing off a series of questions on the respiratory and circulatory systems. Satisfied with the high percentage of correct answers, Rebecca then asked, "Before

I give out the quiz, are there any questions?" When there were none, she added, "So everybody understands?" Again, there was silence. Rebecca told the students to close their books and distributed the quiz papers. That afternoon, she corrected the quiz. The results were an unpleasant shock; a large number of students received D's and F's. During a post-lesson conference with her cooperating teacher, she wailed, "How could this happen? They certainly knew the answers during our review session!"

This incident underscores the difficulty of gauging the extent to which all members of a class really understand what is going on. As we mentioned earlier, teachers sometimes get fooled because they call only on volunteers—the students most likely to give the correct answers. In this case, Rebecca's cooperating teacher had kept a "map" of the verbal interaction between teacher and students and was able to share some revealing data: during a 15-minute review, Rebecca had called on only *six* of the 19 children in the class, and all of these had been volunteers. Although this allowed Rebecca to maintain the smooth flow of the interaction, it led her to overestimate the extent of students' mastery. Moreover, as Rebecca's cooperating teacher pointed out to her, questions that try to assess comprehension by asking "Does everyone understand?" are unlikely to be successful. There's no accountability built into questions like this; in other words, they don't require students to demonstrate an understanding of the material. In addition, students who do not understand are often too embarrassed to admit it. (They may not even realize they don't understand!) Clearly, you need to find other ways to assess if your class is "with" you.

STRATEGIES FOR MANAGING RECITATIONS AND TEACHER-LED DISCUSSIONS

Recitations and teacher-led discussions pose formidable challenges to teachers. You need to respond to each individual's learning needs, while maintaining the attention and interest of the group; to distribute participation widely, without dampening the enthusiasm of those who are eager to volunteer; to assess students' understanding without embarrassing those who don't know the answers; to allow students to contribute to the interaction, while remaining "on course."

This section of the chapter considers six strategies for meeting these challenges. As in previous chapters, research on teaching, discussions with the four teachers, and observations of their classes provide the basis for the suggestions. Although there are no foolproof guarantees of success, these strategies can reduce the hazards associated with recitations and teacher-led discussions. (Table 10-1 provides a summary of the suggestions.)

Distributing Chances to Participate

Early in the school year, I watched Fred introduce the topics that his Contemporary World Issues class would be studying during the coming year. He explained that students would be examining a variety of cultures, looking at how people make a living in each culture.

TABLE 10-1
STRATEGIES FOR MANAGING RECITATIONS

Strategy	Example
Distribute chances to participate	Use patterned turn-taking Pick names from a cup Check off names on a seating chart
Provide time to think	Extend wait time to three seconds Tell students you don't expect an immediate answer Allow students to write a response
Stimulate and maintain interest	Inject mystery and suspense Inject humor and novelty Challenge students to think
Provide feedback to students	When answer is correct and confident, affirm briefly When answer is correct but hesitant, provide more deliberate affirmation When answer is incorrect, but careless, make a simple correction When answer is incorrect but student could get answer with help, prompt or backtrack to simpler question If student is unable to respond, don't belabor the issue
Require overt responses	Have students write answers, physically display answers with manipulative materials, respond chorally
Use a steering group	Observe the performance of a sample of students (low and average achievers) in order to know when to move on

Okay, let's think about what goes into making a living. Make a list of the five most important elements in our economic system that have a bearing on your own life. I'm going to do this too. [Students began to write. After a few minutes, Fred continues.] Okay, let's see if we can develop a good answer, a consensus. Let's go around the room and each person give one thing.

In this situation, Fred chose to use a "round-robin" technique, which allowed him to give everyone a chance to participate. Since he didn't have to deliberate each time he called on someone, this strategy also enabled him to keep the pace moving. Watching him, I recalled a study by McDermott (1977) of first-grade reading groups. McDermott found that turn-taking in the high-achievement group proceeded efficiently in round-robin fashion, with little time lost between readers. In the low-achievement group, however, the teacher allowed the students to bid for a turn, and so much time was devoted to deciding who would read next that students spent only one-third as much time reading as students in the top group.

Sometimes, teachers prefer to use a pattern that is more subtle than the round-robin, so that students do not know exactly when they will be called on. Donnie often uses this approach (described earlier in the section on interaction routines, Chapter Four):

After a review of solving equations with two unknowns, Donnie tells her students to open their textbooks to the oral exercises on page 351. She tells them: "Everyone in here will get a chance to answer a problem. Okay, Kevin has his hand raised, so let's start with him. Decide if the ordered pairs are solutions to the equation." [She goes through the oral exercise, rapidly calling on students.]

After class, when I discussed this lesson with Donnie, I asked her if she had used some system for calling on students. She explained:

I used a pattern. I started with Kevin, and then went diagonally to the back of the room, then across, and down. I find that using a pattern like that helps me to keep track of who I call on, and it helps me make sure I get to everyone. And it's less obvious than just going up and down the rows. This way, kids are not so aware of who I'm going to call on next. So they don't sit there and try to work out the answer to the problem they know they're going to get. Sometimes, they'll try to figure out the pattern, and they'll say, "Wait a minute, you missed me," but it's like a game.

Instead of a pattern, some teachers use a list of names or a seating chart to keep track of who has spoken, placing a tick mark by the name of each student who participates. Other teachers use a "coffee mug technique," pulling students' names from a coffee mug, and placing the slips of paper on the side after the student has responded. Whichever system you choose, *the important point is to make sure that the interaction is not dominated by a few volunteers.*

It's also important to make sure that males and females have equal opportunity to participate. A recent view of the literature (Grossman and Grossman, 1994) reports that "teachers demonstrate a clear bias in favor of male participation in their classes":

Teachers are more likely to call on a male volunteer when students are asked to recite; this is also true when they call on nonvolunteers. When students recite, teachers are also more likely to listen to and talk to males. They also use more of their ideas in classroom discussions and respond to them in more helpful ways. . . . This pattern of giving more attention to males is especially clear in science and mathematics classes. (p. 76)

Similarly, *How Schools Shortchange Girls* (1992), a study commissioned by the American Association of University Women (AAUW), reports that males often demand—and receive—more attention from teachers. In one study of ten high school geometry classes (Becker, 1981), for example, males called out answers to teacher questions twice as frequently as females. The same result was obtained in a more recent study (Jones and Wheatley, 1990) of 30 physical science and 30 chemistry classes: whereas the female students appeared "self-conscious and quiet," the males were "more aggressive in calling out responses and tended to use louder tones of voice when seeking the teacher's attention" (p. 867).

Why would teachers allow male students to dominate classroom interaction by calling out? Morse and Handley (1985) suggest three possible reasons: (1) the behavior is so frequent that teachers come to accept it; (2) teachers expect males to be aggressive; and (3) the call-outs may be perceived by teachers as indicators of interest. Whatever the reasons, Morse and Handley's study of junior high science classes found that the trend towards male dominance became even greater as students moved from seventh to eighth grade.

Sandy is one science teacher who does not allow the boys to "grab the floor":

> I find that the boys are often faster at responding than the girls. Boys will call out the answers even if they're not sure, while the girls will sit and think before they give an answer. I really have to stay aware of that and make sure that the girls get an opportunity to respond.

The following vignette illustrates one strategy Sandy uses to ensure that girls have the opportunity to participate:

SANDY: Listen really carefully. [She writes an equation on the board. Pointing to the equation, she turns to the class and continues.] A student was asked to produce 30 grams of O_2 gas. How many grams of $KClO_3$ must the student use to do this? [There is no response.] Can I say that if the student needs to produce 30 grams of O_2 gas she would need to start with 30 grams of $KClO_3$?

STUDENTS: [in chorus] No-o-o.

SANDY: Why not? [Students raise their hands. A few boys start to call out.] Wait, raise your hand. [She calls on a girl who has not raised her hand.] Janice.

JANICE: Because oxygen is different. [Several boys start to call out again. Sandy shakes her head to indicate that they should wait.]

SANDY: Okay, Janice. Because O_2 is a different chemical, but what is the relationship between moles of O_2 and moles of $KClO_3$?

JANICE: [She shrugs. Again, boys start to call out.]

SANDY: Look back at the board. Does the equation reveal anything to you about the relationship?

JANICE: [Her eyes light up.] It's a two-to-three ratio.

SANDY: Super!

Although greater participation by males may be a common phenomenon, it does not hold true across all contexts. In the urban high school where Donnie teaches, for example, it's not considered "cool" for a boy to act too smart or too interested in learning:

> The boys may try to "take over" in basic skills, but not in the more advanced math classes like algebra or geometry. In these classes, it's the girls who want to respond. As you get to eleventh or twelfth grade, there are fewer and fewer boys in these classes and they're not the leaders. We're really losing a lot of our males. . . .

Whatever the pattern, teachers need to be sensitive to gender differences in participation and use strategies to ensure that both males and females have opportunities to participate. Listen to Carmen:

> I try really hard to make sure that boys and girls have an equal opportunity to answer. I try to alternate—to call on a girl, then a boy. And if I don't get any volunteers from girls (or boys), I'll say something like, "What's wrong with the women (or the men) in this class? Let's hear from some of you!"

Sometimes, distributing participation is difficult because students are reluctant to speak and there are too *few* volunteers. At other times, distributing participation is problematic because there are too *many* volunteers. The more teachers stimulate interest in a particular lesson, the more students want to respond. This means greater competition for each turn (Doyle, 1986), and "bidding" for a chance to speak can become loud and unruly. One useful strategy is to allow several students to answer one question. In the following interaction, we see Carmen increase participation by not "grabbing" the first answer and moving on to a new question. It was the beginning of class, and Carmen was reminding students about the paper sculptures they had begun a week earlier:

CARMEN: [Students come in, go to their seats, and chat quietly.] I'm waiting. [Students stop talking.] Okay, what did we do last week? [Students begin to call out. Carmen shoots her arm into the air, a clear signal to raise hands. Students raise their hands, and Carmen calls on a volunteer.] Latitia.

LATITIA: We did stripes on long papers.

CARMEN: Right. But not only stripes. What else? Edwin.

EDWIN: Zigzags. [She nods and signals for another student to respond.]

STUDENT: I did hearts and clubs and diamonds. [Again Carmen nods and signals to another student.]

STUDENT: All kinds of designs.

CARMEN: Now why are we doing designs? Zenia.

ZENIA: We're going to build things.

CARMEN: What are we going to build? [She nods at a student to answer.]

STUDENT: Sculptures.

CARMEN: Yes, paper sculptures. Now remember, you don't have to color every strip with designs. What else could you do with the paper strips?

STUDENT: Fold the end and twist it.

CARMEN: What else? Timmy?

TIMMY: Make a circle. All kinds of shapes.

STUDENT: Bend it.

STUDENT: You could cut.

CARMEN: If you cut, what could you do with the pieces?

STUDENT: You could make those rings, like at Christmas.

During one visit to Donnie's class, I watched her distribute participation widely by specifying that each student should give only one possible answer to the problem:

DONNIE: Today we start a new adventure—equations with two variables. Our answers are going to be ordered pairs. I'm going to put this up here, $x + y = 3$. [She writes the equation on the board.] Now, if I ask you to give me all the possible answers, what would you say? [There are lots of hands up.] Okay, give me *one*, Shameika.

SHAMEIKA: (0,3).

DONNIE: [She writes that on the board.] Okay, give me another. Sharif.

SHARIF: (1,2).

DONNIE: Another. Tayeisha.

TAYEISHA: (2,1).

Another strategy is to have each student write a response and share it with one or two neighbors. This allows everyone to participate actively. You might then ask some of the groups to report on what they discussed.

One final thought: While you're thinking about ways to distribute participation, keep in mind the suggestions made in Chapter Three for counteracting the action zone phenomenon: (1) move around the room whenever possible; (2) establish eye contact with students seated farther away from you; (3) direct comments to students seated in the rear and on the sides; and (4) periodically change students' seats so that all students have an opportunity to be up front.

Providing Time to Think Without Losing the Pace

Envision this scenario: You've just asked a well-formulated, carefully worded, higher-level question designed to stimulate critical thinking and problem solving. And you're met with total silence. Your face begins to feel flushed, and your heart beats a little faster. What to do now?

One reason silence is so uncomfortable is that it's hard to interpret: Are students thinking about the question? Are they asleep? Are they so muddled they're unable to respond? Silence is also troubling to teachers because it can threaten the pace and momentum of the lesson (Arends, 1988). Even a few seconds of silence can seem like eternity. This helps to explain why many teachers wait less than *one second* before calling on a student (Rowe, 1974). Yet research demonstrates that if you extend *wait time* to three or four seconds, you can increase the quality of students' answers and promote participation. After all, if you're asking a thought-provoking question, you need to give students time to think.

Sometimes it's helpful to tell students that you don't expect an immediate answer. This legitimates the silence and gives students an opportunity to formulate their responses. During a visit to Fred's class, I saw him indicate that he wanted everyone to think for a while before responding:

> We've been talking about how you can use indicators to decide if a person will be a liberal or conservative, a Republican or a Democrat, and some people came to me after school and said they thought that maybe I was encouraging you all to make stereotypes. I'm really glad they brought that up. You should not do an assignment in an unthinking, unquestioning way. So let's talk about this. First, these people obviously thought it was bad to stereotype people. Why? Why is it bad to stereotype people? *Before you answer, think.* [There's a long pause. Fred finally calls on a student to respond.]

Allowing students to write an answer to your question is another way of providing them with time to think. Written responses also help to maintain students' engagement, since everyone has to construct a response. In addition, students who are uncomfortable speaking extemporaneously can read from their written papers. In the following example, we see Sandy use this strategy:

> Sandy is introducing the concept of chemical equilibrium. She has drawn a diagram on the board showing the relative concentrations of A+B and C+D over time. She asks, "Where is equilibrium established? At Time 1, Time 2, or Time 3? Jot it down and write a sentence explaining why you chose T1, T2, or T3." She walks around the room, looking

at students' papers. With a little laugh, she comments: "I see a lot of correct answers, and then the word 'because.' "

During our conversation about her lesson, Sandy recalled an incident that underscored the value of having all students write a response to a question:

> I had this girl in my honors class, who came to see me about the second week of school. She was obviously upset about how she was doing; she wanted to drop the class. She started to cry. "Everyone is so much smarter than I am." I asked her how she had come to that conclusion, and it was clear that she was equating response time with ability. I find that a lot of the girls do that. She says, "I'm just in the middle of figuring it out, and the other kids are already answering." She says, "I like it when you ask us to write our answers down first. But when I have to respond orally I'm intimidated."

Once you have selected someone to respond, it's also important to provide that student with an opportunity to think. This is another kind of wait time, and research has documented that here, too, teachers often jump in too soon (Rowe, 1974). Sometimes they provide the answer themselves or call on another individual. This is particularly tempting if other students are waving their hands. Watch the way Donnie deals with this situation during a lesson on linear measurement:

DONNIE: Okay, so how are you going to figure this out? Eugene.
EUGENE: You have to know how many inches are in a mile.
DONNIE: And how are you going to figure *that* out? [Eugene is silent, but Ebony is waving her hand.]
EBONY: Ooh, ooh, Miss, I know, I know how to do it.
DONNIE: [very softly] Wait a minute, Ebony, give him a chance. Let him think.

Stimulating and Maintaining Interest

In previous chapters, we have discussed Kounin's classic study (1970) of the differences between orderly and disorderly classrooms. One finding of that study was that students are more involved in work and less disruptive when teachers attempt to involve nonreciting individuals in the recitation task, maintain their attention, and keep them "on their toes." Kounin called this behavior "group alerting." Observations of our four teachers reveal that they frequently use group-alerting strategies to stimulate attention and to maintain the pace of the lesson. For example, watch how Carmen generates interest in the upcoming lesson on sculpture by creating a sense of quiet excitement:

CARMEN: Okay, I'm going to cut the clay. How do you think I'm going to cut the clay?
STUDENTS: With a knife.
CARMEN: No. . . . Let me show you. You're going to love it. I cut it with a wire. Look. [Carmen takes the wire and cuts the large chunk of clay into brick-like slabs.]
STUDENTS: Oooh . . .
CARMEN: Each of you will get a chunk. This is really nice clay, good quality. I put a lot of water in it. It really feels good. . . .

Students' interest can also be maintained if you inject some humor or novelty into the recitation itself. During a lesson on portraits, Carmen talked about the various colors that people come in:

CARMEN: We all come in different shades and colors. How would I go about making the skin tone of a black person? [She points to the various cups in front of her, containing brown, black, yellow, pink, white, and orange paint.] What color would I start with?

STUDENTS: Brown.

CARMEN: Okay, we'll start with brown. [She pours some brown into a little paper cup.] If the person's skin tone is darker, what could you add?

STUDENTS: Black.

CARMEN: Let's try that. [She adds a little black and then paints a stripe on a piece of paper to show what tone she has created.] Now, what if you want to go lighter? Let's say you're more like butterscotch or cappuccino. [Students laugh at the terms.] What would you add?

STUDENT: Yellow.

CARMEN: Okay. [She adds some yellow and shows the students what they would get.] Look at yourselves. You may want to paint on your skin in order to match, like make-up. Don't worry. It's not toxic.

Challenges to students can also be a way of encouraging students to think and to pay attention. Here are a few examples:

FRED: Please listen to this now. . . . Most Americans don't understand this at all; they don't have a clue. I want you to understand this.

DONNIE: You need to fix this in your minds because we're going to use this later. . . . Now this is not really a trick question, but you'll have to think. . . .

SANDY: This usually isn't covered in a first-year chemistry course. As a matter of fact, it's a problem that I asked on my honors chemistry test. But I know you guys can do it. I have confidence that you can do it. Just take it apart, step by step.

These challenges are reminiscent of the behavior of "Teacher X," one of the subjects in Hermine Marshall's (1987) study of three teachers' motivational strategies. Marshall found that Teacher X frequently used statements designed to challenge students to think: "I'm going to trick you," "Get your brain started . . . You're going to think," "Get your mind started," "Look bright-eyed and bushy-tailed" (stated, according to Marshall, "with enthusiasm and a touch of humor"). This frequent use of statements to stimulate and maintain student attention was in sharp contrast to the typical statements made by the other two teachers in the study (e.g., "The test will be on Thursday" or "Open your books to page 382"). In fact, Teacher Y and Teacher Z *never* used the strategy of alerting students to pay attention, and they rarely challenged students to think. The vast majority of their directives were attempts to *return* students to the task *after* attention and interest had waned.

Another way of engaging students is to make room for personal knowledge and experience. Bracha Alpert (1991) studied students' behavior during classroom recitations and discussions in three high school English classrooms. She found that in two classrooms, students tended to be resistant: they mumbled, refused to answer, and argued. In the third classroom, no signs of student resistance were apparent; instead, students in this class actively participated in discussions. Alpert concluded that the resistance was created by the teachers' tendency to emphasize factual, formal, academic knowledge, without any attempt to relate students' per-

Donnie challenges students to think during a lesson on triangles.

sonal life experiences to what was being taught. She provides some examples of this approach: "What's the significance of the dream [in the poem]?" "What is the tone of the poem?" or "What's being implied [by the author] in that scene?" In sharp contrast, the third teacher encouraged students to relate their personal experiences to the literary works they read. For example, when discussing why the literary character is so angry, he asked students to think of things that made them angry. He also asked them questions that promoted their involvement with the literary works—for example, "Do you feel sorry for any of the characters?" "Do you want Eliza to marry Freddy?"

Although it is easier to do this in subjects like English, social studies, and art, observations indicate that Sandy and Donnie also try to relate topics to students' own personal experiences. For example, when Sandy is introducing acids and bases, she'll begin by inviting students to tell her everything they already know about the topic. Her invitation usually leads to a discussion about fish tanks and pools, and once, they talked about what could happen if a child for whom you were babysitting drank Drano (a base) and why you couldn't use vinegar (an acid) to neutralize it! Similarly, when Donnie teaches about circles in geometry, she talks in terms of bicycles; each spoke of the tire is a radius, and the place where the chain touches the gear is the point of tangency.

Providing Feedback Without Losing the Pace

As we discussed in Chapter Seven, the BTES (Fisher et al., 1980) study documented the importance of providing feedback to students:

> When more frequent feedback is offered, students pay attention more and learn more. Academic feedback was more strongly and consistently related to achievement than any of the other teaching behaviors. (p. 27)

But how can you provide appropriate feedback while maintaining the pace and momentum of your lesson? Barak Rosenshine (1986) has reviewed the research on effective teaching and has developed a set of guidelines that may be helpful. According to Rosenshine, when students give correct, confident answers, you can simply ask another question or provide a brief verbal or nonverbal indication that they are correct. If students are correct but hesitant, however, a more deliberate affirmation is necessary. You might also explain *why* the answer is correct ("Yes, that's correct, because . . . ") in order to reinforce the material.

When students provide an incorrect answer, the feedback process is trickier. If you think the individual has made a careless error, you can make a simple correction and move on. If you decide that the student can arrive at the correct answer with a little help, you can provide hints or prompts. Sometimes it's useful to backtrack to a simpler question you think the individual can answer, and then work up to your original question step by step. Watch Sandy:

> Students are stuck on the question: "Given the following balanced equation, what volume of H gas can be produced from the decomposition of two moles of H_2O?" Their faces are blank, and there's absolute silence. Sandy asks: "Well, what is the volume of one mole of *any* gas at STP (standard temperature and pressure)?" All hands shoot up. Sandy calls on a student to respond. "22.4 liters." Sandy continues: "Do you know the relationship between moles of H_2O and moles of H gas produced?" Again, there are lots of hands, and a student replies: "It's a one-to-one relationship. The equation shows you that." Suddenly there is a lot of hand-waving, and students begin to call out, "Ooh, I see." "Oh, I got it." With a smile, Sandy motions for them to calm down and wait: "Okay, hold on, let's go back to the original question. Given the following balanced equation, what volume of H gas can be produced from the decomposition of two moles of H_2O?"

There are times when students are simply unable to respond to your question. When that happens, there's little point in belaboring the issue by providing prompts or cues; this will only make the recitation or discussion sluggish. Donnie sometimes allows students in this situation to "pass." This practice not only helps to maintain the pace, it also allows students to "save face." Meanwhile, she makes a mental note that she needs to reteach the material to the individuals having difficulty.

> Donnie is reviewing homework problems on the Pythagorean theorem. "Okay, moving on to #14." She moves over to Edward and looks as though she's going to call on him. He signals that he doesn't want to answer that question. "Don't call on you? Okay. I'll come back." She moves away and calls on someone else.

The most problematic situation for teachers is when students' answers are clearly incorrect. Saying "No, that's not right" can be uncomfortable, yet students deserve to have accurate feedback. As Sandy emphasizes, "It's really important to be clear about what's correct and what's not. The students have to know that the teacher will not leave them thinking the wrong thing." Rather than directly correcting students, however, Sandy prefers to help them discover their own errors:

> I have difficulty saying "Your answer is wrong," but I usually don't have to. I can ask them to explain their reasoning. Or I can take the part of the answer that is correct and work with it. I can ask a question about their response. "How does the graph show that?" "So you're saying it would have to be like this . . . " I like students to find their *own* mistakes and correct them.

Similarly, Donnie will ask, "How did you arrive at that answer?" And Fred will tell students: "That answer doesn't make sense to me. How did you figure it out?" Sometimes, he compliments students on making a "really good mistake": "I love mistakes. That's how we all learn."

Monitoring Comprehension: Requiring Overt Responses

A simple way to determine how well your students understand the material is to have them respond overtly to your questions. Earlier, we saw how Sandy had her students write down their responses to her question, so she could circulate and see what they were writing. Fred and Donnie also use this strategy:

> Fred's students have just read an article about the "Nacirema" people. [They later learn that the Naciremas are Americans—spelled backwards.] When the students are finished reading, Fred asks them to make ten valid inferences about these people, providing supporting evidence for each inference. "Now, before you begin, I want to see if you understand what to do or if you're clueless about this assignment. Take this piece of paper and write down: 'In Nacirema culture, kids cry when they lose their rac.' Now this is a valid inference. Write down one, two, or three pieces of evidence for this valid inference." He circulates throughout the room and checks to see what students are writing.

> Donnie's students have been learning about the properties of circles. At the end of the period, Donnie tells her students to take out a piece of unlined paper, a compass, a ruler, and a pencil. She tells the students: "Now this is to check on your ability to apply the terms that we've been going over, not just regurgitate the definitions. I will repeat the directions two or three times. This also checks your ability to listen and follow directions. [One boy calls out, "My worst quality," and everyone laughs.] Draw a circle with a radius of two inches. [She pauses to give the students the chance to do so.] Call the center of the circle Point P. . . . From the center, going due south draw radius PA. Label it. . . . The next thing you're going to do is draw a chord, but listen, the chord you're going to draw is going to bisect PA and go in an east-west direction. . . . "

Another way of quickly assessing students' comprehension is to ask them to put their thumbs up or down to indicate agreement or disagreement with a particular statement. You can also assess students' comprehension by having them respond chorally rather than individually. This allows you to scan the room and see who's having difficulty. This can be particularly helpful in a drill situation.

Monitoring Comprehension: Using a Steering Group

Another way of checking on students' understanding is to observe a "steering group." This is a sample of students whose performance is used as an indicator that the class is "with you" and that it's all right to move on to a new topic (Lundgren, 1972). Be careful, however, about choosing students for the steering group. If you select only high achievers, their performance may lead you to overestimate the comprehension of the class as a whole.

During one discussion with Donnie, she indicated that one boy in her algebra class was a key member of her steering group:

> I have this one boy who's average in ability. He generally sits in the back of the room, and when he doesn't understand, he gets a certain look on his face. I can tell he's confused. But when he *does* understand, the "light goes on." When I see the light is on with him, I can be sure most of the other kids understand.

MODERATING STUDENT-CENTERED DISCUSSIONS

Thus far, the chapter has examined three major problems associated with recitations and teacher-led discussions and has provided some suggestions for avoiding these problems. We have considered these two subsettings together because they share a number of features. In both the recitation and the teacher-led discussion the teacher is in charge, determining the content, the participants, and the pacing. Now we turn to a third type of verbal interaction, the *student-centered discussion*. Here, students have an increased opportunity to interact directly with one another, while the teacher acts as a facilitator or moderator.

Consider this example observed in Fred's IPLE class (Institute for Legal and Political Education). The topic was the deficit, and Hope had just asked a key question: "Why doesn't the government just print more money to pay off the debt?" Fred noted that this was an important question, and he attempted to provide an explanation. Hope wasn't convinced. Other students joined in:

SUSAN: I think I got it now. You know how they say that everyone can't be a millionaire. There's got to be some poor people? It's like that.

JOHN: Yeah, like when I play *Monopoly*. I buy every property, so I go into bankruptcy. So I take out a loan, and I'm ruining the game because I'm not playing with the money I'm supposed to have. It's like cheating.

LORIE: Yeah, that money doesn't really exist.

HOPE: What do you mean? If the government prints the money, it does exist. [A number of students begin talking at the same time.]

FRED: Hold on. Stuart, then Roy, then Alicia.

STUART: The money's worth a lot because there's only a little. If there were a lot, it would only be worth a little.

HOPE: I still don't understand. So what, if it's only worth a little.

ROY: Pretend there's this gold block sitting in Fort Knox and it's worth $10, but there's only one $10 bill. Now if we make up ten $10 bills, each will only be worth $1.00.

HOPE: So what? I can still use it to buy stuff. [A few students start to jump in, but Fred intervenes.]

FRED: Alicia hasn't had her chance to talk.

ALICIA: I think I got it now. Let me try. There's this diamond, and we both want it. . . . [She continues to explain, but Hope is still confused.]

FRED: Let's see if I can help out here. . . .

As we can see from this excerpt, Fred essentially stays out of the interaction, except for making sure that students have an opportunity to speak when the interaction gets excited. In contrast to the recitation, or even many teacher-led discussions, students speak directly to one another. They comment on one another's contributions; they question; they disagree; and they explain.

Providing opportunities for student-student discussions means that teachers have to give up their role as *leader* and assume the role of *facilitator.* This can be difficult for teachers who are used to dominating or at least directing the conversation. Even Fred, who encourages and values student-centered discussions, sometimes feels frustrated at not playing a larger role in the conversation:

> I really like having kids asking other kids questions, asking one another for supporting evidence, debating issues directly. But even so, sometimes I really get ticked off that I can't get a word in. During some discussions, I'm dying to say something. Sometimes, I'll just say, "Teacher prerogative," and jump in.

Acting as a facilitator rather than a leader does not mean abdicating responsibility for guiding the interaction. This became very clear during a conversation with Fred, when he described some of the problems he tries to anticipate and avoid:

> First of all, a discussion like this can be an opportunity for some kids to show how smart they are and to get air time, so it's important to watch out that kids don't pontificate and monopolize. Second, you have to listen carefully and ask yourself, "Where is this going?" I often have an end goal in mind, and I try to make sure that the discussion doesn't get too far afield. Occasionally, I'll jump in and say something like, "I think we're losing the focus here" or "I think you're arguing over semantics." Also, a lot of times kids state opinions as fact, and I think it's important not to let them get away with that. I'll interject and ask them to provide supporting evidence. Or I'll ask for clarification: "Is that what you meant to say?"

In addition to these suggestions, there are several other guidelines worth keeping in mind (Gall and Gillett, 1981):

1 *Limit the size of the group.* It's difficult to have a student-centered discussion with a large number of participants. Fred's IPLE class has only 12 students, so group size wasn't too much of a problem here, but in a more typical class, only a small percentage of the students would have an opportunity to speak. In his larger classes, Fred sometimes uses the "fishbowl" method, in which five or six students carry on the discussion in the middle of the room, while the rest of the class sits in a large circle around them and acts as observers and recorders. Another solution is to divide the class into small discussion groups of five, with one student in each group acting as a discussion leader.

2 *Arrange students so they can make eye contact.* It's very difficult to speak directly to someone if all you can see is the back of a head. If at all possible, students should move their desks into an arrangement that allows them to be face-to-face.

3 *Teach discussion skills.* Just as you need to teach students the skills for work-

TABLE 10-2
DISCUSSION SKILLS FOR PARTICIPANTS

- Talk to each other, not just to the moderator.
- Don't monopolize.
- Ask others what they think.
- Don't engage in personal attack.
- Listen to others' ideas.
- Acknowledge others' ideas.
- Question irrelevant remarks.
- Ask for clarification.
- Ask for reasons for others' opinions.
- Give reasons for your opinions.

Adapted from Gall, M. D., and Gillett, M. (1981). The discussion method in classroom teaching. *Theory Into Practice, 19*, 101.

ing in small groups, it is important to prepare students for participating in a student-centered discussion. Gall and his colleagues (1976; cited in Gall and Gillett, 1981) have developed a list of skills that may be helpful (see Table 10-2).

FINAL THOUGHTS

This chapter has focused on three different patterns of verbal interaction—recitations, teacher-led discussions, and student-centered discussions. It's important not to get them confused—to think that you're leading a discussion when you're actually conducting a recitation. As Sandy comments:

> A lot of beginning teachers get these two mixed up. They've been told they're supposed to ask a lot of questions, so they do, but often the questions are yes/no questions or questions that elicit short answers without a lot of depth: What do all atoms have in common? How many protons are in this atom? In discussions, the majority of the questions are critical thought questions, and the response time is longer. You're trying to develop an idea or draw a conclusion. You're not just reviewing; you're working toward a conceptual goal.

Also keep in mind the criticisms that have been leveled against recitations, and reflect on how frequently you dominate the verbal interaction in your classroom. Ask yourself whether you also provide opportunities for student-centered discussion, during which you serve as a facilitator (rather than a questioner) and encourage direct student-student interaction. Reflect on the level of thinking you require from students. The classroom recitation can serve a number of useful functions, but *overuse* suggests that your curriculum consists largely of names, dates, facts, and algorithms (Cazden, 1988).

SUMMARY

This chapter began by examining some of the major criticisms of recitation, as well as the useful functions it can serve. We then distinguished recitations from teacher-led discussions and considered the hazards these two subsettings present to teachers. Next, the chapter suggested a number of strategies for using recitations and teacher-led discussions successfully in your classroom. Finally, we looked at an example of a student-centered discussion and briefly considered a number of guidelines for managing this type of verbal interaction.

Characteristic Pattern of a Recitation

- I-R-E (teacher initiation, student responses, teacher evaluation)
- Quick pace
- To review material, to elaborate on a text

Criticisms of Recitation

- The teacher plays a dominant role, the student a passive one.
- There is a lack of interaction among students.
- Recall is emphasized over higher-level thinking skills.
- Recitation promotes public evaluation which can lead to negative interdependence.
- Recitation format sometimes conflicts with students' cultural background.

Five Functions of Recitation

- Provides opportunity to check on students' comprehension
- Offers an opportunity to push students to construct more complete responses
- Involves students in presentation of material
- Allows for contact with individuals in a group setting
- Helps to maintain attention level

Characteristics of a Teacher-Led Discussion

- I-R (or even I-R-R-R)
- Student-initiated questions
- Student comments on contributions of peers
- Slower pace
- Intended to stimulate thinking, to foster problem solving, to examine implications

Three Hazards of Recitations and Teacher-Led Discussions

- Unequal participation
- Losing the pace and focus
- Difficulty in monitoring comprehension

Strategies for Successful Use of Recitations and Teacher-Led Discussions

- Distribute chances for participation:
    Use some type of patterned turn-taking.
    Ensure that males and females have equal opportunity to participate.

- Provide time to think about answers before responding.
- Stimulate and maintain interest:
    Inject mystery/suspense elements into your questions.
    Use humor, novelty.
    Make room for personal knowledge and experience.
- Provide feedback without losing the pace.
- Monitor comprehension by requiring overt responses.
- Monitor comprehension by observing a steering group.

Moderating Student-Centered Discussions

- Acts as facilitator rather than questioner.
- Ensure that some students don't monopolize.
- Make sure the discussion stays on track.
- Ask students to provide supporting evidence for opinions.
- Limit group size.
- Arrange students so they have eye contact.
- Teach discussion skills.

When planning your lessons, think about the extent to which you use recitations, teacher-led discussions, and student-centered discussions in your classroom. Think about the level of the questions you ask: Are all of your questions low level, factual questions that can be answered with a word or two, or are your questions designed to stimulate thinking and problem solving? Ask yourself if you consistently dominate the interaction, or if you also provide opportunities for real discussion among students.

ACTIVITIES

1. Visit a classroom and observe a recitation. On a seating chart, map the verbal interaction by placing a check in the "seat" of each student who participates. Analyze your results and draw conclusions about how widely and fairly participation is distributed in this class. For example:

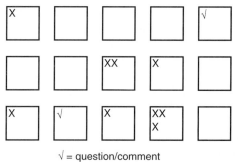

√ = question/comment
X = response to a question

2. Your colleague has asked you to help him figure out why his students are not paying attention in class. He would like you to observe him and offer feedback. What follows is a session you observed. Using what you know about distributing participation, stimulating and maintaining interest, and monitoring comprehension, identify the trouble spots of his lesson and provide three specific suggestions for improvement.

When you enter the class, Mr. B is perched on a stool in front of the room with the science book in his hand.

MR. B: Who remembers what photosynthesis is? [No response.] Do you remember yesterday when we looked at green plants and we discussed how a plant makes its own food? [Mr. B. notices that Thea is nodding.] Thea, do you remember about photosynthesis?

THEA: Yeah.

MR. B: Well, can you tell the class about it?

THEA: It has something to do with light and chlorophyll.

MR. B: Good. Tom, can you add to this? [Tom was drawing in his notebook.]

TOM: No.

MR. B: Tom, Thea told us that photosynthesis had to do with light and chlorophyll. Do you recall our discussion from yesterday when we defined photosynthesis?

TOM: Sort of.

MR. B: What do you mean? Didn't you write down the definition with the rest of the class? Look in your notebook and tell me the definition. [Tom starts to page through his notebook. Many of the students have begun to whisper and snicker. Some are looking in their notebooks.] How many of you have found the page where we defined photosynthesis? [Seven students raise their hands.] Good. Would somebody read to me that definition? Thea.

THEA: Photosynthesis is the process of forming sugars and starches in plants from water and carbon dioxide when sunlight acts upon chlorophyll.

MR. B: Excellent. Does everyone understand? [A few students nod.] Good. Tomorrow we will be having a quiz about plants and photosynthesis. Tom, will you be ready for the quiz?

TOM: Sure, Mr. B.

MR. B: Okay, now lets all turn to page 135 in our science texts and read about the uses of plants.

3. Monitoring students' comprehension is sometimes problematic. Choose one of the following topics (or think of one in your own content area) and suggest two different ways a teacher could elicit overt participation in order to determine student understanding:

    a. Main characters and their traits
    b. Characteristics of parallelograms
    c. Symbols for chemical ions
    d. Types of woodworking joints
    e. Foreign language vocabulary words
    f. Longitude and latitude

    g. States and capitals

    h. Types of clouds

    i. Fat content of various products

REFERENCES

The AAUW Report: How schools shortchange girls. (1992). Washington, D.C.: The AAUW Educational Foundation and National Education Association.

Alpert, B. (1991). Students' resistance in the classroom. *Anthropology and Education Quarterly, 22,* 350–366.

Arends, R. I. (1988). *Learning to teach.* New York: Random House.

Becker, J. R. (1981). Differential treatment of females and males in mathematics classes. *Journal for Research in Mathematics Education, 12*(1), 40–53.

Carter, K. (March–April 1985). Teacher comprehension of classroom processes: An emerging direction in classroom management research. Paper presented at the annual meeting of the American Educational Research Association, Chicago, Illinois.

Cazden, C. B. (1988). *Classroom discourse: The language of teaching and learning.* Portsmouth, NH: Heinemann.

Doyle, W. (1986). Classroom organization and management. In M. C. Wittrock (Ed.), *The handbook of research on teaching* (3rd edition). New York: Macmillan, 392–431.

Farrar, M. T. (1988). A sociolinguistic analysis of discussion. In J. T. Dillon (Ed.), *Questioning and discussion—A multidisciplinary study.* Norwood, NJ: Ablex.

Fisher, C. W., Berliner, D. C., Filby, N. N., Marliave, R., Cahen, L. S., and Dishaw, M. M. (1980). Teaching behaviors, academic learning time, and student achievement: An overview. In C. Denham and A. Lieberman (Eds.), *Time to learn.* Washington, D.C.: U.S. Department of Education.

Gall, M. D., and Gillett, M. (1981). The discussion method in classroom teaching. *Theory Into Practice, 19,* 98–103.

Good, T., and Brophy, J. E. (1994). *Looking in classrooms.* (6th edition). New York. HarperCollins.

Grossman, H., and Grossman, S. H. (1994). *Gender issues in education.* Boston: Allyn and Bacon.

Hoetker, J., and Ahlbrand, W. P. Jr. (1969). The persistence of the recitation. *American Educational Research Journal, 6,* 145–167.

Jackson, P. W. (1968). *Life in classrooms.* New York: Holt, Rinehart & Winston.

Jones, M. G., and Wheatley, J. (1990). Gender differences in teacher-student interactions in science classrooms. *Journal of Research in Science Teaching, 27,* 861–874.

Kagan, S. (1989-1990). The structural approach to cooperative learning. *Educational Leadership, 47*(4), 12–15.

Kounin, J. S. (1970). *Discipline and group management in classrooms.* New York: Holt, Rinehart, & Winston.

Lundgren, U. (1972). *Frame factors and the teaching process.* Stockholm: Almqvist and Wiksell.

Marshall, H. H. (1987). Motivational strategies of three fifth-grade teachers. *The Elementary School Journal, 88*(2), 135–150.

McDermott, R. P. (1977). Social relations as contexts for learning in school. *Harvard Educational Review, 47,* 198–213.

Mehan, H. (1979). *Learning lessons: Social organization in a classroom.* Cambridge, MA: Harvard University Press.

Morine-Dershimer, G. and Beyerbach, B. (1987). Moving right along. . . In V. Richardson-Koehler (Ed.), *Educators' handbook, A research perspective*. New York: Longman, 207–232.

Morse, L. W., and Handley, H. M. (1985). Listening to adolescents: Gender differences in science classroom interaction. In L. C. Wilkinson and C. B. Marrett (Eds.), *Gender influences in classroom interaction*. Orlando, FL: Academic Press.

Philips, S. (1972). Participant structures and communicative competence: Warm Springs children in community and classroom. In C. Cazden, V. John, and D. Hymes (Eds.), *Functions of language in the classroom*. New York: Teachers College Press.

Roby, T. W. (1988). Models of discussion. In J. T. Dillon (Ed.), *Questioning and discussion—A multidisciplinary study*. Norwood, NJ: Ablex, 163–191.

Rosenshine, B. V. (1986). Synthesis of research on explicit teaching. *Educational Leadership, 43*(7), 60–69.

Rowe, M. B. (1974). Wait-time and rewards as instructional variables, their influence on language, logic, and fate control: Part 1: Wait time. *Journal of Research in Science Teaching, 11*, 291–308.

Stodolsky, S. S. (1988). *The subject matters: Classroom activity in math and social studies*. Chicago: University of Chicago Press.

FOR FURTHER READING

Cazden, C. B. (1988). *Classroom discourse: The language of teaching and learning*. Portsmouth, NH: Heinemann.

Grossman, H., and Grossman, S. H. (1994). *Gender issues in education*. Boston: Allyn and Bacon.

Morine-Dershimer, G., and Beyerbach, B. (1987). Moving right along . . . In Virginia Richardson-Koehler (Ed.), *Educators' handbook, A research perspective*. New York: Longman, 207–232.

Philips, S. U. (1983). *The invisible culture: Communication in classroom and community on the Warm Springs Indian Reservation*. New York: Longman.

PART IV

BEYOND THE CLASSROOM ENVIRONMENT

Chapter Eleven

Working with Families

"His parents actually admitted they can't control him at home, and yet they expect *me* to control him at school!"

"Do you believe they had the nerve to suggest that Sara be allowed to pass the course even if she has a failing average?"

"Joseph hasn't handed in homework for five days, and when I call to talk about it, they tell me it's *my* problem!"

Comments like these can be heard in almost any teachers' room. It's not unusual for preparation periods, lunch time, and after-school meetings to become "gripe sessions" about parents' lack of cooperation, their unrealistic demands, and their irresponslblllty.

Similarly, when parents get together, they often voice complaints about their children's teachers:

"How can she teach them anything if she can't even control the class?! She shouldn't be a teacher if she can't make them behave."

"She just doesn't understand what's at stake here. Sara really needs to pass this course so she can graduate. It's not her fault she's failing. I think the teacher just has it in for her."

"He gives way too much homework—it's ridiculous that there should be one hour of homework in just one class!"

As these comments indicate, parents and teachers are often at odds with one another. Indeed, Sara Lawrence Lightfoot (1978) has written: "One would expect that parents and teachers would be natural allies, but social scientists and our own experience recognize their adversarial relationship. . . ." (p. 20).

This "adversarial relationship" is unfortunate. Researchers have documented many advantages of close communication and collaboration between families and teachers. For example, parent involvement in their children's schooling is associated with higher academic achievement, better attendance, more positive student attitudes and behavior, and greater willingness to do homework (e.g., Becher, 1984; Epstein, 1984; Haynes, Comer, and Hamilton-Lee, 1989; Henderson, 1987; Henderson, Marburger, and Ooms, 1986; Rich, 1988).

From a classroom management perspective, there are real benefits to working closely with families. First, *knowing about a student's home situation provides insight into the student's classroom behavior.* Listen to Donnie:

> It was the very first day of school—when everyone is still being really good—but this one girl was really loud and hyperactive. It was clear that everyone disliked her. She seemed completely unable to control herself. I checked into her home situation as soon as I had a free period. I found out that her mother had kicked her out of the house; she said she couldn't handle all the kids. The girl had tried to commit suicide, but now she was really trying to get her act together. She had gotten a part-time job, and she was living with an aunt. This girl had really been thrown out into the world, and school is her haven. Actually, when I think about what she's facing, I'm really impressed by how well she's doing.

As Donnie's example illustrates, it's easier to understand why Johnny sits with his head down on his desk if you're aware that he spent the night in a homeless shelter; Carla's belligerence makes sense if you know that her mother just lost her job and her father is absent; and Jana's anxiety about getting all A's is understandable if you appreciate how much her parents pressure her to succeed. Furthermore, insights like these can help you decide what course of action to take when dealing with a student's problems. You're better able to judge if a suggestion that a parent proofread term papers is inappropriate because the parent can't read, or if a note home will lead to benefits or to beatings. (The issue of child abuse is discussed in Chapter Twelve.)

Second, *when families understand what you are trying to achieve, they can provide valuable support and assistance.* Most parents want their children to succeed in school and will do what they can to help. But they can't work in a vacuum. They need to know what you are trying to achieve and how you expect children to behave in your classroom. Familiarizing parents with your curriculum, routines, and policies minimizes confusion, misinterpretations, and conflict.

Third, *families can help to develop and implement strategies to change students' behavior.* Working together, parents and teachers can bring about improvements in children's behavior that would be impossible working alone. Fred shares this example:

> I had this kid in my U.S. History II class who wasn't doing any work at all. It was his senior year, and I think he just decided he didn't have to do anything any more. His parents didn't have a clue about what to do. We all sat down and worked out a plan. They were to call me at 10:30 every Friday morning. If the report on their son was good, he got the car keys, got to go out with his friends, got to go to the ballgame. If the report was bad, the weekend did not exist. We told him, "We really care about you and if this is what we have to do to get you through senior year, then so be it." The kid tested the plan once, and there was no weekend for him. After that, he really started to perform

and ended up with a B for the year. Plus, there was an additional payoff. His parents were able to give him all kinds of good strokes because he started taking responsibility.

Given the obvious benefits of communication and collaboration between families and teachers, why is the relationship often so detached and distant? Why, at times, is it even strained and distrustful? In the next section of this chapter, we examine three barriers to close working relationships—teacher reluctance to involve parents, parent reluctance to become involved, and the changing nature of families. We then turn to our teachers and to the literature on parent involvement in order to suggest ways that families and schools can work together to educate adolescents.

BARRIERS TO FAMILY-TEACHER COOPERATION

Teacher Reluctance to Involve Families in Schooling

A primary reason for teachers' reluctance to work with families is the *extra time and energy that are required.* Teaching is physically and emotionally exhausting, and reaching out to parents is sometimes viewed as one more burdensome task. Epstein and Becker (1982) remind us how much time it takes to make just one call home: "If a teacher telephones 30 parents and talks for 10 minutes to each, the teacher spends 5 hours voluntarily on the telephone with parents" (p. 103). And that's for just one class! Since this is obviously in addition to planning lessons and activities, grading papers, organizing cooperative learning groups, and creating tests, it's understandable if teachers wonder whether the extra time required is worth the trouble. Furthermore, there are few external rewards to encourage teachers to spend time working with parents (Epstein and Becker, 1982), and teachers often lament the lack of support from their principals or other teachers.

In addition, *teachers' perceptions of families* undoubtedly contribute to the reluctance to seek greater parental involvement. Some teachers recognize that time is often a scarce commodity for parents, limited by responsibilities at work, household chores, and caring for other family members. These teachers question whether it is fair to ask already burdened parents to spend time working with their teenage children on academic activities or assisting with behavior problems (Epstein and Becker, 1982). As Sandy told us:

> Some parents are just overwhelmed. One poor, single mother I know just doesn't have the time or energy to become more involved. She's worried about keeping her job and making ends meet. Her plate is just too full; she can't handle anything else. It's not that she doesn't care. But the fact that her kid is not doing his homework is just not her highest priority right now. Knowing this is important. Once you know you're not going to get parent involvement, you can figure out another approach.

Other teachers have been burned by encounters with angry, irresponsible, or apathetic parents. They would tend to agree with Anne Walde and Keith Baker (1990), who wrote that "far too many parents—and not just disadvantaged ones—simply don't give a damn. For them, school is a free babysitting service" (p. 322). Walde and Baker argue that many parents are not concerned with their child's education, do not want to be involved, or lack the skills needed to support their children. They describe numerous encounters with parents to support their assertion. Here is one example:

Teacher: John isn't doing his homework.
Parent: I know he isn't. He watches TV all the time and doesn't do his homework. I just don't know what to do.
Teacher: Why don't you turn the TV off?
Parent: Oh, he'd never let me do that!

Another reason for teachers' reluctance to involve parents in schooling has to do with *the level of authority and autonomy teachers enjoy within their classrooms.* As public servants, teachers are often exposed to criticism. Parents may blame them for children's problems (Vernberg and Medway, 1981) or question their professional competence (Power, 1985). It's not surprising that teachers sometimes become guarded and protective of their "turf." Lightfoot (1978) writes:

The only sphere of influence in which the teacher feels that her authority is ultimate and uncompromising seems to be with what happens *inside* the classroom. Behind the classroom door, teachers experience some measure of autonomy and relief from parental scrutiny. . . . (p. 26)

Lightfoot concludes that teachers who are "more confident of their skills, expertise, and abilities" (p. 30) will be more likely to reach out to parents, and recent research supports her contention. In a study of factors that facilitate parent involvement, Hoover Dempsey, Bassler, and Brissie (1987) found that *teacher efficacy* (teachers' beliefs that they can teach and that their students can learn) was the factor most strongly related to parent involvement.

Parent Reluctance to Become Involved in Schooling

It is well recognized that family involvement in schools declines as students move from elementary to middle school and junior high, and that by high school, it has practically disappeared (Rioux and Berla, 1993). During one conversation with Donnie, she explained the decline in parent involvement this way:

Once kids leave elementary school, parents seem to feel it's time to cut the cord. They think the kids need to be on their own more, and that school should be the kids' responsibility. Also, they feel they can't help anymore because they don't know the content. They tell me, "I don't know algebra or geometry" or "I don't understand these new ways of teaching math." They're scared off by the content and feel they can't offer assistance.

In addition to this general, pervasive trend, there are more specific reasons why families may resist involvement. Some adults have unhappy memories of their own experiences as students. Listen to this father describe his reasons for not participating more fully in his son's schooling:

> They expect me to go to school so they can tell me my kid is stupid or crazy. They've been telling me that for three years, so why should I go and hear it again? They don't do anything. They just tell me my kid is bad.
>
>   See, I've been there. I know. And it scares me. They called me a boy in trouble but I was a troubled boy. Nobody helped me because they liked it when I didn't show up. If I was gone for the semester, fine with them. I dropped out nine times. They wanted me gone. (Finders and Lewis, 1994, p. 51)

Like this father, some adults remember school as an oppressive institution, not as a "place of hope" for their children (Menacker, Hurwitz, and Weldon, 1988). As sociologist Willard Waller (1932) wrote more than 60 years ago, "Each generation of teachers pays in turn for the sins of the generation that has gone before" (p. 59).

Other families believe that schooling should be "left to the experts" (Greenwood and Hickman, 1991). They may think they are showing their support for teachers by staying out of the way (Froyen, 1992); they may suspect that efforts to seek their involvement are merely attempts to shift responsibility (Froyen, 1993) and resent being asked to do the "teacher's job"; or they may feel they have little to offer teachers who have had years of training and experience.

Still other families feel guilty when their teenage children have difficulties in school. They may become defensive and uncooperative when teachers try to discuss their youngster's problem or may be too embarrassed to disclose troubles they are having at home. Rather than deal with the child's problem, these families may try to deny what is occurring and to avoid communication with the teacher (Froyen, 1992).

Finally, some families are unnerved by the "threatening monolith" we call school (Lightfoot, 1978, p. 36). In the main office, high counters serve as barricades to the principal, and there are few spaces in which parents can sit and chat or speak privately with teachers. Overprotective administrators discourage "invading" parents from visiting classrooms or making contact with teachers. If parents are poor, uneducated, or have limited proficiency in English, these barriers to involvement are even more intimidating. Margaret Finders and Cynthia Lewis (1994) interviewed Latino parents and parents in two low-income Anglo neighborhoods about family involvement in schooling. They report that fear was a common theme among the parents they interviewed. One mother expressed her discomfort this way:

> Parents feel like the teachers are looking at you, and I know how they feel, because I feel like that here. There are certain things and places where I still feel uncomfortable, so I won't go, and I feel bad, and I think maybe it's just me. (p. 53)

Another mother conveyed the anxiety she feels because of the linguistic and cultural mismatch between home and school:

[In] the Hispanic culture and the Anglo culture things are done different and you really don't know—am I doing the right thing? When they call me and say, "You bring the plates" [for class parties] do they think I can't do the cookies, too? You really don't know. (p. 52)

The Changing Nature of the Family

In 1955, 60 percent of American households consisted of a working father, a homemaker mother, and two or more schoolage children (Hodgkinson, 1985). Teachers sent letters home addressed to "Dear Parents," reasonably confident that two parents would read them, and schools scheduled "Parent Conferences" with the expectation that parents were the primary caregivers of their children.

Times have changed. Consider this entry from the journal of a sixth-grade student teacher:

One boy in my class is very bright . . . but he never turned in assignments or participated in class discussions. He tended to annoy the students around him by doing strange things.

Two weeks ago he missed 2 days of school. Last week he missed 4. Some students saw him playing outside over the weekend, but he wasn't in school at all this week. There were no phone calls, and the social worker had to look into it.

His uncle came to school today and told us that the father dropped him off with the grandparents Monday and hasn't been heard from since. He is officially a "missing person." The mother lives in another state and doesn't want the boy. His parents apparently went through a very messy divorce. Now this boy is tossed around with no one who wants him. And we as teachers were concerned that he didn't do his spelling homework!

Stories like these have become all too common. The typical family of the 1950's now represents *less than 10 percent of our households* (Hodgkinson, 1985). The number of single-parent families has increased to a total of 9.7 million, almost all headed by women (Carlson, 1991), and more than half of the children born today will spend at least part of their childhood years in a one-parent home (O'Neil, 1991). The significant adults in many children's lives are not their parents at all, but grandparents, aunts, uncles, brothers, sisters, or neighbors (Davies, 1991). The "stay-at-home" mother is vanishing; indeed, in 1993, almost 60 percent of all children younger than six had mothers in the labor force (*The State of America's Children,* 1994). Many children come from non-English speaking homes, and their families are unfamiliar with schools in the United States (Epstein, 1988).

The changing nature of the American family has made communication and collaboration more difficult than ever. Nonetheless, research has found that it is *teachers' attitudes and practices—not the educational level, marital status, or work place of parents—that determine whether families become productively involved in their children's schooling* (Epstein, 1988). In other words, it's the teacher who makes the difference. For this reason, you must not only understand the barriers to parent involvement, you must also be aware of the ways that families and schools can work together.

OVERCOMING THE BARRIERS: FOSTERING COLLABORATION BETWEEN FAMILIES AND SCHOOLS

Providing cookies for bake sales, attending school plays and athletic events, showing up for parent conferences, signing and returning report cards—these are the traditional ways parents have been involved in their children's schooling. But families and teachers can collaborate in other ways as well. Joyce Epstein and her colleagues at Johns Hopkins University (Epstein, 1984; Epstein and Becker, 1982; Epstein and Dauber, 1991) have studied comprehensive parent involvement programs and have identified different types of family-school collaboration. Four of Epstein's categories provide a framework for our discussion.

Type 1: Helping Families to Fulfill Their Basic Obligations

This category refers to the family's responsibility to provide for children's health and safety, to supervise and guide children at each age level, and to build positive home conditions that support school learning and behavior (Epstein and Dauber, 1991). Schools can assist families in carrying out these basic obligations by providing workshops on parenting skills; establishing parent-support groups; holding programs on teenage problems (e.g., drug and alcohol abuse, eating disorders); communicating with families through newsletters, videotapes, and home visits; and referring families to community and state agencies when necessary.

Asking teachers to assume responsibilities for the education of *families,* in addition to the education of *children,* may seem onerous and unfair. Not surprisingly, some teachers hesitate to become "social workers," a role for which they are untrained (Olson, 1990). Others feel resentful and angry at parents who do not provide adequate home environments; in particular, teachers may "write off" parents who are poor and minority, believing these families cannot or will not assist in their children's education (Olson, 1990).

Although these attitudes are understandable, you need to remember that your students' home environments shape their chances for school success. As the number of distressed, dysfunctional families grows, assisting families to carry out their basic obligations becomes increasingly critical. Indeed, James Coleman, professor of education and sociology at the University of Chicago, notes:

> Traditionally, the school has needed the support and sustenance provided by the family, in its task of educating children. Increasingly, the family itself needs support and sustenance from the schools . . . in its task of raising children. (Olson, 1990, p. 20)

Furthermore, research on parent involvement indicates that *most families want to become more effective partners with their children's schools.* Epstein comments: "Our data suggest that schools will be surprised by how much help parents can be if the parents are given useful, clear information about what they can do, especially at home" (Brandt, 1989, p. 27). Although there are certainly a few families who cannot be reached, it appears that most parents are deeply concerned about their children's education; they simply do not know how to help.

What can you, as a teacher, realistically do to assist families in carrying out their basic obligations? Although you will probably not be directly involved in planning parent education workshops, writing newsletters, or creating videotapes, you can play an important, *indirect* role. You can let families know about available materials, motivate and encourage them to attend programs, bring transportation problems to the attention of appropriate school personnel, and help families to arrange car pools (Greenwood and Hickman, 1991).

In Carmen's school, parent support groups are available through EPIC—Effective Parenting Information for Children (Hayes, Lipsky, McCully, Rickard, Sipson, and Wicker, 1985). EPIC provides teachers with training and manuals designed to prepare children to become responsible adults. It also offers opportunities for families to get together to share concerns and to discuss topics like communicating with adolescents, discipline, resisting peer pressure, and home/school cooperation. A similar program, the Parent Involvement Corps (PIC), was established at Donnie's school some years ago. Designed for parents of ninth-grade students, the program was intended to welcome parents to school, to help them feel comfortable there, to teach parenting skills, and to inform parents of their rights. Although PIC was a one-year, grant-funded program, it led to the creation of a permanent Parent-Teacher Association, which the high school had sorely needed. If programs like EPIC and PIC exist in your school, you can make sure families are aware of them, even if you are not directly involved; if you see a family with special needs, you can alert school personnel involved in these programs about the situation.

You can also educate families about relevant community and state agencies. Donnie, for example, advises families who have no health insurance where they can obtain medical and dental attention. When it became clear that one of her students was bulimic (at prom time!), Donnie worked with the family to find an agency that could provide the necessary psychological and medical assistance.

In addition to playing this indirect assistance role, there are times when it may be appropriate to work *directly* with families. Fred reports that he often needs to provide parents with some perspective on "this unique creature called 'teenager': "They haven't had 150 kids, and it's often a revelation for them to learn that they're not the only parents having problems." Similarly, Sandy tells us that a lot of her interactions with parents involve helping them to communicate more effectively with their teenage children:

> Many times, I find that my discussions with parents begin with the problems their children are having in chemistry class, but move on to more general problems. You start talking about grades, and the next thing you know you're talking about curfews and dating. Many of the parents have no control over their 15- and 16-year-olds. They'll say to me, "I just don't know what to do. He or she is the same way at home. I'm at a loss." I acknowledge their frustration and the difficulty of working with teenagers. (It helps that I have teenagers too!) I tell them, "You're not alone. Many 15- and 16-year-olds behave

this way, and many parents feel this way." I try to provide some perspective and give them some tips about communication. I try to encourage them to set some limits. I find that a lot of parents don't like to set limits; they don't want confrontations with their kids, and they need encouragement to monitor what their kids are doing.

Sometimes I encounter overbearing parents who put too much pressure on their kids. Their expectations are unrealistic. Ninety-five on a test is not good enough; they want their child to have the highest test grade in the class. I tell them, "Wait a minute, we both want what's best for your child; we want him to work to his utmost ability, but utmost ability is not perfection on every test." I remember one situation, where a girl in my class was putting out very little effort. She got a 79 on the first test, which was far below her ability. After I spoke with her, she started working a lot harder, and her grade on the next test was 89. I told her how proud I was of her, and said something like, "Your parents must have been delighted." She got this funny look on her face, and I knew something was wrong. I found out that they had made only one comment: "Why wasn't it an A?" They didn't give her any praise at all. I decided I needed to speak with them about the situation. I told them, "Look, your daughter went from doing no work and getting a 79 to working hard and getting an 89, and you didn't even acknowledge the improvement. She's going to figure out that she might as well do no work and get 79's, since working hard and getting 89's doesn't get her any approval." I tried to help them see that as soon as they asked why she hadn't gotten an A, she was absolutely deflated. Parents like this need to understand the importance of acknowledging improvement, instead of holding out for the perfect grade.

Type 2: Fulfilling the Basic Obligations of Schools—Communicating with Families

Epstein's second category of family-school involvement refers to the school's obligation *to communicate about school programs and children's progress.* Communications include report cards and progress reports, memos and notes, open houses and parent-teacher conferences, and phone calls. This is certainly the most commonly accepted way to work with parents, and there is no doubt that these communications are essential. The crucial question, however, is not only whether these communications occur, but *when they occur, whether they are being understood, and whether they lead to feelings of trust and respect or alienation and resentment.*

All of the teachers stress the importance of communicating with parents in a way that promotes a feeling of partnership. Donnie comments:

Sometimes I see parents in the market, or in church, or downtown. When I do, I acknowledge them, and I invite them to call and talk about their children. I tell them, "We've got to work together. We're partners."

Fred echoes Donnie's message:

Sometimes teachers don't invite contact. They'll only call if there is a problem. But some parents need that initial encouragement. If you can make that initial contact, then the parent will usually continue the contact. It's important to make parents understand that you're both on the same side. You're both working in the best interests of the kid. When you make that clear, even the most irate parent turns into a pussy cat. I tell them, "Listen, everything I do is designed to be the best for your kid. But if you're concerned about something, let me know. Feel free to call." I tell my parents: "We need to work together as a team. And your kids need to know we're working together."

Research on family-school communication supports the importance of partnership. A study by Lindle (1989), for example, indicates that maintaining a professional, businesslike manner is not the best way to gain the respect and support of parents. In fact, parents view "professionalism" as *undesirable*; they express dissatisfaction with school personnel who are "too businesslike," "patronizing," or who "talk down to us." Rather than a professional-client relationship, parents prefer an equal partnership, characterized by a "personal touch." (Sometimes, partnership is threatened by the use of educational jargon that parents may find difficult to understand; see Figure 11-1.)

It is clear that Donnie, Carmen, Sandy, and Fred are able to establish productive partnerships with families, and the next few sections of this chapter describe some of the ways they do this. It should be noted, however, that as a "special" teacher, Carmen has considerably less contact with parents than the other teachers. If you are teaching a subject like art, music, physical education, or home economics, you too may find yourself less involved with parents than the teachers of core academic subjects.

Phone Calls   Given the hectic lives that people lead, one of the main problems about telephone calls is making the connection! At the beginning of the school year, all four teachers find out when and how to contact the families of their students. Some businesses have strict policies about employees' receiving phone messages, and a call during work hours may result in a reprimand. Some parents work at night, and a call in the morning will interrupt much needed sleep; others may not have a phone at all, and you'll need to send a note home asking them to call you. (Donnie and Sandy both send notes home in plain, white envelopes—without the school's return address. This way there is less chance that a wary teenager will remove the letter from the pile of mail before the parent ever sees it!) All of the teachers also let parents know when they can receive telephone calls during the school day. Donnie even gives parents her home phone number; she says that no parent has ever abused the information.

To get the information she needs, Sandy has her students fill out a card with their parents' home and work numbers on the first day of school. She also asks students to indicate if their parents are permitted to get telephone calls at work. In addition, when Sandy has to call a parent, she'll often make a "pre-call," asking when it would be a convenient time to call and reassuring the parent that there's no earth-shattering problem. She's especially careful about checking the school personnel records to see which parent should be contacted:

A majority of my students come from divorced homes. If the parents are not sharing joint custody, you cannot talk to the noncustodial parent. If the parents are sharing custody, then the record tells which parent the student is residing with, and I call that parent. Sometimes, the records will indicate if calls are to be made to both parents or if written communications are to be done in duplicate for both parents.

FRANK AND ERNEST®   By BOB THAVES

FIGURE 11-1
The use of educational jargon sometimes impedes communication. *(Frank & Ernest reprinted by permission of NEA, Inc.)*

Before calling a parent about an academic or behavior problem, Sandy always gives her students notice:

> I say something like, "I know you want to be treated like an adult, but sometimes we need to work together with mom or dad to ensure your success. We need some help here. We can't solve this alone." I never use the telephone call as a threat or punishment. And I always wait 24 hours before calling. That way, the student can tell the parent that the call is coming (or about how the 75 they said they got on the test was really a 55!). When I talk with parents, I'm really careful about how I phrase things, so that I don't promote a negative reaction. Instead of saying, "Your son is disrupting the class," I'll say something like "We have to help your son control his behavior so that he can learn some chemistry." If the kid is disrespectful, I'll say, "I'm calling you about this because I know you wouldn't approve of this. I know you'd want to hear." In this way, you're conveying the idea that the parent will be supportive of you and that you don't think the kid comes from a family that would approve of such behavior.

During one meeting, I asked the four teachers to share some of the ideas they have for ensuring telephone contacts with parents are productive. Here are their responses:

> When the office receives a telephone call for you from a parent, and you're in class, have the secretary ask when would be a good time to call back.

> Even if a call comes during your free period, have the office take the message and say you'll call back. That gives you time to shift gears and prepare for the call. You can check your record book so that you are familiar with the student's progress.

> If a parent is calling with a complaint, try very hard not to get defensive. Listen and try to understand the parent's frustration. Respond by expressing your concern and assuring the parent that you are really committed to finding a solution.

> If a parent calls to complain that a child is upset about something ("He says you're picking on him" or "She says you're embarrassing her in front of the class"), acknowledge the student's perception. Convey your regret that the student has that perception. For example: "Gee, I'm really sorry that she has that perception. What specifically has she said, so that I can figure out what's going on? Help me to understand, because I don't want her to feel that way." Don't start out defensively: "I don't pick on kids."

For chronic callers (parents who call three times a week) make it clear that it's important for you and the child to work the problem out. Explain that the frequent calls are embarrassing the student.

If the telephone call is difficult, and there's a danger of your becoming defensive, have another person in the room help monitor your tone of voice. He or she can tap you on the shoulder or make a face if you begin to get hostile or defensive.

If a parent is out of control, suggest that you talk again at a later time, so that you both have a chance to calm down.

If parents ask you to call every week with a report on their child's progress, suggest that they call you instead. (After all, you may have 150 students to think about, while they have only one!) Designate a day and time for them to call (e.g., on Fridays, during your prep period).

A few additional words of caution are in order. First, be careful about using telephone calls to discuss sensitive issues or problems. Talking on the telephone doesn't allow you to "soften" your messages with smiles, gestures, or body language; nor do you have access to parents' nonverbal language in order to judge reactions (Lemlech, 1988). For this reason, telephone calls are more likely to lead to misinterpretations than face-to-face interactions. Second, although it's important to contact parents about serious problems, frequent phone calls about minor misbehaviors can be annoying. Furthermore, the practice can convey the message to both parents and children that the school can't deal with problems that arise; it's like saying, "Wait till your parents find out!"

It's also important to emphasize that phone calls should not be reserved for problems. As Donnie reminds us:

Teachers shouldn't just call when there's something bad. It's really important to call parents to give good news, to say "Your kid is really doing well," to tell them about something terrific that happened. Sometimes, when I do that, the student will come in the next day and say, "You called my house! And you didn't say anything bad about me!" And I'll tell them, "I had nothing bad to say!" I'll also let parents know what's coming up, the things that are going on. If you do that, then you've laid the foundation for a good relationship, and parents are more open later on. If you do have to call about a problem, they're less likely to be hostile or defensive.

Report Cards   Report cards have been the traditional way of communicating with families about a child's progress in school. Unfortunately, they are often not very informative. What exactly does it mean when a student receives a C in Spanish? Is she having problems with vocabulary, with comprehension, or with conversation? Is another student's D in mathematics due to difficulties with problem-solving, or is it merely a result of careless computational errors? Since many high schools use computerized report cards, it is not always possible for the teacher to elaborate on grades with a personalized narrative. Donnie tells us:

On our report cards, you can pick from nine little statements, like "the student is disruptive," "comes late," "is doing well," "is working at or above grade level," "has missed tests." But you're only allowed to check two! And they're so impersonal, I'm not sure that they really communicate much of anything.

Another common problem with report cards is timeliness. If you rely solely on report cards to communicate with parents about a student's progress, two months might pass from the time a problem first appears until parents learn about it. In order to avoid this problem, some schools require teachers to send out progress reports midway through each marking period. Specific policies vary from district to district. Sandy explains what happens at Highland Park High School:

> Progress reports have to be sent out mid-marking period for all seventh and eighth graders. In grades nine through twelve, we only have to send home a progress report if a student is in danger of receiving a D or an F for the marking period, but I send them out for other reasons too, like attendance or behavior or for commendable progress. I also tell students that I'm sending a progress report home and I show it to them. I believe they have the right to know.

> Sometimes, showing students the progress reports encourages them to clean up their act. For example, Edward had a 75 average because he had two assignments missing. When I told him I was sending home a progress report, he asked me to just report the 75 average and leave off the part about the two missing assignments. He said his mother "would kill" him if she found out he wasn't doing his homework consistently. He promised he'd never miss another assignment. I decided he was serious, and so I agreed, but I told him that if she asked, I'd have to tell her. He never missed another assignment.

Although Sandy is conscientious about sending home progress reports, she also believes that any serious problems should be dealt with sooner:

> Teachers should not rely on progress reports to tell parents about serious problems. Teachers need to contact parents if a problem develops. All of my students' parents know if their child has a D or an F before progress reports. I send progress reports because I have to, but my parents already know. Relying on progress reports is not very smart, since probably 50 percent of the kids take them out of the mail before their parents ever see them!

Back-to-School Night   For many parents, open house or back-to-school night is the first opportunity to meet you and to see the classroom. It's also the first opportunity *you* have to show parents all the great things you've been doing and to tell them about the plans you have for the future. As Fred says,

> I always put on a show for back-to-school night. I feel good about what happens in my room, and I want the parents to feel good about what's happening, too. I outline my objectives and the course syllabus; I describe my expectations for kids and for parents, and I talk about what they can expect from them. I usually talk about why I teach history; I give a little propaganda speech about what I'm trying to accomplish and how they can help. But it's always been a fun night. I believe that the parents have to laugh, just like the kids. The bell always rings when I'm halfway through; there's never enough time, but I talk with the parents at the coffee hour afterwards.

If you don't feel quite as enthusiastic as Fred, don't feel bad. Even teachers as experienced as Sandy sometimes feel nervous about back-to-school night. In fact, Sandy tells us:

> I hate back-to-school night! The one good thing is that I always get so nervous that I talk really fast and finish early. That leaves plenty of time for people to ask questions.

Keep in mind that first impressions *do* matter, so you need to think carefully about how you will orchestrate this event. Here are some guidelines that emerged during my discussions with Donnie, Fred, Sandy, and Carmen:

> Greet people at the door, introduce yourself, and find out who they are. DO NOT AS-SUME THAT THE STUDENT'S LAST NAME IS THE SAME AS THE PARENTS' LAST NAME, OR THAT BOTH PARENTS HAVE THE SAME LAST NAME.

> Make sure your presentation is succinct and well organized. Parents want to hear about your goals, plans, and philosophy, as well as the curriculum and policies about home-work and absences.

> If parents raise issues that are unique to their child, let them know in a sensitive way that the purpose of open house is to describe the general program. Indicate that you're more than happy to discuss their concerns during a private conference. You may want to have a sign-up sheet available for this purpose.

> Listen carefully to questions parents have. Provide an opportunity for parents to talk about *their* goals and expectations for their children in the coming school year. This can begin the two-way communication that is so crucial for family-school collaboration.

> Provide a sign-up sheet for parents who are able to participate in classroom activities (e.g., as a guest speaker or chaperone on field trips).

> Display the books and materials used in your courses.

> If refreshments are being served after the class meetings, go and join in conversations with parents. Clustering with the other teachers separates you from parents and conveys the idea that there is a professional barrier.

> PREPARE!

Parent-Teacher Conferences   Schools generally schedule one or two formal parent-teacher conferences during the school year. (See Figure 11-2 for Calvin's reaction to the prospect of such a conference.)

Interestingly, these meetings are often a source of frustration to both teachers and parents. Parents resent the formality of the situation (Lindle, 1989) and find the limited conference period frustrating. As one mother puts it, "Ten minutes is ridiculous, especially when other parents are waiting right outside the door. I need time to tell the teacher about how my child is at home, too" (Lindle, 1989, p. 14).

Teachers, too, are sometimes unhappy with these formal conferences. They agree with parents that the brief time allotted often precludes meaningful exchange. Furthermore, teachers complain about the lack of attendance: "The parents you *don't* need to see show up, while the ones you desperately *want* to talk with don't

Calvin and Hobbes

by Bill Watterson

FIGURE 11-2
Parent-teacher conferences provide a way of communicating with families. *(Calvin and Hobbes © Watterson. Dist. by Universal Press Syndicate. Reprinted with permission. All rights reserved.)*

come." Interestingly, Donnie doesn't mind that the parents of good students come to parent conferences:

> If there's a real problem, I've already contacted the parents by the time parent conferences come along. We've already met. So I think it's nice to see the ones whose kids are doing well. It's nice to be able to give positive reports. And parents want reassurance that all is going well.

Before a conference, it's important to prepare carefully. For example, Sandy looks over each student's grades, computes a current average, notes any trends in academic performance or behavior, and jots down a few key words to use when she's talking to parents. It's also useful to have a few samples of students' work to show parents.

Conferences can be tense—especially if you're meeting with family members for the first time—so our four teachers begin by trying to put parents at ease. They suggest leading with something positive: "Your son is a delight to have in class" or "Your daughter appears to be really interested in the topics we've been studying." Next, problems or weaknesses can be broached—not as character flaws ("she's lazy"), but as problems that need to be solved ("She's having difficulty getting her assignments in on time. What can we do about this?"). Donnie puts it this way:

> I might tell parents, "We have a problem. Your son's performance is going down. Can you help me to understand? Is there anything going on that I should know about?" I stress that we have to work together. I explain that if I understand more about the home situation, then I'll know better how to approach the student. Maybe there's been a death in the family, or the father moved out, or a move is imminent. All this helps me to be more effective.

Sandy also tries to enlist parents' assistance in dealing with problems; however, she cautions teachers not to make demands that are impossible for parents to carry out:

> Don't say things like, "You have to get your child to participate more in class." Be reasonable. If you're talking about a 17-year-old senior, what are the chances that a parent can do that? On the other hand, you *can* say, "Joanne is very quiet in class. Is this her normal behavior?"

Although they try to provide parents with substantive information, our teachers emphasize the need *to listen.* All four teachers always allow time for parents to ask questions and to express their concerns, and they solicit parents' suggestions. A conference should be a two-way conversation, not a monologue. *It's also critical not to assume that poor parents, uneducated parents, or parents with limited English proficiency have nothing of value to offer.* One mother in the study by Finders and Lewis (1994) expressed her frustration this way:

> Whenever I go to school, they want to tell me what to do at home. They want to tell me how to raise my kid. They never ask what I think. They never ask me anything.

Finally, our teachers stress the importance of not closing doors to further communication. If a conference is not going well, you might suggest another meeting, perhaps with the department supervisor or a guidance counselor on hand to mediate the discussion.

In addition to these formally scheduled conferences, our teachers look for chances to have more casual face-to-face meetings. Sandy, for example, strikes up conversations with families at school plays, choir concerts, and football games. As Carmen walks to school, she frequently stops to talk with the parents and students she meets on the street. Donnie makes a point to chat with parents she meets at the supermarket and at church. Informal encounters like these can help break down the barriers that too often exist between families and teachers.

Type 3: Family Involvement in School

At the high-school level, most family involvement in school consists of attendance at student performances, athletic events, or other programs. Family involvement may also take place "behind-the-scenes"; for example, parents may engage in fundraising activities, interview prospective teachers and administrators, prepare breakfast on "Teacher Appreciation Day," participate on committees developing discipline and attendance policies, and chaperone social events.

Participation in classroom activities is far less common, but involving even a few parents can provide considerable support and enrich the curriculum. When Fred's Contemporary World Cultures classes study religions, for example, parents of different faiths come in to explain their religious beliefs; in his IPLE class, parents who are lawyers sometimes share their expertise; and his history classes may be visited by survivors of Nazi concentration camps. In Sandy's chemistry classes, parents speak on scientific or environmental issues; parents who are faculty members at Rutgers University have set up tours of the chemistry labs there. Donnie holds a "mini-career day," when successful, former students share their career experiences and communicate the message, "You can do this too."

If you decide to invite parents to participate in your classroom, you need to think carefully about how to recruit them. Sometimes parents don't volunteer simply because they're not sure what would be expected or how they could contribute. Back-to-school night offers a good opportunity to make a direct, in-person appeal and to explain the various ways parents can assist.

If you're teaching in a district where there has been little parent involvement in school, special efforts will be needed to change the situation. At Carmen's school, for example, a sit-down dinner was held on Back-to-School Night this year, in order to entice parents to come and to make them feel welcome. At New Brunswick High School, a committee has been established to consider ways of making the school more "parent-friendly." As a result of the committee's efforts, teams of teachers have visited neighborhood churches on Sunday mornings to invite parents to the high school. As Donnie puts it,

> Parents were complaining that they don't feel welcome. Well, the point of these trips is to say, "We want you to visit. This is *your* school; come in and see what's going on. If you can, volunteer, work in the library, help kids with homework. We welcome you.

Type 4: Family Involvement in Learning Activities at Home

Epstein's fourth type refers to the ways families can assist their children's learning at home (Epstein and Dauber, 1991). At the secondary level, this kind of involvement often creates considerable anxiety for parents. As Donnie mentioned earlier, some parents are scared off by the subject matter. Sandy agrees:

> At the elementary level, parents often help with homework, read to their children, and monitor their studying. But at the high-school level, the first thing out of a parent's mouth is "I can't do calculus. I can't do chemistry. There's no way I can help."

Parents are not the only ones who wonder how they can help with their teenagers' homework assignments. Some teachers also question whether parents can really be useful, given their "highly variable instructional skills" (Becker and Epstein, 1982, p. 86). Indeed, in a survey of teachers' attitudes toward parental involvement in learning activities at home (Becker and Epstein, 1982) about half of the 3,700 respondents had serious doubts about the success of such efforts. Furthermore, some teachers believe that it's unfair to ask already overworked parents to assume teaching responsibilities.

Although our four teachers acknowledge that parents may not have familiarity with the subject matter, they are convinced that parents can play an extremely important role by monitoring their children's schoolwork, providing support and encouragement, and setting limits. Fred tells us:

> I find that parents really want to help their kids, but they often don't have a clue about what to do. They're really receptive to suggestions. Sometimes I suggest that parents help by checking the spelling on their kids' papers. Maybe I'll suggest they check that the kid has done the homework. Maybe I'll explain the requirements for a research paper, and suggest they check to see the requirements are met. I'll suggest they ask to see the kid's papers. A lot of times kids put their papers in the garbage and never show them to their parents.

Similarly, Sandy tells parents not to worry if they don't know chemistry; they can still help to structure their child's environment:

If a kid is having trouble with chemistry, 99 percent of the time, the problem is not with the *subject,* but with the *time spent* on the subject. Parents can monitor the time spent on homework. They can say, "Doing chemistry in front of the TV is not working." They can say, "You have to do your homework before you go out." They can suggest that their child call a friend if they're having trouble. They can make sure their child comes in for help after school. I'll tell them, "I want your child in here two days a week so I can help with the chemistry. But you have to see that they get here."

It is important to recognize that this view of the parental role may conflict with some families' beliefs about the importance of independence and self-sufficiency. A mother in the study by Finders and Lewis (1994) explains why she stays out of her daughter's schooling:

It's her education, not mine. I've had to teach her to take care of herself. I work nights, so she's had to get up and get herself ready for school. I'm not going to be there all the time. She's gotta do it. She's a tough cookie. . . . She's almost an adult, and I get the impression that they want me to walk her through her work. And it's not that I don't care either. I really do. I think it's important, but I don't think it's my place. (p. 52)

As Finders and Lewis (1994) comment, "This mother does not lack concern for her child. In her view, independence is essential for her daughter's success" (p. 52).

CONCLUDING COMMENTS

In 1976, Ira Gordon (1976), a well-known advocate of parent education and involvement, wrote these words:

We believe, with good evidence, that virtually all parents want a better life for their children than they have had. . . . We know that parents, when properly approached, want to be involved in the education of their children. . . . We have found that parents, regardless of region, race, or economic status, respond when the school reaches out to them in positive, nonthreatening, nonscolding, nonmanipulative ways. (p. 10)

This chapter has described different ways that teachers can reach out to families. The suggestions vary considerably in terms of how common they are and how much time and energy they demand. As you get to know your students and their family situations, you will be able to decide which practices are most appropriate and most feasible.

As you consider the various alternatives, remember Gordon's message. This is an age of single parents, of mothers who work outside of the home, of grandparents, aunts, and neighbors who care for children, of increasing numbers of families whose cultural backgrounds differ from that of most teachers. Family-school collaboration has never been more difficult—but it has never been more important.

SUMMARY

This chapter began by discussing the benefits to working closely with families. I then examined the barriers to family-teacher cooperation and stressed that teachers' attitudes and practices—not the educational level, marital status, or work place of parents—determine whether families become productively involved in their children's schooling. Finally, I presented strategies for overcoming the barriers and for fostering collaboration between families and schools.

Benefits of Working Closely with Families

- Knowing about a student's home situation provides insight into the student's classroom behavior.
- When families understand what you are trying to achieve, they can provide valuable support and assistance.
- Families can help to develop and implement strategies for changing behavior.

Barriers to Family-Teacher Cooperation

- Teachers are sometimes reluctant to involve families in schooling because of:
    The extra time and energy that are required
    Their perceptions that families are too overburdened, apathetic and irresponsible, or lack the skills needed
    The level of authority and autonomy teachers enjoy within their classrooms
- Parents are sometimes reluctant to become involved in schooling because:
    They have unhappy memories of school
    They believe schooling should be left to the experts
    They feel guilty if their children are having problems
    They find schools intimidating and threatening places
- The changing nature of the family:
    The number of single parent families has increased
    The "stay-at-home" mother is vanishing
    The significant adults in children's lives may not be parents, but grandparents, neighbors, aunts, or uncles
    Many children come from non-English–speaking homes

Fostering Collaboration between Families and Schools

- Schools can assist families in carrying out their basic obligations by providing parent education, establishing parent-support groups, and referring families to community and state agencies.
- Teachers need to communicate about school programs and students' progress through memos and notes, phone calls, report cards, progress reports, and face-to-face interactions (e.g., Back-to-School Night, parent conferences).
- Family members can serve as volunteers in classrooms.
- Families can assist their children at home on learning activities:
    supervising homework
    providing encouragement and support
    setting limits

Like Ira Gordon, I believe most parents will be supportive and helpful if schools reach out to them in welcoming ways. In this age of single parents, mothers who work outside the home, and children who come from diverse cultural backgrounds, meaningful family-school collaboration has never been more difficult, but it has never been more important.

ACTIVITIES

1. In getting ready for the school year, you have decided to send a letter to the family of each student in your classes. The point of the letter is to introduce yourself, describe the curriculum, highlight a few upcoming projects, and explain your expectations in terms of homework, behavior, and attendance.

Select a subject you might actually teach (e.g., American History, Algebra I, Spanish, Home Economics I, World Literature, Physical Education, etc.), and write such a letter. As you write, think about the need to create a warm tone, to be clear and organized, to avoid educational jargon, and to stimulate interest about school.

2. Last week you conducted a parent conference with Mrs. Lewis, Joey's mother. During the conference you described his disruptive behaviors and what you've done to deal with them. You also explained that he is in danger of failing your class because he rarely does homework and has gotten poor grades on most quizzes and tests. Mrs. Lewis seemed to accept and understand the information; however, the next day, an irate *Mr.* Lewis called. He told you that he had never seen his wife so upset and that he wants another conference as soon as possible to get to the bottom of the problem. He also intimated that the problem might be due to a personality conflict between you and his son. Although the phone call caught you off-guard, you scheduled the conference for two days later.

Consider the following questions:

a. What will you do to prepare for the conference?

b. How will you structure the meeting so that you can state your information in a productive way without being defensive?

c. What sort of follow-up might you suggest?

3. Anita is extremely "forgetful" about doing homework assignments. She has received innumerable zeros and regularly has to stay for detention to make up the work. You have called her mother to report on this behavior and to ask for assistance, but her mother does not want to get involved. As she puts it, "I've got all I can do to handle her at home. What she does with school work is your responsibility!"

Interview two experienced teachers about what they would do in a case like this, and then formulate your own course of action based on what you learn.

REFERENCES

Becher, R. M. (1984). *Parent involvement: A review of research and principles of successful practice.* Washington, D.C.: National Institute of Education.

Becker, H. J., and Epstein, J. L. (1982). Parent involvement: A survey of teacher practices. *The Elementary School Journal, 83*(2), 85–102.

Brandt, R. (1989). On parents and schools: A conversation with Joyce Epstein. *Educational Leadership, 47*(2), 24–27.

Carlson, C. G. (1991). *The parent principle: Prerequisite for educational success. Focus 26.* Princeton, NJ: Educational Testing Service.

Davies, D. (1991). Schools reaching out: Family, school, and community partnerships for student success. *Phi Delta Kappan, 72*(5), 376–380, 382.

Epstein, J. (1984). *Effects on parents of teacher practices in parent involvement.* Baltimore: Johns Hopkins University, Center for Social Organization of Schools.

Epstein, J. L. (1988). How do we improve programs for parent involvement? *Educational Horizons,* 58–59.

Epstein, J. L., and Becker, H. J. (1982). Teachers' reported practices of parent involvement: Problems and possibilities. *The Elementary School Journal, 83*(2), 103–113.

Epstein, J. L., and Dauber, S. L. (1991). School programs and teacher practices of parent involvement in inner-city elementary and middle schools. *The Elementary School Journal, 91*(3), 289–305.

Finders, M., and Lewis, C. (1994). Why some parents don't come to school. *Educational Leadership, 51*(8), 50–54.

Froyen, L. A. (1992). *Classroom management: The reflective teacher-leader* (2nd edition). New York: Macmillan.

Gordon, I. J. (1976). Toward a home-school partnership program. In I. J. Gordon and W. F. Breivogel (Eds.), *Building effective home-school relationships.* Boston: Allyn and Bacon, 1–20.

Greenwood, G. E., and Hickman, C. W. (1991). Research and practice in parent involvement: Implications for teacher education. *The Elementary School Journal, 91*(3), 279–288.

Hayes, T. F., Lipsky, C., McCully, T., Rickard, D., Sipson, P., and Wicker, K. (1985). *EPIC—Effective parenting information for children.* Buffalo, NY: EPIC.

Haynes, N. M., Comer, J. P., and Hamilton-Lee, M. (1989). School climate enhancement through parent involvement. *Journal of School Psychology, 27,* 87–90.

Henderson, A. T. (1987). *The evidence continues to grow: Parent involvement improves student achievement.* Columbia, MD: National Committee for Citizens in Education.

Henderson, A. T., Marburger, C. L., and Ooms, T. (1986). *Beyond the bake sale: An educator's guide to working with parents.* Columbia, MD: National Committee for Citizens in Education.

Hodgkinson, H. (1985). *All one system: Demographics of education, kindergarten through graduate school.* Washington, D.C.: Institute for Educational Leadership.

Hoover-Dempsey, K. V., Bassler, O. T., and Brissie, J. S. (1987). Parent involvement: Contributions of teacher efficacy, school socioeconomic status, and other school characteristics. *American Educational Research Journal, 24*(3), 417–435.

Lightfoot, S. L. (1978). *Worlds apart: Relationships between families and schools.* New York: Basic Books.

Lindle, J. C. (1989). What do parents want from principals and teachers? *Educational Leadership, 47*(2), 12–14.

Menacker, J., Hurwitz, E., and Weldon, W. (1988). Parent-teacher cooperation in schools serving the urban poor. *Clearing House, 62,* 108–112.

Olson, L. (April 4, 1990). Parents as partners: Redefining the social contract between families and schools. *Education Week,* 17–24.

O'Neil, J. (1991). A generation adrift? *Educational Leadership, 49*(1), 4–10.

Power, T. J. (1985). Perceptions of competence: How parents and teachers view each other. *Psychology in the Schools, 22,* 68–78.

Rich D. (1988). Bridging the parent gap in education reform. *Educational Horizons, 66,* 90–92.

Rioux, J. W., and Berla, N. (1993). Innovations in parent and family involvement. Princeton Junction, NJ: Eye on Education.

The State of America's Children Yearbook, 1994. Washington, D.C.: Children's Defense Fund.

Vernberg, E. M., and Medway, F. J. (1981). Teacher and parent causal perceptions of school problems. *American Educational Research Journal, 18,* 29–37.

Walde, A. C., and Baker, K. (1990). How teachers view the parents' role in education. *Phi Delta Kappan, 72*(4), 319–320, 322.

Waller, W. (1932). *Sociology of teaching.* New York: John Wiley and Sons.

FOR FURTHER READING

Henderson, A. T., Marburger, C. L., and Ooms, T. (1986). *Beyond the bake sale: An educator's guide to working with parents.* Columbia, MD: National Committee for Citizens in Education.

Phi Delta Kappan (January 1991). Special section on parent involvement, J. L. Epstein (guest editor), 72(5).

Rich, D. (1987). *Teachers and parents: An adult-to-adult approach.* Washington, D.C.: National Education Association.

Strengthening partnerships with parents and community. (October 1989). *Educational Leadership, 47*(2).

Swap, S. A. (1987). *Enhancing parent involvement: A manual for parents and teachers.* New York: Teachers College Press.

Chapter Twelve
_____

Helping Students with Serious Problems

In Chapter Eleven, I described recent changes in the American family—the increase in the number of single parents, the vanishing "stay-at-home" mother, and the growing population of ethnic groups who do not speak English. I pointed out that these changes make it more difficult to achieve close family-teacher communication than in earlier years. But other societal trends will also affect you as a teacher. Consider these statistics:

> Poverty afflicts American children more than any other age group, with 22 percent of all children living below the poverty line (Children's Defense Fund, 1994); African-American children are particularly affected: 44 percent live in poverty (Joint Center for Political and Economic Studies, 1990; cited in O'Neil, 1991).

> Growing numbers of children are victims of physical conditions associated with learning problems—low birthweight, maternal smoking, prenatal alcohol exposure, prenatal exposure to drugs, lead poisoning, child abuse and neglect, and malnutrition (O'Neil, 1991).

> It is estimated that there are 28.6 million children of alcoholics in the United States; 6.6 million are less than 18 and most are enrolled in our schools (Newsam, 1992).

> The United States ranks first among industrialized nations in rates of teenage pregnancy; about 80 percent of teen mothers drop out of school (Reynolds, 1989).

> The number of children exposed to violence is increasing. In one survey of elementary school children on Chicago's south side, 26 percent reported having seen someone shot; 29 percent had witnessed a stabbing (O'Neil, 1991).

> One-fourth of all youngsters between the ages of 10 and 17 (a total of at least 7 million nationwide) are growing up in circumstances that limit their development, compromise their health, impair their sense of self, and thereby restrict their futures (Children's Defense Fund, 1994).

The message in these alarming statistics is clear: Large numbers of America's youth are at risk—for school failure, substance abuse, physical problems, psychological and emotional disorders, abuse and neglect, teenage pregnancy, and violence. (For a chilling picture of the plight of America's children, see Table 12-1.) Moreover, *when these youngsters come to school, their problems come with them.* This means teachers have to deal with issues that were unimaginable in an earlier era—issues that require knowledge and skills far beyond those needed to be an effective instructor.

How can you provide extra support for the at-risk students who may be in your classroom? *First, you need to be alert to the indicators of potential problems.* As an adult immersed in adolescent culture, you will probably develop a good idea of

TABLE 12-1
ONE DAY IN THE LIFE OF AMERICAN CHILDREN

3	children die from child abuse.
9	children are murdered.
13	children die from guns.
27	children—a classroomful—die from poverty.
30	children are wounded by guns.
63	babies die before they are one month old.
101	babies die before their first birthday.
145	babies are born at very low birthweight (less than 3.25 pounds).
202	children are arrested for drug offenses.
307	children are arrested for crimes of violence.
340	children are arrested for drinking or drunken driving.
480	teenagers get syphilis or gonorrhea.
636	babies are born to women who had late or no prenatal care.
801	babies are born at low birthweight (less than 5.5 pounds).
1,115	teenagers have abortions.
1,234	children run away from home.
1,340	teenagers have babies.
2,255	teenagers drop out of school each school day.
2,350	children are in adult jails.
2,781	teenagers get pregnant.
2,860	children see their parents divorce.
2,868	babies are born into poverty.
3,325	babies are born to unmarried women.
5,314	children are arrested for all offenses.
5,703	teenagers are victims of violent crime.
7,945	children are reported abused or neglected.
8,400	teenagers become sexually active.
100,000	children are homeless.
1,200,000	latchkey children come home to houses in which there is a gun.

Reprinted with permission of Childrens Defense Fund, from The State of America's Children Yearbook, 1994.

what typical teenage behavior is like. This allows you to detect deviations or changes in a student's behavior that might signal the presence of a problem. In *Teacher as Counselor: Developing the Helping Skills You Need* (1993), Jeffrey and Ellen Kottler suggest you learn to ask yourself a series of questions when you notice atypical behavior:

> What is unusual about this student's behavior?
> Is there a pattern to what I have observed?
> What additional information do I need to make an informed judgment?
> Who might I contact to collect this background information?
> What are the risks of waiting longer to figure out what is going on?
> Does this student seem to be in any imminent danger?
> Who can I consult about this case?

During one meeting, the teachers talked about how they try to be alert to problems their students might be experiencing. Carmen told us how she stands by the door when her classes enter, so that she can greet each student:

> I only see my kids 40 minutes a week, so I don't get to know them as well as their regular teachers do. I just don't have the continuous interaction that would allow me to detect subtle changes. Even so, I keep an eye out for problems. I look at the kids when they enter and while I'm taking attendance, and if I see someone who's upset or who looks funny, I'll make a mental note about it. Then, when everyone's working, I'll go over and ask, "Are you okay? Is there anything I can help you with?" Even if they say no, I still keep an eye on them. Later, I'll ask the classroom teacher if something's going on.

Sandy also watches her students carefully. Note how she tries to distinguish between problems that warrant immediate action and those that do not, and how she collects additional information:

> I watch for changes in students' behavior. If I see anything that looks like drug abuse, I report it immediately. If it doesn't seem like a drug problem, I generally approach the student and ask what's going on. If the kid seems depressed, I'll say something like, "Hey, you seem a little down today. Are you having a problem? Do you want to talk?" We all have bad days, and adolescents have wide swings of mood; it's the nature of the beast. A day or two of strange behavior doesn't necessarily mean there's a big problem. Adolescents aren't very good at masking their emotions, and most of the time they're upset because they had a fight with their mother, or the dog had to be put to sleep, or their boyfriend or girlfriend broke up with them. But if a kid is acting weird or seems depressed for longer than a few days, I check with other teachers to find out if they're seeing anything unusual too. If they've also noticed problems, I go to the principal or the vice-principal; often they know if something is going on at home. If there appears to be a real problem, I'll report it.

As Sandy's last comment suggests, *a second way you can help students with serious problems is to be informed about the various special services that are available and to know how to obtain access to those services.* Keep in mind these words of Maynard Reynolds, a leading special educator:

It is too much to ask that a beginning teacher know about all of the problems he or she will encounter in teaching; but it is not too much to ask that the beginning teacher recognize needs for support and assistance when challenging problems arise, and to understand that it is a sign of professionalism to seek help when needed rather than a sign of weakness. (Reynolds, 1989, p. 138)

Since specific resources and reporting procedures vary from district to district, it is essential that you learn about the special services in your own school and find out if there are special referral forms. Depending on the situation, you may want to consult with the principal or vice-principal, student assistance counselor, school social worker, substance awareness coordinator, nurse, guidance counselor, or member of a "core team" (a group of teachers, staff, student assistance personnel, and administrators who identify, refer, and support at-risk students experiencing problems). Some schools, like New Brunswick High School (where Donnie teaches), Roosevelt (where Carmen teaches), and South Brunswick High School (where Fred teaches), even have "School-Based Youth Services Programs" (SBYSP), centers in the school where outside agencies provide a wide variety of support services to students and their families. Gail Reynolds is the director of the SBYSP at New Brunswick High School. She explains about "School-Base":

We have five main programs in New Brunswick: counseling services—which include substance abuse programs; a teen parenting program; health screening and services; employment training; and recreation. Our largest service is the counseling program. We've got trained social workers and psychologists who work with the students who have the most difficult problems and who need longer term interventions than the guidance office could provide. We also run groups for kids who are acting out, who don't have any impulse control, who come from really chaotic families, who are really depressed.

In addition to the counseling, we provide health screening and services. We have a co-ordinator who's a social worker and a nurse right here in the school. They make assessments, refer kids to the Eric B. Chandler Health Center [a nearby health clinic] or to Planned Parenthood as needed, set up the appointments for them, and actually get the kids there and back.

In our teen parenting program, we run two groups—one on life skills preparation (getting ready for the world of work) and one on child development and parenting skills. We also have a child care center right here in the school that can accommodate up to 19 infants and toddlers; we have a van, and every morning we pick up the mothers and their babies and bring them here, and we bring them home every night.

Having all these programs right here in the school is the best way for us in New Brunswick. We found that if we have the programs off-site, the kids just don't follow through. We used to make referrals to a counseling center nearby and set up the appointment, but then the kid wouldn't go, so what good does it do? This way, the programs are immediately available to them. The kids are comfortable in school; they know you; they trust you. Of course, the down side is that a lot of kids are super sensitive about their friends seeing them come to School-Base. It's hard to maintain strict confidentiality in a school setting. But that's one reason why we have recreation and employment programs. We're trying to send the message that you don't have to have a problem to come here.

A third way of helping is to develop communication skills that will allow you to work more effectively with troubled or disaffected youngsters. Although your job is not to be a counselor or a therapist, you *can* learn to listen and to talk to students in ways that have been shown to be effective in counseling situations. Thomas Gordon, a clinical psychologist and author of *Teacher Effectiveness Training* (*T.E.T.*) (1974; see Chapter Six), emphasizes the importance of knowing how to talk with students who are experiencing problems:

> Talk can cure, and talk can foster constructive change. But it must be the right kind of talk. How teachers talk to their students will determine whether they will be helpful or destructive. The effective teacher, like the effective counselor, must learn how to communicate acceptance, must acquire some specific communication skills.

This chapter begins by examining some of the serious problems teachers may encounter in today's high schools—substance abuse, violence, abuse and neglect, eating disorders, and depression/suicide. We then move on to a discussion of the communication skills that you can use to help students who are experiencing problems. These skills include attending and acknowledging, active listening, asking open-ended questions, and problem solving. As you will see, this chapter not only describes the experiences of our four teachers, it also draws upon the wisdom of counselors who work directly with troubled students in each of the three districts, New Brunswick, Highland Park, and South Brunswick.

WHAT ARE THE PROBLEMS? AND WHAT CAN YOU DO?

Substance Abuse

After more than a decade of decline in the use of alcohol and other drugs by adolescents, the trend appears to be reversing. The facts are not encouraging (NJ Alcohol/Drug Resource Center and Clearinghouse, 1994):

> Nearly nine out of ten high school seniors report experimenting with alcohol; almost three out of ten have abused alcohol (i.e., consumed five or more drinks in a row at least once during the past two weeks).

> Three out of four adolescents report a pattern of regular drinking; nearly 100,000 children aged 10 or 11 report getting drunk once a week.

> Significant alcohol, inhalant, and cigarette use is reported as early as fourth grade, and alcohol experimentation increases from 6 to 17 percent between fourth and sixth grades.

As these statistics suggest, alcohol remains the number one drug of choice among adolescents. But there has been a sharp rise in marijuana use (which ranks second), and an increase in the use of stimulants, LSD, and inhalants (Center of Alcohol Studies, 1994). In fact, during the time I was writing this chapter, a front-page headline of *The New York Times* proclaimed: "Survey Reports More Drug Use By Teen-Agers" (Janofsky, December 13, 1994). The article cited a University of Michigan study of nearly 50,000 students from 420 high schools across the country. The findings? One in three seniors, one in four sophomores, and one in eight eighth graders said they had smoked marijuana at least once within the last year. These were all increases over the previous year's results. The study also found that the percentage of students at these grade levels who reported using cocaine, crack, hallucinogenic drugs, heroin, and stimulants at least once in the last year was marginally higher for the second consecutive year. (For a summary of the drugs most frequently used by teenagers, their street names, how they are taken, and their effects, see Table 12-2.)

In response to the growing problem of substance abuse, many schools have established Student Assistance Programs (SAPs) and have hired full-time Student Assistance Counselors (SACs). Note that the initials "SA" do *not* stand for Substance Abuse. The wording is deliberate. Although SAPs focus on identifying and helping students at risk for alcohol and other drug problems, they generally adopt a broad-based approach. There are two good reasons for this strategy. First, it's less stigmatizing to go to a Student Assistance Counselor than a Substance Abuse Counselor. Second, drug problems usually occur in conjunction with other problems—depression, abuse, academic difficulties, family problems, pregnancy (Gonet, 1994).

To a large extent, SACs rely on teachers to refer students who might be having problems with alcohol and other drugs or who might be at risk for such problems. But teachers may be particularly reluctant to make referrals about suspected drug use. Five different reasons for this reluctance emerged during my conversations with teachers and counselors. Carol Lowinger, the Student Assistance Counselor in Fred's school, believes that some teachers think drug use is just not all that serious:

> Some teachers have a tendency to minimize the situation—especially if it involves alcohol or pot. They just don't consider pot to be a "real" drug. They think, "Oh, all kids do this; it's not that big a deal."

In addition, Carol speculates that some teachers feel it's not their role to get involved, while others want to play the role of confidante:

> Sometimes, teachers are overwhelmed by all the responsibilities of teaching. They feel like they have more than enough to do without getting involved in students' personal problems. They tell themselves, "It's not my role to report this; I'm here to teach." But other times, teachers don't refer because they want to try to help the kid themselves. You know, a lot of teachers really like the role of mediator, caretaker, trusted confidante. They *like* the fact that a student is confiding in them about a problem, and sometimes they make a pact of confidentiality with the student: "You can tell me your secret. I won't tell anybody." But if the kid is in serious trouble, that can be a problem. First of all, they don't really have the training to help the way a counselor could. Second, they might be sending a message to the kid that it's not okay to go to a counselor or a mental health professional—and that's *not* a message we want to send. We want kids to see that we all need a variety of people in our lives, people who can help us in many different ways. We don't want kids to think that one person is all they need, and if they have the teacher they don't need to go to anybody else. Third, they could actu-

ally be serving as a "professional enabler"—they're allowing the kid to continue behavior that could be self-destructive. That's not helpful to the kid. What you've got to do is say to the kid, "I care too much about you to allow this to continue. We've got to get help for you."

Another reason for teachers' reluctance to refer is the belief that they are "turning kids in" when they would rather "give the kid a break" (Newsam, 1992). Sandy herself comments on this attitude:

> Some teachers are afraid to report suspected drug use because they don't want to create a hassle *for the kid.* They don't want to get the kid in trouble. They may also be afraid that reporting kids will ruin their relationship with students. But I haven't found that to be the case. Sometimes, the kid will come back and say, "Why did you do that?" But I say, "This is too big for us. We need more help." Sometimes, I'll even have kids come to tell me about a problem with a friend. They know I'll find help. *That's what they want.*

Finally, teachers may be reluctant to report suspected drug use because they are unsure about the indicators. Tonia Moore, the Student Assistance Counselor in Sandy's school, is very sensitive to this problem:

> Teachers tell me, "I have no idea what substance abuse looks like. It wasn't a part of my training. I wouldn't know when to refer a student." I tell them, that's okay. You can't tell substance abuse just by looking. There has to be a chemical screening. But you can see changes in behavior. You know enough about kids to know when somebody's behavior has changed, or if their behavior is different from all the other kids. You don't need to *know* the student is using; you just need to *suspect* that there may be drug use or a problem related to drug use.

What are the behaviors that might lead you to suspect drug use and to make a referral? Table 12-3 shows the behavior checklist used at South Brunswick High School. Many schools use forms very similar to this one. Keeping your school's behavior checklist handy can help you stay alert to the possibility that students are using drugs or living with addiction in their families.

It's important to distinguish between situations in which a pattern of behavior problems suggests possible *drug use outside of school* and situations in which a student appears to be *under the influence of drugs during school, at school functions, or on school property.* When you see students who might be "under the influence," you cannot wait to fill out a behavior checklist; you need to alert the appropriate personnel as soon as you possibly can. Fred shares this experience:

> A few years ago, I had this really bright kid in my first-period class. He was a star football player; he could have gone to college anywhere. But then he got into drugs. I remember one day in particular when he came into class high. I didn't realize it at first, because he just sat down quietly and everything seemed okay. But then he got up to sharpen his pencil, and I could see that he was walking funny. He was actually *leaning* to one side. It looked like he was going to fall over. I never saw anyone walk like that. I gave the rest of the class an assignment and asked him to come with me out into the hall. I tried to be really discreet; I didn't want everyone watching and talking about him. I planned to call a hall monitor, but the principal happened to be walking by just at that minute, so he took him to the nurse.

TABLE 12-2
COMMONLY USED DRUGS

Category	Name	Street name	How it's taken	Effects
Depressants	Alcohol (beer, wine, "hard liquor")		Swallowed	Depresses the central nervous system (CNS), slowing down bodily functions; decreases pulse and breathing; affects motor coordination and speech; diminishes ability to concentrate and impairs judgment; lowers inhibitions; chronic, heavy use can damage nearly every organ and system in the body
	Barbiturates and tranquilizers	*Barbiturates:* barbs, barbies, blues, candy, courage pills, dolls, downers, goofballs, reds, sleepers, yellow jackets; *Tranquilizers:* downers, sleepers, tranks	Swallowed, injected	Depress the CNS; relax muscles; slow breathing; lower blood pressure; produce drowsiness; may produce relaxation and feeling of well being; may lead to poor judgment, lack of motivation, and concentration
	Inhalants (aerosols, gases, solvents, amyl and butyl nitrite)	gas, glue, poppers, rush, laughing gas	Inhaled	Depress the CNS; produce alcohol-like effects—a loss of inhibitions, slurred speech, lack of coordination, weakness, giddiness, and slowed reflexes; may cause confusion and mood swings; some inhalants cause delusions and hallucinations
Stimulants	Amphetamines and diet pills	Uppers, speed, crank, meth, crystal, glass, bennies, Black Beauties, pep pills	Swallowed or injected. "Ice," one of the strongest amphetamines, is smoked in a pipe.	Stimulate the nervous system; speed up heart and breathing rates; raise blood pressure; decrease appetite; increase alertness; may produce sleeplessness, dizziness, anxiety, excitability, hallucinations; interfere with vision, judgment, and coordination

	Drug	Slang/Names	How Used	Effects
	Cocaine and crack (cocaine already in smokeable form)	"C," coke, cola, flake, gold dust, rock, snow, white, stardust	*Cocaine:* sniffed or snorted; can also be injected into veins; *Crack:* smoked	Stimulate the primary central nervous system; similar to the effects of amphetamines; initially, can lead to feelings of euphoria, alertness, increased mental energy, and sense of well being; dependence can lead to loss of energy, insomnia, sore throat, nosebleeds, headaches, sinus problems and runny nose, lost sex drive, trembling, nausea, constant licking of lips, sniffling of nose
Hallucinogens	LSD: psilocybin (found in mushrooms); PCP (synthetic); mescaline (found in peyote cactus buttons); LSA (found in some morning glory seeds)	*LSD:* acid, barrels, blotters, flats, Lucy in the sky with diamonds, mellow yellow, sugar cubes; *Mescaline:* mesc, buttons, moon; *PCP:* angel dust, cyclones, ozone; *Psilocybin:* magic or sacred mushrooms	Usually swallowed, but can also be inhaled, smoked, and injected	Increase pulse and heart rate; increase blood pressure and temperature; may cause nausea, chills, convulsions; affect perceptions and judgment; may cause hallucinations; affect moods (may feel excited, peaceful, panicky)
	Marijuana (a very mild hallucinogen; the psychoactive ingredient in THC, tetrahydro-cannabinal); hashish is a more potent form of marijuana	pot, grass, tea, mary jane, weed; a marijuana or hashish cigarette—reefer, joint, roach (butt of a joint)	Typically smoked in cigarette form; can also be sprinkled in food and ingested	Increase in heart rate, reddening of eyes, dryness in mouth and throat; temporary impairment of short-term memory; alters sense of time, reduces ability to concentrate; feelings of euphoria and relaxation

TABLE 12-3
THE REFERRAL FORM USED IN SOUTH BRUNSWICK

STUDENT ASSISTANCE PROGRAM
BEHAVIOR CHECKLIST

The goal of the Student Assistance Program is to help students who may be experiencing problems in their lives. These problems can be manifested in school through any combination of behaviors. The following is a list of typical behaviors students having problems may exhibit. While most students engage in many of the behaviors at one time or another, the student who may be having trouble will show a combination or pattern of these behaviors.

Student:_____   Grade:_____

Staff
Member:_____   Date:_____

Academic Performance
____Drop in grades
____Decrease in participation
____Inconsistent work
____Works below potential
____Compulsive overachievement
    + (preoccupied w/ school success)

School Attendance
____Change in attendance
____Absenteeism
____Tardiness
____Class cutting
____Frequent visits to nurse
____Frequent visits to counselor
____Frequent restroom visit
____Frequent request for hall passes

Social Problems
____Family problems
____Run away
____Job problems
____Peer problems
____Constantly borrowing money
____Relationships problems

Physical Symptoms
____Staggering/stumbling
____Incoherent
____Smelling of alcohol/marijuana
____Vomiting/ nausea
____Glassy, bloodshot eyes/dark
____Poor coordination
____Slurred speech
____Deteriorating physical appearance
____Sleeping in class
____Physical Injuries
____Frequent physical complaints
____Dramatic change in musculature

Extracurricular Activities
____Lack of participation

____Increasing noninvolvement
____Decrease in motivation
____Dropping out missing practice(s)
____Not fulfilling responsibilities
____Performance changes

Disruptive Behavior
____Defiance of rules
____Irresponsibility, blaming, lying, fighting
____Cheating
____Sudden outburst, verbal abuse
____Obscene language, gesture
____Attention-getting behavior
____Frequently in wrong area
____Extreme negativism
____Hyperactivity, nervousness
____Lack of motivation, apathy
____Problem with authority figures

Atypical Behavior
____Difficulty in accepting mistakes
____Boasts about alcohol/or drug use, "partying bravado"
____Erratic behavior
____Change of friends
____Overly sensitive
____Disoriented
____Inappropriate responses
____Depression
____Defensive
____Withdrawn/difficulty relating
____Unrealistic goals
____Sexual behavior in public
____Seeking adult advice without a specific problem
____Rigid obedience
____Constantly seeks approval

Other
____Students talking about alcohol or other drugs

TABLE 12-3 (continued)
THE REFERRAL FORM USED IN SOUTH BRUNSWICK

____Possession of drugs/alcohol or other drugs

____Involvement in thefts and assaults

____Vandalism

____Talking about involvement in illegal activities

____Possession of paraphernalia

____Having beeper

____Bragging about sexual exploits

____Mentions concerns about significant other's alcohol or other drug use, gambling

____Staff knowledge of addiction in family

Additional Comments:

In New Jersey, teachers are legally required to report "as soon as possible" a student who appears to be under the influence of drugs. Tonia Moore explains one of the reasons for mandating an immediate response:

> It used to be that teachers would come to me at the end of the day and say, "I was really worried about X today. I think he was really on something." That's no good. *I need to know at the time.* After all, that student could fall down the stairs, or the student could leave the building during lunch time and get killed crossing the street. *We have to deal with the problem immediately.* It can really be a matter of life and death.

Make sure you know to whom you're supposed to refer students who appear to be under the influence of drugs. In Fred's school, teachers call the assistant principal, who comes to the classroom and accompanies the student to the nurse. In Sandy's school, teachers send students to the nurse, who then contacts the Student Assistance Counselor. In Donnie's school, teachers call a security guard who takes the student to the nurse.

Since you cannot be sure that a student is using drugs just by looking, it's important not to be accusatory when you talk with the student. Sandy describes how she usually handles this situation:

> If I see a kid with his head down on the desk, I'll go over and ask real quietly, "Do you need to see the nurse?" Usually they'll say, "No, I'm just tired," or "No, I'm bored." I'll tell them, "But this is chemistry! This is supposed to be fun." Usually, the head stays up after that. But if the head goes back down, I'll say, "I think you need to see the nurse. You don't seem to be feeling well." I'm not confrontational, and I try to show the kid that I'm acting out of concern. Sometimes I'm wrong, and it turns out that the kid just stayed up until 4:00 A.M doing a term paper. That's fine. It's better to err on the side of caution.

Making a referral can be difficult, but you need to remember that turning away and remaining silent can send the message that you condone the behavior—or that you don't care enough to do anything. You also need to remember that referral is not the end of your responsibility. Listen to Fred:

> The referral is not the end of your job. You still have to stay involved. I try to let the kid know that he can come and talk to me. But I also let him know that I care enough not to tolerate drugs in my class, that I won't cut him any slack, and that I won't make excuses for him.

Violence

Stories about kids shooting other kids, about stabbing incidents, and about teachers being killed in the crossfire are appearing in newspapers with increasing frequency—and the stories are supported by studies of school violence. In a study of 720 public school districts conducted by the National School Boards Association (1994; see Portner, 1994), 82 percent of the districts reported that school violence had increased in the past five years. Furthermore, the report indicated that violence is no longer confined to schools in inner cities, but affects rural and suburban districts as well. For many youngsters, schools are still the safest place in their lives, but "for many, the symbol of the little red schoolhouse as a safe haven has been replaced by the yellow and black sign, Danger Zone" (Curcio and First, 1993).

Violence in schools—fights, assaults, and threats—is often related to drug use, and both violence and drug use may be related to the presence of gangs. According to Donnie, gang activity in New Brunswick was intense about five years ago, when the city's adolescents were divided into "uptown" and "downtown" gangs:

> What you saw was that the kids who lived in the projects stayed together and kept up a feud with the kids on the other side of Livingston Avenue. They'd fight about drugs, about somebody from one side of town going out with a girl from the other side of town, about somebody "ratting" on somebody else. Whenever there was a gang fight over the weekend or at night, the kids would all come in buzzing the next day. One year, a kid got killed in a gang fight, and there was a tremendous amount of tension that spilled over into the school. It would simmer down, and then every year, there'd be a big memorial to him that would re-kindle all the trouble. But it seems as if the main kids who were involved have moved on. Things have been a lot quieter the last few years.

Although many schools and districts deny gang presence, educators who have studied gangs (Goldstein, Harootunian, and Conoley, 1994; Lal, Lal, and Achilles, 1993) report that gang activity has infiltrated schools throughout the country. Indeed, Kodluboy and Evenrud (1993) contend that "gang activity is present within the boundaries of virtually every major school district in America" (p. 257).

It's not easy to identify a gang, since teenagers frequently "run in packs" and try to look and act just like everyone else. Nonetheless, there are some indicators that can help you decide if gangs are present in your school. These are summarized in Table 12-4. In addition, remember that the key to gang activity is negative behavior. Kenneth Trump, coordinator of the Youth Gang Unit of the Cleveland Public Schools, explains:

> Kids who sit together in the lunch room don't constitute a gang. But when groups start assaulting other students or creating an atmosphere of fear and intimidation, they become a gang. In short, groups of students reach gang status when their behavior, either individually or collectively, is disruptive, antisocial, or criminal. (1993, p. 40)

How can you, as an individual teacher, cope with school violence? Unfortunately, there's no easy answer, but it helps to think in terms of prevention, intervention, and reporting. Obviously, the best approach is to prevent violence by creating an atmosphere of respect, order, and community. During one conversation with

TABLE 12-4
SIGNS OF GANG PRESENCE
(ADAPTED FROM LAL, LAL, AND ACHILLES, 1993)

Gathering or hanging out:	Gang members may establish territory (e.g., in the lunch room, on playing fields, and in bleachers). Once these areas are claimed, other students will stay away.
Nonverbal and verbal signs:	Gang members often have special ways of signaling one another and conveying messages: "Flashing"—the use of finger and hand signs "Monikers"—nicknames emphasizing a member's particular attribute (e.g., "Shooter" uses a gun well; "Lil Man" is short)
Graffiti:	Signs, symbols, and nicknames on notebooks, papers, clothing, and walls; graffiti advertises the gang and its members and may contain challenging messages to other gangs; when graffiti is crossed out, that constitutes a direct challenge from a rival gang.
Stance and walk:	Unique ways of standing and walking that set them apart: "Standing duck-footed"—feet are pointed outward "Holding up the wall"—leaning back with one hand in the pocket and one foot against a wall
Symbols:	Tatoos, earrings, colors, scarves, bandannas, shoelaces, caps, belts (change over time)

Fred, he emphasized this point:

> I think we've been pretty successful at creating a sense of community in this school. I worked on a committee of kids, teachers, and parents that met about a year-and-a-half ago to come up with a statement of beliefs, a set of expectations for living in a civil society. [See Table 12-5.] We said, "If you don't hold to these, then you are not a member of this community." They're not really rules, they're the standards we hold to as members of a community. When somebody violates those standards, we don't just say "you were fighting and that's a bad thing," but "you violated the standards of the community."
>
> I think this statement has really helped a lot. There's not a lot of fighting here, and we've got 1300 people crowded into a building that was meant to house a lot less. We've also had committees of parents, kids, and teachers work on resolving racial and ethnic problems. The message is clear: We're a community, and we need to learn to live together peacefully and civilly.

Another violence prevention effort that is being tried in all three districts is the establishment of SAVVY programs—Students Against Violence and Victimization of Youth. Since 1992, SAVVY has trained high school students in violence-prevention skills that they then teach to third, fourth, and fifth graders. One hope is that by the time these youngsters get to high school, they will have developed nonviolent

TABLE 12-5
SOUTH BRUNSWICK HIGH SCHOOL'S STATEMENT OF BELIEFS

SOUTH BRUNSWICK HIGH SCHOOL
Statement of Beliefs

South Brunswick High School is a learning community that exists to serve the needs of each individual student within a group setting. To support the proper learning environment, we, the staff and students, acknowledge the importance of the following statements that connect us to each other.

As a citizen of South Brunswick High School, I will:

1 Support each person's right to learn.
2 Be courteous and considerate to other people.
3 Refrain from labeling individuals and groups.
4 Accept the fact that we are all unique individuals with similarities and differences.
5 Avoid physical fighting, verbal assault, and will not encourage these behaviors in other people.
6 Treat others with respect.
7 Take responsibility for my own choices.

U.S. Department of Education Blue Ribbon School Award 1990–1991.

ways of resolving their conflicts. Another hope is that the high school students involved with the program will also develop some new ways of thinking about and responding to violence.

For the last several years, New Brunswick and South Brunswick have run a collaborative program, bringing high school students from both districts together for the training. But Gail Reynolds admits that it's not easy to get New Brunswick High School students committed to this program:

> It's hard to get the New Brunswick kids involved because they don't really buy the concept of nonviolence. This year only six kids have stuck with the training; we had hoped for a lot more. I think programs like this have to start earlier, so kids can see nonviolence as a real alternative. That's one of the potential benefits of SAVVY—it allows us to get to the younger kids.

Another violence-prevention effort that has become increasingly popular in recent years is peer mediation (Miller, 1994; Smith, 1993). Designed to help students learn to resolve conflict in nonviolent, constructive ways, these programs are operated by students who are trained to mediate disputes between other students. Mediators do not hand down solutions, but guide the disputants to negotiate their own solutions. So far, anecdotal evidence suggests that peer-mediation programs can substantially reduce violent incidents. Some researchers, however, believe that peer mediation has more impact on the *mediators* than on the antagonists (Miller, 1994). If this is so, it means that high-risk students—not just the "good kids"—must be trained and used as mediators.

In addition to learning about or becoming involved in long-term prevention efforts like these, teachers can help to prevent violence by being observant, especially in hallways, cafeterias, stairwells, and locker rooms—areas where violence is most likely to erupt. Chester Quarles, a criminologist who specializes in crime prevention, suggests that teachers attempt to make eye contact whenever they pass students in the halls:

> The subliminal message being exchanged is that "I know who is here and I know who you are. I can remember your features. I can identify you." The influence of careful observation is a strong criminal deterrent for everyone that you observe. . . . Observant teachers . . . can decrease the probability that any of the people they encounter will commit a delinquent act against another that day. (1989, pp. 12–13)

Despite efforts at prevention, school violence does occur—and sometimes it occurs right in front of you. What do you do if you're on the scene when a fight erupts? I asked the teachers that question one evening, as we talked about the increasing incidence of violence in schools. They were unanimous in their response:

1. *Get help.* All four teachers stressed the importance of immediately calling for other teachers and for the principal or vice-principal. Once other people are there to help, it's easier—and safer—to get the situation under control.

2. *Tell students to stop.* Often, students don't want to continue the fight, and they'll respond to a verbal command. But sometimes, they're too out of control. Then it's necessary to go to Step 3.

3. *Intervene physically*—but *only* if the age, size, and number of combatants indicate that it's safe to do so, and when there are three or four people to help.

4. *Disperse other students.* There's no need for an audience, and you don't want onlookers to become part of the fray.

As we discussed the issue of fighting in school, the teachers repeatedly stressed the fact that *fights are fast.* They can erupt quickly—so you don't have a lot of time to think through a response—and they're usually over in less than 30 seconds (although that can seem like a lifetime). Interestingly, there was also amazing unanimity among the teachers on the issue of fights among girls versus boys. As Carmen put it: "Teachers shouldn't think that fighting is only going to happen among boys. Girls fight too—and girl fights are terrible. Girls kick, pull earrings, bite, scratch, and when you try to stop it, they turn on *you.*"

Finally, it's important to remember that you must report violent acts. Every school system needs to have a violent-incident reporting system that requires you to report what happened, when and where it happened, who was involved, and what action was taken (Blauvelt, 1990). Remember that assault and battery, possession of a weapon on school property, and vandalism are *crimes*—not just violations of school rules—and they must be reported to the police (Blauvelt, 1990).

Abuse and Neglect

During one conversation with Carmen, she emphasized the difficulty of detecting abuse and neglect among older students:

> Older kids hide their problems more than younger kids. If you ask about a bruise, they're likely to say they were in a fight at school or they fell. I think they don't want to "tattle" on their families. They feel like they have to be loyal.

In a similar vein, Donnie comments:

> At the high-school level, abuse and neglect are not as obvious as they are at the elementary level. Kids cover up more. But it's clear that a lot of them live in situations that are really awful. Teachers have to watch really carefully and listen to all the conversations that you're not supposed to hear. That way you can learn about what's going on in kids' lives and in the community.

As Donnie and Carmen point out, abuse of adolescents is often well hidden. Furthermore, adolescents just don't seem as vulnerable as younger children: they may have as much strength or weight as adults; they seem able to run away from abusive situations; and they appear to have more access to potential help outside the family (Tower, 1987). For these reasons, it's easy to think that abuse and neglect are not problems at the high-school level. But adolescents still need protection. Consider the following situation, which Donnie shared during one meeting:

> A number of years ago, I had a 16-year-old football player in my class. I noticed that he seemed really quiet, which was unusual for him. I asked him to come see me after school. When he came in, I said, "You don't seem yourself. Is everything okay?" To my amazement, he started to cry. It turned out he had been seduced by a 35-year-old woman living next door. Obviously, she didn't tie him down, but having sex with a minor constitutes sexual abuse. It was the last thing I expected. I figured he had broken up with his girlfriend, or he was having a problem on the football team. I was really hit between the eyes, and I was furious. I kept thinking, "How could she do that? He's just a kid." I had difficulty thinking straight. I thought, "Now what do I do?" I was the first person he had told. It was after school, and the psychologist was gone, the counselor was gone. But I convinced him to go with me to the principal. The office took over from there.

It has been estimated that almost two million school-age youngsters are victims of child abuse and neglect each year (Parkay and Stanford, 1992). In order to protect these youth, most states have laws requiring educators to report suspected abuse to the state's "child protective service." Although definitions of abuse vary, states generally include nonaccidental injury, neglect, sexual abuse, and emotional maltreatment. It is essential that you become familiar with the physical and behavioral indicators of these problems. (See Table 12-6.)

Teachers are often reluctant to file a report unless they have absolute proof of abuse. They worry about invading the family's privacy and causing unnecessary embarrassment to everyone involved. Nonetheless, it's important to keep in mind that *no state requires the reporter to have absolute proof* before reporting. What most states do require is reasonable "cause to suspect" or "belief" that abuse has occurred (Michaelis, 1993). If you are uncertain whether abuse is occurring, but have reasonable cause, you should err in favor of the youngster and file a report. Waiting for proof can be dangerous; it may also be illegal. If a child is later harmed, and it becomes clear that you failed to report suspected abuse, both you and your school district may be subject to both civil and criminal liability (Michaelis, 1993).

It's also important to learn about the reporting procedures in your state (*before* you are faced with a situation of suspected child abuse). Some states, like New Jersey, require teachers to file a report directly to the state's child protective service in order to avoid unnecessary delays. Other states allow teachers to report the suspected abuse to a school administrator or a nurse who then makes the actual call.

States also vary with respect to the form and content of reports required. Generally, however, you should be prepared to provide the student's name, age, address, and sex; the parents' names and addresses; the nature and extent of injury or condition observed; evidence of prior injuries; and your own name and telephone number (Tower, 1987).

This variation underscores the importance of becoming familiar with the procedures and resources in your own school. The best way to do this is to speak with people who can provide guidance and direction—experienced teachers, the principal, the school nurse, members of the Core Team, and the Student Assistance Counselor.

Eating Disorders

During a visit to one of Fred's honors classes in late April, I was shocked by the emaciated appearance of one of his female students, Sara. Her eyes and cheeks were sunken in, and her arms looked like twigs. I couldn't take my eyes off her. After class, Fred shared the story:

> This kid is a straight A student—she'll probably be valedictorian or salutatorian of her class. Everything she does is perfect. I don't think she's ever gotten less than 100 on any test or assignment I've given. And she's a fantastic soccer player. As a matter of fact, she's being recruited by a number of schools that want her to play soccer. To me, it looks like she couldn't even kick the ball. But I know that she practices every day, and she runs too.
>
> A couple of Sara's friends have come to talk with me after school—they're worried about her too. They say that she insists she's fat and that she hardly eats. She seems to be particularly obsessed about not eating anything with fat in it—no pizza, no cheese, no cakes or cookies, and, of course, no meat of any kind. Apparently, all they ever see her eat is bagels and lettuce!
>
> I've talked with Sara—I've told her that I'm really worried about her, but she insists that she's fine and that everyone's overreacting. I've also reported the situation to the school psychologist and the SAC [Student Assistance Counselor], and I know that they've called Sara's parents. I even called her parents myself. But her parents don't acknowledge that there's a problem. It's just so sad, but what else can we do?

Given our society's obsession about thinness, it's not surprising that teenage

TABLE 12-6

PHYSICAL AND BEHAVIORAL INDICATORS OF CHILD ABUSE AND NEGLECT

Type of child abuse or neglect	Physical indicators	Behavioral indicators
Physical abuse	Unexplained bruises and welts: —on face, lips, mouth —on torso, back, buttocks, thighs —in various stages of healing —clustered, forming regular patterns —reflecting shape of article used to inflict (electric cord, belt buckle) —on several different surface areas —regularly appear after absence, weekend or vacation Unexplained burns: —cigar, cigarette burns, especially on soles, palms, back or buttocks —immersion burns (sock-like, glove-like, doughnut shaped on buttocks or genitalia) —patterned like electric burner, iron, etc. —rope burns on arms, legs, neck or torso Unexplained fractures: —to skull, nose, facial structure —in various stages of healing —multiple or spiral fractures Unexplained lacerations or abrasions: —to mouth, lips, gums, eyes —to external genitalia	Wary of adult contacts Apprehensive when other children cry Behavioral extremes: —aggressiveness —withdrawal Frightened of parents Afraid to go home Reports injury by parents
Physical neglect	Consistent hunger, poor hygiene, inappropriate dress Consistent lack of supervision, especially in dangerous activities or long periods Constant fatigue or listlessness Unattended physical problems or medical needs Abandonment	Begging, stealing food Extended stays at school (early arrival and late departure) Constantly falling asleep in class Alcohol or drug abuse Delinquency (e.g., thefts) States there is no caretaker
Sexual abuse	Difficulty in walking or sitting Torn, stained or bloody underclothing Pain or itching in genital area Bruises or bleeding in external genitalia, vaginal or anal areas Venereal disease, especially in pre-teens Pregnancy	Unwilling to change for gym or participate in PE Withdrawal, fantasy or infant behavior Bizarre, sophisticated, or unusual sexual behavior or knowledge Poor peer relationships Delinquent or run away Reports sexual assault by caretaker

TABLE 12-6 (continued)

PHYSICAL AND BEHAVIORAL INDICATORS OF CHILD ABUSE AND NEGLECT

Type of child abuse or neglect	Physical indicators	Behavioral indicators
Emotional maltreatment	Habit disorders (sucking, biting, rocking, etc.) Conduct disorders (antisocial, destructive, etc.) Neurotic traits (sleep disorders, speech disorders, inhibition of play) Psychoneurotic reactions (hysteria, obsession, compulsion, phobias, hypochondria)	Behavior extremes: —compliant, passive —aggressive, demanding Overly adaptive behavior: —inappropriately adult —inappropriately infant Developmental lags (physical, mental, emotional) Attempted suicide

Source: Child Abuse and Neglect: A Professional's Guide to Identification, Reporting, Investigation and Treatment. Trenton, NJ: Governor's Task Force on Child Abuse and Neglect, October 1988.

girls often become concerned about body image. But Sara's intense preoccupation with losing weight goes way beyond ordinary concern. Sara seems to suffer from *anorexia nervosa,* an eating disorder that generally begins during adolescence and primarily afflicts white females, although it's increasing among black females and does occur among males (Gonet, 1994). Anorexic adolescents literally starve themselves; even so, they continue to feel fat and may actually perceive that they are becoming heavier. Sara's involvement in running and soccer is also typical; in an attempt to lose weight more quickly, anorexics may combine excessive physical exercise with dieting.

Another eating disorder is *bulimia nervosa,* in which individuals starve themselves, then binge (often on high-calorie or high-sugar foods), and finally purge themselves (by inducing vomiting). Individuals with bulimia may be underweight, overweight, or average, but they share an intense fear of gaining weight. They may also feel they have lost control over their lives; thus, they seek to control their eating and their weight (Gonet, 1994).

Of the two eating disorders, bulimia is more common, while anorexia is more severe and can actually be fatal. But both are long-term illnesses that require treatment; they will not go away by themselves. This means you need to be alert to the signs of eating disorders and report your concern to the appropriate person in your school. Too often, teachers overlook eating disorders, since concern about weight is a "normal pathology" in our society. Furthermore, the young women who most frequently suffer from eating disorders are often good students who cause no problems in class. Naomi Wolf, author of *The Beauty Myth* (1991), recalls how no one in her school tried to intervene when she was an anorexic teenager:

There were many starving girls in my junior high school, and every one was a teacher's paragon. We were allowed to come and go, racking up gold stars, as our hair fell out in fistfuls and the pads flattened behind the sockets of our eyes. . . . An alien voice took mine over. I have never been so soft-spoken. It lost expression and timbre and sank to a monotone, a dull murmur the opposite of strident. My teachers approved of me. They saw nothing wrong with what I was doing, and I could swear they looked straight at me. My school had stopped dissecting alleycats, since it was considered inhumane. [But] there was no interference in my self-directed science experiment: to find out just how little food could keep a human body alive. (p. 202)

Suicide/Depression

Suicide among adolescents is an increasingly serious problem. In 1950, persons 15 to 24 years of age committed less than 6 percent of all suicides; by 1980, this proportion had grown to 20 percent. Today, suicide is second only to automobile accidents as the leading cause of death among young people in this age group (Underwood and Dunne-Maxim, 1993).

Although adolescent suicides are often triggered by some kind of stress such as breaking up with a friend, arguments with parents, or school problems, suicide is *not* the result of a single event. Most suicide victims have had a long history of problems, all of which contributed to the final event (Underwood and Dunne-Maxim, 1993). Risk factors include biological factors, substance abuse, depression, aggressiveness, and child abuse—but it is normal for many individuals to experience one or more of these risk factors and not be suicidal.

Some of the warning signs that indicate the potential for suicide are listed in Table 12-7. As you look over this table, keep in mind that suicidal intent is often well hidden; conversely, it is normal for individuals to exhibit one or more of these indicators and not be suicidal. Nonetheless, if you see signs of suicide, if the youngster communicates an intent to commit suicide (in writing or verbally), or if you receive a report of such signs from another student, you should immediately communicate the information to the principal or the Student Assistance Counselor. Many

TABLE 12-7
SIGNS OF SUICIDE POTENTIAL
(ADOPTED FROM KOTTLER AND KOTTLER, 1993)

Use of drugs or alcohol

Extensive preoccupation with death fantasies

Absence of a support system

A specific plan for committing suicide

Available means to carry out the plan (e.g., loaded gun; bottle of sleeping pills at home)

A history of self-destructive acts

A gesture that may be interpreted as a cry for help

History of relative having committed suicide

Significant mood changes from depression to elation

Noticeable, negative changes in appearance or academic performance schools have a Crisis Management Team that will be responsible for meeting with the student to determine the extent of the problem. You should not take it upon yourself to counsel the student and to give assurances that "life will get better."

Hopefully, your school has a Crisis Management Team that can coordinate the school's responses when a suicide occurs. The school's task is to deal with the grief of the members of the school community. Students need to accept the reality of the loss and to begin to work through the pain of grief (Underwood and Dunne-Maxim, 1993). It's essential that the school not ignore the suicide, but make sure it is talked about in a structured, controlled manner. The crisis team or mental health consultants should be brought in to help members of the school community deal with their feelings.

TALKING WITH STUDENTS WHO HAVE PROBLEMS

As I've stressed earlier, it is not your job to be a school counselor, therapist, or confidante for all your students. You have neither the time nor the training to serve in those roles. Nonetheless, there will be instances in which students will reach out to you for understanding. A student might confide her fears about being pregnant; another might tell you about his alcoholic parents; still another might want to talk about her feelings of inadequacy and isolation. What will you do? In many cases, the appropriate response is to put the student in touch with a special service provider who has the expertise needed to intervene. Listen to Sandy:

> Sometimes students will try to trap you into inappropriate confidentiality. They'll say, "I need to tell you something, but you have to promise not to tell anyone else." Right away, I tell them, "I can't promise that, because if this is too big for us to handle, I need to tell people who can help. We have a school psychologist, a student assistance counselor, a principal, a guidance counselor, a nurse. All these resources are here to help you. If you tell me what's bothering you, I can get you to the right person." Sometimes, the kid will say, "I don't want to tell that person; I don't *know* them." Then I say, "Okay, you can tell *me,* and I'll tell them."

In addition to getting professional help for a student with a serious problem, you can also be helpful by having some basic communication skills. These allow you to help students to express their feelings, gain clarity, and (hopefully) resolve their own problems.

Attending and Acknowledging

Giving a student your complete, undivided attention is the first and most basic task in being helpful (Kottler and Kottler, 1993). It is rare that individuals are fully attentive to one another. Have you ever tried to talk with someone who was simultaneously organizing papers, posting papers on the bulletin board, or straightening rows of desks? Divided attention like this communicates that the person doesn't really have time for you and is not fully paying attention.

Attending and acknowledging involve both verbal and nonverbal behaviors.

Even without saying a word, you can convey that you are totally tuned in by orienting your body toward the student, establishing eye contact, nodding, leaning forward, smiling, or frowning. In addition, you can use verbal cues. Thomas Gordon (1974) recommends "empathic grunting"—the little "uh-huhs" and phrases (e.g., "Oh," "I see," "Mmmmm") that communicate, "I'm really listening." Sometimes, when a student needs additional encouragement to talk more, you can use an explicit invitation, what Gordon calls a "door opener"—"Tell me more," "Would you like to say more about that?" "Do you want to talk about it?" "Want to go on?"

One of the hardest ideas for teachers to accept is that a person can help another simply by listening. But Kottler and Kottler (1993) remind us that attending can be a powerful helping tool:

> You would be truly amazed at how healing this simple act can be—giving another person your full attention. Children, in particular, are often so used to being devalued by adults that attending behaviors instantly tell them something is different about this interaction: "Here is a person who seems to care about me and what I have to say." (p. 40)

Active Listening

Attending and acknowledging communicate that you are totally engaged, but they do not convey if you really *understand*. Active listening takes the interaction one step further by having you reflect back what you think you heard. This feedback allows you to check out whether you are right or wrong. If you're right, the student knows you have truly understood. If you're off target, the student can correct you, and the communication can continue. Examples of active listening appear in Table 12-8.

If you're new to active listening, you may find it useful to use the phrase, "You feel . . ." when you reflect back what you heard. Sometimes, novices feel stupid, as if they're simply parroting back what the person just said. (In fact, when I was first learning to do active listening, a student became really annoyed and demanded to know why I kept repeating what he had said!) As you gain more skill, however, you are able to *paraphrase* what you hear, and the interaction becomes far more subtle.

Keep in mind that active listening is not easy. Student teachers with whom I work often want to reject it out of hand; they find it unnatural and awkward, and they would much prefer to give advice, not simply communicate that they understand. But knowing that someone really understands can be profoundly important, especially to teenagers who so often feel misunderstood. In addition, active listening provides an opportunity for students to express their feelings and to clarify their problems. It can also help to defuse strong feelings without taking the responsibility away from the student for solving the problem.

Questioning

When people tell us their problems, we often want to ask them questions in order to find out more information. Kottler and Kottler (1993) caution teachers to be careful

TABLE 12-8
EXAMPLES OF ACTIVE LISTENING

Student: Wait till my mom sees this test grade. She's gonna flip out.
Teacher: You think she'll be really mad at you, huh?
Student: Yeah, she expects me to come home with all A's.
Teacher: Sounds like you're feeling really pressured.
Student: Well, I am. You'd think that getting a B was like failing. My mom just doesn't understand how hard this is for me.
Teacher: So you think a B is an okay grade in a tough course like this, but she thinks that you can do better.
Student: Yeah, she has this thing that if I come home with a B I'm just not working.
Teacher: That's rough. I can see how that would make you feel like she doesn't appreciate the efforts you're making.

Student: I can't believe I have to be home at 12:00! It's crazy! All my friends have a later curfew—or they don't have any curfew at all!
Teacher: So you think your parents are a lot stricter than the other kids' parents.
Student: Well, they are! I mean, I know it's 'cause they care about me, but it's really a pain to have to be home earlier than everyone else. I feel like a dork. And besides, I think I'm responsible enough to have a later curfew.
Teacher: So you're not just embarrassed, you're mad because they don't realize how responsible you are.

Student: All along my boyfriend's been telling me he'll stick by me if I get pregnant, and then it happens, and he's gone.
Teacher: You feel really abandoned.

Student: I don't want to go to School-Base [for mental health counseling]. Only crazy kids go to School-Base!
Teacher: Going to School-Base is kind of embarrassing. . . .
Student: Yeah. My friends are gonna give me a really hard time.
Teacher: You think they're going to say you're crazy.
Student: Yeah. I wanna go, but I don't want people to make fun of me.
Teacher: I can understand that. It's really rough when people make fun of you.

Student: I had the worst nightmare last night! I mean, I know it was just a dream, but I just can't get it out of my head. This bloody guy with a knife was chasing me down this alley, and I couldn't get away.
Teacher: Nightmares can be so scary.
Student: Yeah, and I know it's babyish, but I just can't shake the feeling.
Teacher: Sometimes a bad feeling from a nightmare stays with you a long time. . . .

---

about this practice:

The problem with questions, as natural as they may come to mind, is that they often put the child in a "one down" position in which you are the interrogator and expert problem solver. "Tell me what the situation is and I will fix it." For that reason, questions are used only when you can't get the student to reveal information in other ways. (p. 42)

Sandy also warns beginning teachers about the use of questions:

I don't ask too many questions. I prefer to let them talk themselves out. Questions can open up situations you're not prepared to deal with. After all, you're not a counselor; you're more like a *conduit:* you hear about problems and you try to put them in touch with someone who has the knowledge and the skill to help. Twenty-five years ago I didn't realize that. I was only three or four years older than my students and I thought I could help them solve their problems. But they don't need teachers to solve their problems for them. They need teachers who can *help them solve their own problems* or who can get them expert help for solving their problems.

If you must ask questions, they should be open-ended—requiring more than a one-word response. Like active listening, open-ended questions invite further exploration and communication, whereas close-ended questions cut off communication. Compare these questions:

What are you feeling right now? vs. *Are you feeling angry?*
What do you want to do? vs. *Do you want to tell your boyfriend?*

Kottler and Kottler point out one notable exception to the rule of avoiding questions whenever possible: when it is important to get very specific information in a potentially dangerous situation, such as when a student is discussing suicide. Then it would be appropriate to ask specific questions: Have you actually tried this? Will you promise not to do anything until we can get you some help?

Problem Solving

We have already discussed problem solving in Chapter Six, when we discussed Gordon's no-lose method of solving classroom conflicts. But you can also use this approach when students have their own problems that they confide in you. A problem-solving approach helps students define their problem, specify their goals, develop alternative solutions that might be constructive, narrow the choices to those that seem most realistic, and put the plan into action (Kottler and Kottler, 1993).

Not too long ago, Donnie used a problem-solving approach when a female student told her she was pregnant and asked if she should get an abortion.

First, the student needed to clarify the situation: Was her boyfriend available or not available? Were her parents supportive or not supportive? Was she using drugs or not using? Also, she needed to think about what resources were available to her? All of these factors play a role in making a decision about what to do.

Then, she needed to figure out what her values and priorities were—does she want to go to college? How does she feel about giving the baby up for adoption? Finally, I tried to help her figure out the alternatives—adoption, abortion, staying single and keeping the kid, getting married and keeping the kid.

I don't give advice in situations like this—I wouldn't know what kind of advice to give. But I *can* try to help kids clarify the situation. They're confused, and as an outside party who can think clearly, I can help them see alternatives they haven't thought of, to talk about the resources that are available to them. My goal is to help them make the best possible decision for themselves.

CONCLUDING THOUGHTS

The problems that students bring to school can seem overwhelming, especially for beginning teachers who are coping with basic issues of survival. And in fact, there may be students whose problems are so great, you really cannot help. As Fred reminds us, "There's failure in this business. These problems transcend the classroom, and there's only so much an individual teacher or the school can do." Sandy echoes this thought:

> When the school has done everything it can, and you know the child is still hurting, you feel so helpless. It's infuriating when you can't do anything. But when this happens you just have to say, "I tried. Now I need to let go."

"Letting go" means recognizing that you may not be able to change a student's life; it *doesn't* mean abandoning your responsibility for making that student's time in school as productive and meaningful as possible. Carol Lowinger, the SAC at Fred's school, believes that, to some extent, teachers need to treat troubled students "like everyone else":

> Sometimes teachers think, "These kids are going through a hard time; I'll give them a break." But out of this sense of caring, they give kids breaks they shouldn't get. Kids need to be held accountable. They have to learn to live in the real world where you can't hide behind your problems. You have to learn to cope, and you *mustn't* learn "I *don't have* to cope." I'm not saying that we shouldn't give them some leeway if their problems are really great; obviously, we need to be flexible and supportive. But they still need to be responsible for their current behavior. If we always bail kids out, we're enabling. That's not helpful—and it's even dangerous.

When students have serious problems, it's more important than ever to create a classroom that is safe, orderly, and humane. You may not be able to change youngsters' relationships with their families, but you can still work to establish positive teacher-student relationships. You may not be able to provide students with control over unstable, chaotic home lives, but you can allow them opportunities to make decisions and to have some control over their time in school. You may not be able to do anything about the violence that permeates the neighborhoods in which they live, but you can structure classroom situations to foster cooperation and group cohesiveness. In Fred's words, "You can show them you care enough about them not to let them them slough off. You can still keep teaching."

SUMMARY

Because large numbers of America's youth are at risk for school failure, substance abuse, physical problems, psychological and emotional disorders, abuse and neglect, teenage pregnancy, and violence, today's teachers have to deal with issues that require knowledge and skills beyond those needed to be an effective instructor. There are three primary ways that teachers can help students with serious problems:

- Teachers need to be alert to the indicators of potential problems.
- Teachers need to be informed about the various special services that are available and to know how to obtain access to those services.
- Teachers need to develop communication skills that allow them to work more effectively with troubled or disaffected youngsters.

The chapter briefly discussed five serious problems teachers may encounter in today's high schools:

- Substance abuse
- Violence
- Abuse and neglect
- Eating disorders
- Depression/suicide

The chapter then outlined communication skills that can be helpful:

- Attending and acknowledging
- Active listening
- Asking open-ended questions
- Problem solving

Sometimes the problems that students bring to school can be overwhelming, especially for beginning teachers who are coping with basic issues of survival. And, in fact, there may be students whose problems are so great, you just cannot help. Nonetheless, you can still try to create a classroom environment that is safe, orderly, and humane. You can show students you care by holding them accountable for their behavior and by continuing to teach.

ACTIVITIES

1. In the school where you are observing or teaching, interview the Student Assistance Counselor, a guidance counselor, or the director of special services to determine the policies for reporting drug abuse. Get copies of the referral forms that are used and compare them with the form shown in this chapter.

2. Reporting suspected abuse and neglect varies from state to state. Find out the policies used in your state. Also find out if your school has particular policies and procedures you are to follow. In particular, get answers to the following questions:

Who is required to report abuse and neglect?
When should you report child abuse? (When you have reasonable cause to suspect? Reasonable cause to believe?)
To what state agency do you report?
What information must be included in the report?

Do you have to give your name when reporting?

3. In the following bits of conversation, students have confided in teachers about problems they are experiencing, and the teachers have responded in ways *not* suggested in this chapter. Provide a new response for each case, using the communication skills discussed in this chapter: acknowledging, active listening, asking open-ended questions, and problem solving.

a. Student: My parents won't allow me to go visit my boyfriend at college for the weekend. They say they trust me, but then they don't show it!

  Teacher: Well, I'm sure they have your best interests at heart. You know, you really shouldn't gripe. After all, a lot of kids don't have parents who care about them. I see a lot of kids whose parents let them do anything they want. Maybe you think you'd like that, but I'm sure you wouldn't. . . .

b. Student: I can't stand my stepmother. She's always criticizing me and making me come home right after school to watch my sister, and making me feel really stupid.

  Teacher: Oh, come on now, Cinderella. I'm sure it's not that bad.

c. Student: My parents want me to go to college, but I really want to join the Marines. What do you think I should do?

  Teacher: Do what your folks say. Go to college. You can always join the Marines later.

REFERENCES

Blauvelt, P. D (1990). School security: "Who you gonna call?" *School Safety Newsjournal,* Fall, 4–8.

Children's Defense Fund (1994). *The state of America's children yearbook 1994.* Washington, D.C.: Children's Defense Fund.

Curcio, J. L., and First, P. F. (1993). *Violence in the schools: How to proactively prevent and defuse it.* Newbury Park, CA: Corwin Press.

Goldstein, A. P., Harootunian, B., and Conoley, J. C. (1994). *Student aggression: Prevention, management, and replacement training.* New York: Guilford Press.

Gonet, M. M. (1994). *Counseling the adolescent substance abuser: School-based intervention and prevention.* Thousand Oaks, CA: Sage Publications.

Gordon, T. (1974). *Teacher Effectiveness Training (T.E.T.).* New York: Peter H. Wyden.

Janofsky, M. (1994). Survey reports more drug use by teen-agers. *The New York Times,* December 13, A26.

Kodluboy, D. W., and Evenrud, L. A. (1993). School-based interventions: Best practices and critical issues. In A. P. Goldstein and C. R. Huff (Eds.), *The gang intervention handbook.* Champaign, IL: Research Press.

Kottler, J. A., and Kottler, E. (1993). *Teacher as counselor: Developing the helping skills you need.* Newbury Park, CA: Corwin Press.

Lal, S. R., Lal, D., and Achilles, C. M. (1993). *Handbook on gangs in schools: Strategies to reduce gang-related activities.* Newbury Park, CA: Corwin Press.

Michaelis, K. L. (1993). *Reporting child abuse: A guide to mandatory requirements for school personnel.* Newbury Park, CA: Corwin Press.

Miller, E. (1994). Peer mediation catches on, but some adults don't. *Harvard Education Letter, 10*(3), 8.

New Jersey Alcohol/Drug Resource Center and Clearinghouse, Center of Alcohol Studies,

Rutgers University (1994). *Facts on adolescent substance abuse.* Clearinghouse Fact Sheet.

Newsam, B. S. (1992). *Complete student assistance program handbook.* West Nyack, NY: The Center for Applied Research in Education.

O'Neil, J. (1991). A generation adrift? *Educational Leadership, 49*(1), 4–10.

Parkay, F. W., and Stanford, B. H. (1992). *Becoming a teacher* (2nd edition). Boston: Allyn and Bacon.

Portner, J. (January 12, 1994). School violence up over past 5 years, 82% in survey say. *Education Week,* 9.

Quarles, C. L. (1989). *School violence: A survival guide for school staff, with emphasis on robbery, rape, and hostage taking.* Washington, D.C.: National Education Association.

Reynolds, M. C. (1989). Students with special needs. In M. C. Reynolds (Ed.), *Knowledge base for the beginning teacher.* Oxford, England: Pergamon Press.

Smith, M. (1993). Some school-based violence prevention strategies. *NASSP Bulletin, 77*(557), 70–75.

Tower, C. C. (1987). *How schools can help combat child abuse and neglect* (2nd edition). Washington, D.C.: National Education Association.

Trump, K. S. (1993). Tell teen gangs: School's out. *The American School Board Journal, 180*(7), 39–42.

Underwood, M. M., and Dunne-Maxim, K. (1993). *Managing sudden violent loss in the schools.* Piscataway, NJ: Governor's Advisory Council on Youth Suicide Prevention.

Wolf, N. (1991). *The beauty myth: How images of beauty are used against women.* New York: Anchor Books, Doubleday.

FOR FURTHER READING

On Substance Abuse

The National Clearinghouse for Alcohol and Drug Information (NCADI)—a communications service of the Office for Substance Abuse Prevention; the nation's primary source of information about alcohol and other drug abuse. Address: The National Clearinghouse for Alcohol and Drug Information, P. O. Box 2345, Rockville, MD 20852; (301)468-2600.

On Violence

Curcio, J. L., and First, P. F. (1993). *Violence in the schools: How to proactively prevent and defuse it.* Newbury Park, CA: Corwin Press.

Hill, M. S., and Hill, F. W. (1994). *Creating safe schools: What principals can do.* Newbury Park, CA: Corwin Press.

Katz, N. H., and Lawyer, J. W. (1993). *Conflict resolution: Building bridges.* Newbury Park, CA: Corwin Press.

Lal, S. R., Lal, D., and Achilles, C. M. (1993). *Handbook on gangs in schools: Strategies to reduce gang-related activities.* Newbury Park, CA: Corwin Press.

The Second Step Curriculum: A violence prevention curriculum. Seattle, Washington: Committee for Children.

On Child Abuse and Neglect

Michaelis, K. L. (1993). *Reporting child abuse: A guide to mandatory requirements for school personnel.* Newbury Park, CA: Corwin Press.

Tower, C. C. (1987). *How schools can help combat child abuse and neglect* (2nd edition). Washington, D.C.: National Education Association.

On Eating Disorders

Bruch, H., Czyzewski, D., and Suhr, M. A. (Eds.) (1988). *Conversations with anorexics.* New York: Basic Books.

Brumberg, J. J. (1988). *Fasting girls: The emergence of anorexia nervosa as a modern disease.* Cambridge, MA: Harvard University Press.

Seid, R. P. (1989). *Never too thin: Why women are at war with their bodies.* Englewood Cliffs, NJ: Prentice-Hall.

On Communication Skills

Gordon, T. (1974). *Teacher Effectiveness Training (T.E.T.).* New York: Peter H. Wyden.

Kottler, J. A., and Kottler, E. (1993). *Teacher as counselor: Developing the helping skills you need.* Newbury Park, CA: Corwin Press.

Index